MYSTERY ON THE MOUNTAIN

Harper & Brothers, Publishers, New York

MYSTERY ON THE MOUNTAIN

The Drama of the Sinai Revelation

THEODOR REIK

TO MIRIAM

Sleep, my child. Sleep, it is late.
The sun is dying, the night at the gate.
Beyond the horizon a vanishing flame.
Death, my child, for you but a name.
You turn your eyes towards morning and light,
Sleep, your days will be blessed and bright.
Sleep, my child. My child, good night.

Sleep, my child. The wind comes and goes.
Whence and whither? Nobody knows.
The roads of the world are dark and wild,
For me, for many, for you, my child.
Lonely and lost, we grope like the blind,
Searching for brothers we cannot find.
Sleep, my child. My child, good night.

Sleep, my child, do not listen to me.
I know the meaning. To you it may be
Like murmuring water, a whispering voice,
Words—my only treasures and joys!
What I acquired will not remain.
Who can inherit? It will be in vain.
Sleep, my child. My child, good night.

Are you asleep, Miriam, my child?—
We are like rivers, now calm and now wild,
And deep within us an ancestor's seed,
Their pride and their pain, their vision, their deed,
Their past now returning to children and heirs.
You are not alone, and your life is theirs.
Miriam, my life—my child, good night!

RICHARD BEER-HOFMANN, *Lullaby for Miriam.*
Translated by Karl Darmstadter

CONTENTS

PART THREE
A Discovery in Archaeological Psychoanalysis

INTRODUCTION

Vision and Revision

A choice anecdote about Anatole France, published not long after his death in memoirs by an intimate friend,[1] seems easily the best way to introduce the story of the long journey I have undergone in preparing the present book. The anecdote presents the renowned author in an amiable conversation with the secretary of a magazine, who asks impatiently why it is necessary for so seasoned a writer to delay so long before correcting galley proofs. The author explains: "I have first to forget what I have written in order to see it with new eyes. Only then do I become aware of what is not immediately understandable and of what is not simple and clear." He adds finally: "You see, *what is natural comes only at the end.*"

The fortunes of the present book and its writer are proofs of the insight offered in this epigram. In the Fall of 1913, I started to write a paper on "The Puberty Rites of Savages"[2] in the hope of throwing light on the extensive material gathered by contemporary anthropologists and historians of religion. As I was reading Freud's *Totem and Taboo,* which had just been issued from the press, a new concept of these periodical festivals of primitive society had formed itself in my thoughts. In the midst of my effort to understand the rites in psychoanalytic terms, certain seemingly irrelevant concerns laid hold of my attention.

These errant thoughts concerned the story of Exodus and of the happenings at Sinai and seemed to hint at a concealed similarity between the puberty ritual of Australian aborigines and the revelation on that famed mountain. Those impressions continued to disturb my thoughts, and to slow my progress in completing my aforementioned paper. Nonetheless, some features in the "central mystery of primitive

vii

society," as Sir J. G. Frazer called the initiation rites, continued to remind me of that other mystery that marks the birth of a new religion. Those ideas emerged and were dismissed. Yet they reappeared. It was in vain that I commanded them to vanish in the crowd of other marginal thoughts. Why should they not disappear like others? Perhaps they would have been in good company.

It was at this stage, when the thoughts were still in the stage of inconclusive hunches and my ideas were as yet, as one says, "half-baked," that I mentioned them to Freud. He listened to me, got up from his chair and searched for an issue of a magazine. If my memory does not fail me, it was the *Mitteilungen der vorderasiatischen Gesellschaft* (*Proceedings of the Near Eastern Society*), to which he regularly subscribed. He showed me a paper there which claimed—with seeming authority—that the Hebrew tribes had, in the Exodus, most probably never been near Mount Sinai or the mountain called by that name today. Apparently, Freud must have felt that it was essential to my theory to insist that the Israelites had camped at Sinai and implied that my theory was too closely connected with the locality of that mountain.

In retrospect, it is evident that the reading of that paper and the skeptical remarks expressed by Freud must have made a great impression upon me. They spurred me to abandon the whole train of thought or plan of research that was directed to a comparison between revelation and primitive initiation. I was half convinced that I had been led astray by a will-o'-the-wisp. Freud's criticism, implied in pointing to the article in the magazine, had completely intimidated me.

I should add, however, that a few months later, to my astonishment, Freud came back to the topic of our conversation and said: "There are far-reaching possibilities in that idea of yours." In the following years he mentioned the plan several times—once in the form of a gentle reproach for my procrastination—but in the meantime I had shelved the project and had turned my interest to other matters. The interest Freud had shown in my researches later on did not, however, go without result. While completing that aforementioned paper on puberty rites I did not fail to include the remark that the report of the covenant of the Hebrews with their God was "a glorified and amended account of an initiation ceremony." I furthermore asserted there that "psychoanalysis enables us to recognize in the Sinai passage a historical counterpart to the important present-day rites of initiation that take place in the bush."[3] If, I said there, "the prohibitions and commands in the puberty rites of the Australian blacks in particular are compared with the Jewish story of the Exodus, the Decalogue and the Book of the Covenant, a striking and hitherto unconsidered similarity becomes apparent." Then follows the remark that I hope "to throw some light on the reason for this in another work." In various papers written in the following years[4] a few results of the research presented in this book are anticipated, yet that hope of completing the grander design still remained unfulfilled.

Returning from the front in the First World War, I was attracted by various problems of general psychology and psychopathology and by questions of psychoanalytic technique. Books dealing with these subjects were foremost in my thoughts and demanded to be written. On a long detour, I returned later to the scientific interest in comparative religion that had absorbed me as a young psychoanalyst. Even when the project of the present book reappeared and regained priority in my thoughts, my resistances put up a desperate rear-guard fight as though this essay were still recalcitrant to be written.

Now after these many years the long-postponed work enters the world, after its author has crossed the line of the biblical age of three-score and ten. Does it matter to anyone but to the author that it was conceived almost a half-century ago, when its author was twenty-five years of age?

In accordance with the demand of psychoanalytic sincerity, it should not be concealed that during that long interval I have followed the pertinent literature with mixed feelings of hope and anxiety. Would someone else discover the concept that explained so much of the mystery of the biblical revelation story? However, I failed to encounter anything of a similar kind. Some scholars seemed to come close to my way of posing the problem, but none quite arrived at my solution. Among psychoanalytic explorers the late Geza Roheim contributed some important analogies between the revelation narrative and reports on Australian initiation, but hardly ventured beyond scholarly investigation of details. It gave me satisfaction to discover that Roheim thought highly of the significance of my early research, declaring that I "was the first to show that Semitic religion is based on the puberty rite."[5]

In the forty-five years since my fateful conversation with Freud, my thoughts have more than once returned to my old undertaking. Thinking of it was always accompanied by a kind of malaise, or uneasy conscience, as though I had not kept a promise to Freud. Yet I knew I had never explicitly promised Freud or anyone else, even myself, to write a book on the Sinai-Exodus events. The commitment

I had made was an unspoken or silent one. When after an interim of more than four decades, I threw myself anew into the study of the materials now grown to gigantic dimensions thanks to the new discoveries of archaeology, it was as though I had come home again. My central ideas had remained intact and fresh although they had been in hibernation for more than forty years.

I began to write this book with the feeling a runner might have when, nearing the finish line, he sees he has lagged behind and fears he may not have time to catch up, he may lose the race. I had to still the voice within myself that murmured: "So little time!"

There can be no doubt that it was lack of moral courage that prevented me from following that early concept to the end. Freud used to say to us, his Viennese students, that many people have psychological talents which might enable them to become good psychoanalysts, but what always proves decisive in the choice of one's profession is character. Within this domain of character, it is moral courage which plays the paramount part. Moral courage gives us power to face unpleasant truths within ourselves and in others, secures us the strength to persevere in ideas which at first appear absurd or repulsive, outrageous or fantastic. In every research it is moral courage which overcomes what Freud once called *"Gedankenschreck,"* fear of adopting and investigating an idea which initially strikes one as bizarre or dangerous. To go to the end with one's ideas against one's own inner resistances amounts to what we call in war "bravery in the face of the enemy."

It was lack of moral courage that had made me desert that plan of my youth and prevented me from following the path I had trod to its final conclusions. That kind of courage sometimes increases with age. It is almost four hundred years since Michel Eyquem de Montaigne wrote: "I speak truth, not as much as I dare, yet I dare a little the more, as I grow older." I too become more courageous with old age as, I hope, this book will prove.

The author in his proper person must now, as modestly as he can, withdraw from the center of the stage and yield place to the narrator who shall give voice to the theme of his book. I have to thank Mrs. Jane Waters, Dr. A. B. Feldman, and Dr. Benjamin Nelson for constructive criticism and editorial help.

The present essay is an attempt at disentanglement of the central strands of the biblical tradition and the opening of an inquiry into the historic meanings and foreseeable future of Judaism. My observations on the latter theme will be dimly foreshadowed here; they will be presented more directly in a sequel to this book which is now in preparation.

Here we are contented to ask questions: Can we resolve the mystery which still surrounds the events of the Exodus from Egypt, the wandering of the Hebrew tribes into the "great and fearful wilderness" and, above all, the revelation? Can we penetrate the mists which still envelop the top of the Sacred Mountain?

I would propose that we take as our first step a too sorely neglected fact. *The Exodus narrative unfolds as a drama founded on historic events* and culminates in Yahweh's descent on Mount Sinai. Why not, therefore, begin our work with an inquiry into the structure and symbolism of the drama? In this spirit, Part I will consider the unfolding of the content of the action, the persons of the play, the elaboration of the plot, and so on. It will not seem odd, therefore, that I occasionally appear to look "behind the screen," to explore what goes on "backstage."

As underneath the lines of a palimpsest, traces of old, erased writings become visible, the outlines of an initiation festival of the Hebrew tribes can be perceived below the biblical narrative. The tradition of such Semitic rites, disavowed very early, was fused with the story of the departure from Egypt and of the Hebrew migration. The drama, as it is presented in the Holy Scripture, is a composite, created and several times recreated from these two elements: an episode in the vicissitudes of some half-nomadic tribes and an earlier initiation ritual that gained world-historic significance when tradition elevated it to the sublime rank of divine revelation. At the end of a very worldly emergency and of profound tribal misery appears the holiest of God's secrets.

In the forty-five years since the plan of this book first occurred to me, an abundance of pertinent literature from the fields of archaeology and higher criticism, of history and theology has emerged, only insufficiently, alas, studied by me. At this point it appears to me imperative to clarify my relation to two works that, standing apart from those scholarly investigations, became important to my research, partly because it follows a different direction: Sigmund Freud's *Moses and Monotheism* and Martin Buber's *Moses*.[6] Different from and often opposed to each other in their aims and methods, both books agree in one essential point: they are focused on the towering, yet problematical figure of Moses. Freud sees the prophet as an Egyptian whose imperishable contribution it was to communicate

to the Jews a newly discovered religion of his native land, monotheism. I am compelled to disagree with my great master on two
counts: (1) I am not persuaded that Moses was an Egyptian; he
seems to me surely to have been a Hebrew. (2) To my mind, it seems
at least questionable to ascribe the origins of *historic monotheism* to
the Egyptians.

Parting company at this point with Freud, with whom I was closely
associated for thirty years, I continue to be loyal to him in aspiring
to a common way of understanding man's nature and culture. Like
him, I have sought to unravel the meanings and varieties of religious
experience and, specifically, to penetrate the not-so-manifest meanings of the Judaeo-Christian heritage. Like him I find it helpful,
even necessary, to probe origins in order fully to understand the
meanings of developed forms. Thus, in the present connection, I
venture into the labyrinth of the early history of the Hebrews looking for clues to the fascination which the Decalogue and the Book of
the Covenant have exerted over the minds of men in the West.
Finally, I remain loyal to Freud in the conviction that psychoanalytic
research into neglected corners of historic tradition is the royal road
to the uncovering of forgotten meanings and tangled emotions in the
life of culture.

Martin Buber's *Moses* belongs to a different genre from that of
Freud. Staunch in his own faith, a sort of latter-day prophet in his
own right, Buber is indifferent to and even critical of psychoanalysis.
Steeped in history and tradition, Buber attempts a daringly fresh
re-creation of the events of Exodus as they were transformed in the
crucible of men's faith and religious imagination. The hero of Buber's
book is the monumental figure of Moses, the prophet, lawgiver, and
statesman.

It will be apparent to the reader that my attempts at the solution
of the great problems pondered by Buber originate in different questions and rest on a basically different interpretation. Yet, if I am not
misled by lifelong convictions, my findings may be found to add
a new dimension to the picture Buber portrays, at least to provide
a complement to his work. In my own paper, I hope, the events of
Exodus and of the Sinai revelation will become intelligible in the
perspective of depth-psychology.

In both books, that of Freud as well as Buber, the gigantic statue
of Moses commands the center of the stage and towers over the heads
of the Hebraic people. In my book, in contrast, Moses appears only
as a foreground figure similar to one on an ancient bas-relief in which

a dominant subject projects only slightly from the background. In the center is the revelation whose mystery I would like to penetrate. The hero of the drama on which the curtain will be raised is the Jewish people, a community and a religion in the making.

I freely admit that my essay may seem to have the character of what the once-renowned Scotsman, Dugald Stewart, used to call "conjectural history" to describe narrations resting on probable inferences concerning the remote past. To escape uncertainty is not given to those who would attempt the reconstruction of the beginnings of Israel's history and religion. In each area, the alternatives lie not between perfect demonstration or total ignorance but between "conjectural histories" of different degrees of plausibility and significance; that is, between conjectural histories in the proper sense and idle and fruitless conjectures. We will not make our way through the thickets of ignorance if we only dare to act on what we know with perfect knowledge. Explorers in search of the concealed truths beneath the biblical tradition will, like the soldiers of Napoleon, remain aware of the fact that from the pyramids forty centuries look down on them. I will be content if the reconstruction comes close to the nature of the reality concealed and revealed in the biblical report.

The aim of this research is, however, located beyond new insights into the beginning of Jewish history and religion. There is an old tradition that the word of God which issued from Mount Sinai was spoken simultaneously in all languages of the earth. In attempting to penetrate the secret of the Sinai revelation, this book tries to determine its significance for the evolution of civilization. Whatever it was that took place on that peninsula more than three millennia ago, it was, according to Winston Churchill, "the most decisive leap forward ever discernible in the human story."[7]

New York
May 1959

THEODOR REIK

PART ONE

The Unfolding of the Drama

1.

The Dramatic Action: The Revelation

Scholars like to make a distinction between natural religions and revelation religions—a classification that is as open to argument as any scientific and "conceptual" discrimination of experience. If we accept it for reasons of utility, we remain aware of the fact that there are shifting frontiers and puzzling transitions. History follows these two views of ultimate religious orientation as far back as possible, tracing the first group through the "animatistic" and the "animistic" phases to the stages when the gods became human and, finally, superhuman. The second group, to which Hebrew religion, Christianity, and Islam belong, is supposed to be founded on historical events in which the Godhead made Himself and His will known to man. These events are characterized by revelation.

The word "revelation" appears to have two meanings. It denotes the process by which God makes known the truth which He requires, and it means the body of truth which God has made known. Revelation is always divine—that means the initiative is always His. The action of self-disclosure depends on His will. It is for Him to bestow the light; the recipients of the revelation promote His purpose by proclaiming and enacting His message. We have thus to distinguish between God's pleasure and man's response. What is the content of revelation? Primarily it is God Himself and His purpose. Revealed truth is sharply contrasted with other ways in which men have gained knowledge of gods and things divine. It is a direct communication from God Himself.

St. Thomas Aquinas (1225–1274) observes with characteristic precision that there is "an *ascent* by the natural light of reason,

3

through created things to the knowledge of God" and "a *descent,* by the mode of revelation, of divine truth which exceeds the human intellect" and is delivered for our belief. "All revelation is self-revelation of God."[1]

Theologians frequently point out that what is revealed to us is not a "body of information concerning various things of which we might otherwise be ignorant. If it is information at all, it is information concerning the nature, mind and purpose of God—that and nothing else."[2] The authenticity of such information cannot be doubted. In the views of theologians, God's knowledge of Himself is the final norm. Archbishop Trench (1807–1886) remarks, with exemplary lucidity, that God's revelation of Himself "is a drawing back of the veil or curtain which conceals Him from man; not man finding out God, but God discovering Himself to man."[3]

Revelations come in different ways and by various media to the believers. The Greeks recognized the words of God in the utterances of the oracles of Delphi. Zoroaster proclaimed that he received the message of Ahura Mazda, and Mohammed construed his visions as the bequest of truth by Allah. Divine words were communicated to the prophets of Israel who announced: "Thus saith the Lord." In contrast to this kind of revelation is the other and rarer case in which the identity and the will of God are declared by Him to a people as, for instance, in the theophany on Mount Sinai. Such a collective experience seems to qualify the insistence of Kierkegaard that the relation of man to God is like the defile of Thermophylae where only one person can pass at a time.

Theology admits that the message communicated takes the intellectual capacity of the hearers into account. A teacher who wants to explain something to a child in kindergarten has to use different language and find different ways of communicating than the teacher instructing a high school student. The divine light remains the same. The forms of enlightenment change.

So-called progressive theology insists, however, that revelation is "neither book nor doctrine, but God Himself in His historical self-attestation. Revelation is event."[4] Otherwise put, revelation is not given in the form of directly communicated knowledge, but through events occurring in the historical experience of mankind. Those events are conceived as "mighty acts" of God and engender in the mind of man reflective knowledge of His power.

If those events are part of history, they cannot be treated as are other occurrences. They have to be looked at as transcendently meaningful. "The essential matter of history," writes the distinguished legal historian, Frederick Maitland, "is not what happened, but what people thought or said about it."[5] This is, of course, especially valid with regard to the historical events considered as revelation.

Let us take another look at the word "revelation." Literally it means an unveiling, the lifting of a cover, the disclosure of something that had been hidden. The difference between disclosing and discovering dare not be overlooked here. I may discover something, but that is not identical with my disclosing it to someone else. I might prefer to keep it for myself, to keep it secret. In the Holy Scripture the term "revelation" is always used in the sense of the disclosure, the unveiling of a mystery.

In certain mystical forms of religion, God is self-sufficient and silent. He is a hidden God (*deus absconditus*). In the prophetic religions He is active and speaks, and He speaks in the first person. Comparative history of religions confirms that God spoke many times and to many people. Indeed, it might be interesting to collect and anthologize all the statements He is declared to have made during the millennia in various places upon His earth. Some of them would sound very different from the sermons preached in His name nowadays. He never made small talk; He was never condescending to people; and what He proclaimed was always worth listening to—which cannot always be claimed for what His constituted ministers of diverse faiths say at the present time. In contrast with great numbers of rabbis and pastors He appears eloquent, but not verbose. His language is terse and concise. He does not say all. Voltaire, who knew the Holy Scripture well, must have had this contrast in mind when he remarked that the way to be boring is to say everything. (*"Le secret d'ennuyer est . . . de tout dire."*)

The Bible is not God's revelation, but the report of it—or rather the *reports* of it, because there were many reporters who told different stories, whose accounts are sometimes distorted, gossipy, and founded on misunderstandings. Those reports show Him—in Renan's words— "revoltingly partial" to a certain people. Toynbee has recently pointed out[6] that it is not incompatible with the historian's point of view to suppose that God has revealed Himself to man, but the historian will be suspicious of any presentation asserting "that a unique and final revelation has been given by God to *my* people in *my* time on *my* satellite of *my* sun in *my* galaxy." Toynbee cannot find any logically necessary connection between the belief that God reveals Himself to His creatures and the belief that He "has chosen to be the recipient of this revelation one creature that happens to be precisely I myself . . ." Nothing could debar a Jew "from believing, in accordance with the theory of probability, that, if there is any chosen people, it is not Israel, but say the Chinese or . . . the Martians." As one can see, it is the old problem of election that perplexes the historian. Devout people would certainly argue that his doubt is irreverent and that Toynbee seeks to espy the ways of the Lord that are dark.

Some may wonder why Toynbee did not prefer a problem which seems to be intellectually more rewarding and whose mundane character is more accessible to scientific inquiry. How did the Hebrew tribes arrive at the conviction that they are the chosen people? What historical, sociological, and psychological factors were responsible for this national conviction? Questions of this sort can be approached without indiscreet, imprudent, and impudent peeping into Yahweh's secrets.

However, even these questions cannot be solved without an inquiry into the nature of the events which led the Hebrew tribes to the belief that God revealed Himself to them at Mount Sinai. The first goal of our research must be to disentangle and elucidate what happened in the Sinai Peninsula around three thousand or more years ago.

The clarification of this central question would at the same time suggest the way to describe the nature of revelation. The theophany on Mount Sinai is not only one of the earliest, but perhaps the most important of the appearances of God. If those Hebrew nomads had not left Egypt and had not listened to the voice from the Holy Mount, our Western civilization would perhaps not exist, or would exhibit very different characteristics. We would revere another kind of religion and would respect another moral code; we would comprise a different "pattern of culture."

Unreflective believers do not recognize any problem here; they accept the biblical account and see in it God's Truth. There is also no problem here for freethinkers. To them the story of Exodus and Sinai is a fairy tale and nothing else. We should perhaps re-evaluate the scope of their "free" thinking.

2.

The Persons of the Drama

The very historians who seek most conscientiously to report precisely what happens in their own lifetime are often altogether unaware of contemporary events which future generations will consider the most impressive of their age. No Roman historian detected the significance of the crucifixion of a certain rabbi who was killed in the same manner as many thousands of others under the government of Tiberius in one of the least important Roman provinces. No Egyptian inscription reports that some despised Hebrew tribes left a border country of Pharaoh's world empire. Who cared about the wandering off of one of those barbaric nomads whom the Egyptians held in contempt? There is no contemporary evidence or proof of that migration, no testimony except the Old Testament. It was a world-shaking event of which the established world recorded no remembrance.

The great religions of our Western civilization, Judaism, Christianity, and Islam, trace their birth back to the chain of those events. Yet no one can say precisely what they were, or when and where they occurred. We know that something happened in that interval between the Exodus of some Hebrew clans from Egypt and their entrance into Canaan, something of such significance and momentum that a new phase of world history has to be dated from that point forward.

The explorer who wishes to find the character of those events has to decide what would be the best approach to the core of the problem. After he has executed his initial research, he will ask himself what is the best way to present the material at his disposal and the conclusions at which he has arrived. The form of this presentation is not only a question of architecture, not only a problem of form or style. Every thinker who is a writer will understand that there is the most intimate connection between the subject matter and its mode of presentation. "One's end," as the poet says, "is in one's beginning."

7

But is the point of departure not already determined? Yahweh revealed Himself to the Hebrews and gave them the Ten Commandments. A new God appeared. A new religion was founded and a new nation was born. Most historians preceding us in their inquiry have begun by putting questions concerning the identity and nature of the God who revealed Himself to Moses and the Children of Israel.

To my way of thinking, the problem of identification of Yahweh is not the most promising approach. My reason for taking this stand is perhaps best expressed through a comparison foreshadowed in the introductory remarks to the present book. The Exodus and the events at the Sinai Peninsula are certainly of a dramatic nature. The scriptural account sometimes even exhibits a *theatrical* character. It is not accidental that the Old Testament report has been used by so many playwrights as raw material.

It will not seem arbitrary, therefore, if the chapters of our own essay appear to be steps in the investigation of the structure and development of a play. We thus begin by supposing that our theme is a play not unique in its subject matter, although surely without parallel in its outcome, the revelation and the events surrounding it. On first view, the leading character doubtless seems to be Yahweh, but we encounter our first difficulty the moment we ask: What is Yahweh's role in the plot? The Hebrews are oppressed by the Pharaoh; Yahweh frees them from the tyrant. Moses has killed an Egyptian and flees to Midian; Yahweh appears to him and orders him to return to Egypt. After having saved them from the persecuting Egyptians, Yahweh reveals Himself to the people and promises them the conquest of Canaan.

Here are certainly highly dramatic events. There are conflicts between the Egyptians and the Hebrews, between Aaron and Moses, between the Hebrew people who revolt against their leader. But what is the part of Yahweh? He appears whenever the plot seems hopelessly involved, clears all difficulties, and saves the people and their leader. He is a "God out of the machine." His appearance in all kind of emergencies, at the court of the Pharaoh, in the desert, and in Canaan, would impress modern audiences as did the theatrical trick of Euripides when he introduced some divinity, borne down from above, to bring the situation to a satisfactory dénouement. No, Yahweh cannot appear as the protagonist of the drama. He can, at best—unseen—speak the curtain line.

Even in the biblical report, Yahweh is not always conceived as the Lord of Heaven and Earth. He is not imaginable as inactive, as a

God in repose and retirement ("a leisurely God"). When we first encounter Him in Genesis, He is extremely absorbed in creating the universe. He appears to rest only at that moment of truly superhuman modesty when He looks at His Creation and sees that it is good. His history from then on, told in the autobiographical Holy Scripture, shows Him in unceasing activity. If it is not the world situation at large, it is His chosen people who keep Him busy. Yet we only *hear* of His activities. *He is never seen acting.*

There are other arguments discouraging the inquirer from starting his exploration with the characterization of the God who revealed himself to the Hebrews. It appears at first blush easy to differentiate this God from the others. There are Zeus and Ra, Marduk and Osiris, Attis and Adonis—each with various attributes, each different from the other. There are the gods of the Phoenicians and the Baalim of the Canaanites—each of them conceived as creators of the universe at one time or another. As skeptics have remarked, it has taken all sorts of gods to make the world.

More careful investigation proves, however, that Yahweh—whatever and whoever he became later on—was not very different from the gods of other nomadic tribes when He first entered the life of the Hebrews in His appearance in the world scene. He was crude and very earthy. He resembled in many respects the gods of other people of the ancient Near East. The only distinctive feature was perhaps His Semitic countenance. He has always kept that, to the eternal dismay of the enemies of the Jews.

It is, however, absurd to assume that "Yahweh" has remained the same over the past four thousand years. Granted that He is eternal, must we suppose that He is eternally the same, that He was as He is? But did He appear to the Hebrews at Canaan in the same form as He does to their more recent descendants in a fashionable synagogue of a great metropolis? A child and the old man who once had been this child are the same person. They retain their identity, but no one will seriously assert that their appearance is unchanged.

Gods were in general not as personalized and individualized four thousand years ago as they are today. Individuality is the result of a highly advanced civilization; this is also true where the individuality of the gods is concerned. The gods of a primitive tribe resemble each other as do the members of a group. The individualization and differentiation of the gods are slow to evolve. If there had not been many similarities between the deities of different nations, we would not understand how it was possible that the ancient world had such a widespread syncretism. There was little difficulty in seeing in the deities of another group a double of one's own god. The prophets of Israel had great trouble in preventing the Hebrews from confusing Yahweh with the Baalim of the neighboring tribes. The early Christian fathers desperately, but often vainly, protested against Greeks and Romans who recognized in Jesus Christ a replica of the young gods in their pantheons who died and were reborn. The features of the national gods and their cults had so much in common that they could occasionally be conceived as "substitutes" for each other.

It does not, therefore, seem promising to approach the problem of the Sinai revelation by way of a discussion of the Hebrew God in His primitive shape. But it is even more difficult to start the exploration with the introduction of Yahweh as He appeared to the Jews later on in His supreme and sublime aspect. He is now invisible and ineffable. His name cannot be uttered. He is unapproachable and unknowable. What can be said or stated about a God whose nature is that nothing can be known about Him? In the old days that were by no means good days, He dwelled on the peak of Mount Sinai or at Mount Horeb. But by and by He rose higher and higher. The sky is not the limit any longer. "The Heaven is my throne and the Earth my footstool."

No, Yahweh's nature does not contribute the most fruitful point of departure for our inquiry into the events at Sinai. To return to our comparison: His appearance, on that peak, though very impressive, would not be satisfactory within a play. It would only escape seeming incongruous in a motion-picture—more literally, in a Hollywood spectacle. Yahweh's revelations would, taken by themselves, strike us as a marvelous feat but not as the unique miracle of the millennia.

In brief: Yahweh is not only almighty, He is also "all-invisible." He appears, but He does not show Himself. He reveals Himself, but He cannot be seen. There is no divine apparition: no memory remains with the audience. A man surveying the world theatre of history, the dramatic story of man, in his imagination cannot re-create the appearance of the Lord in an image. Who is the dramatist who knows how to present the Lord as the play's protagonist?

3.

Moses as Protagonist

The comparison of the revelation with a drama should not be offensive to the believers. Does the Bard not say: "All the world's a stage and all the men and women merely players," leaving us to wonder who is the playwright? Jean-Louis Balzac (1597–1654), who was almost a contemporary of Shakespeare, wrote that God is the author of the spectacle and men are only His actors: "The great dramas played upon this earth are composed in Heaven."[1]

If then we continue to look at the Sinai account as the possible plot of a play we soon resolve our doubt about who has the leading part. It is Moses, a figure of such monumental greatness that Mount Sinai appears in Heinrich Heine's eyes "puny" compared with him.

A poignant insight into the effect of Moses upon the imagination is found in Arnold Schönberg's opera, *Moses and Aaron*, which was performed for the first time during the last festival weeks in the Zurich Stadtheater on June 6, 1957. Absorbed by this work for twenty years, Schönberg died before he finished the last act. Everyone who knows his work—including those who cannot enjoy his music—will recognize that it was the result of a powerful and profound brooding over the biblical story. The composer, who was his own librettist, brings Aaron into contrast and conflict with Moses, whom he presents as the older brother. Aaron, more extroverted and articulate than Moses, is convinced that he is justified in giving his people, whom he loves, the image of the Golden Calf as their god. When Moses remains too long on the mountain, the people become restive, begin to grumble and ask for a god: "What you require are gods of a present, everyday sort!" While Aaron wants to express the idea of God by an understandable image, Moses demands unconditional surrender to the almighty invisible deity. Aaron is convinced that the

11

people will not believe in a god they cannot see. "The Burning Bush and the Tablets are images too," Aaron says. At the end of the second act Moses remains alone, in despair. The prophet of Yahweh is disappointed. "Thou unimaginable God," he says, "unnamable, perplexing God! Do you allow this interpretation? . . . Thus everything I thought was insane and cannot and ought not to be said . . . ?"

Schönberg did not live to complete the third act. At his death, the score remained unfinished on his desk, but sentences written in his handwriting show that he imagined that Moses, although defeated, would triumph at the end. The Elders forewarn the people: "Whenever you leave the wilderness of the desert and when your capabilities have led you to the heights, you shall always be thrown back again from misuse of success into the desert. But in the desert you shall be invincible and there you shall achieve your destiny: union with God." Here is an echo of the voice of the prophets who saw Israel's salvation in the flight from urban civilization to the tents of the nomads.

In this grandiose and inspired vision of the conflict between the two brothers, Schönberg presented the clash between the idol which the crowd needs to worship and the pure idea of deity—the collision between corporeality and spirituality. The heart of the struggle is personified in the opposition between Aaron and Moses. Aaron knows that for the people seeing is believing. Moses hopes that his people, listening to the message coming first from outside and then from within, will believe in the imageless God. In the view of the self-willed and profound composer, the great deed of Moses is not the creation of pure monotheism, but that of the invisible God.

At this point one inevitably recalls the leading idea of Freud's book, *Moses and Monotheism*,[2] to which we have already referred in our introductory pages. Freud was convinced that Moses was an Egyptian of noble lineage, an admirer and follower of the Pharaoh Ikhnaton, whom history has called the first monotheist because he proclaimed the worship of one god only, whose symbol was the sun and whose name was Aton. Ikhnaton tried to remove the cult of all other gods and demanded a high ethical standard from the followers of one god. After Ikhnaton's death a general reaction against his religious reform set in. Moses, Freud imagines, disappointed by the rejection of the high and pure religion of the Pharaoh, chose the Israelites of Goshen as people who would adopt the ideal of monotheism. Freud's theory of Moses' allegiance to Ikhnaton's belief would find a confirmation if newer excavations would unambiguously point to the possibility that a group of Ikhnaton's followers lived at the time of Moses around Mount Sinai where they rigidly and intolerantly continued the cult of Aton.

Many scholars energetically deny that pure monotheism as we now understand it was possible at the time of Moses. They insist that this form of belief is the result of the work of the prophets, many centuries removed from the Mosaic age. Even then, it was a faith often resisted and deserted by the Israelites living in Canaan.

It is furthermore very doubtful that Ikhnaton's creed was what we would call monotheism. What can be conceived as a tendency toward it or an initial phase of a monotheistic idea, henotheism, is to be understood as a phase of the religious development that was general in Western Asia between 1500 and 1200 B.C. As W. F. Albright has emphasized[3] there was a decided movement in that direction favored by the intermingling of different civilizations and facilitated by their communications. Various gods could stand in place of each other—especially when they had similar functions. To paraphrase Coleridge's words concerning the Ancient Mariner, syncretism of this kind "passes, like night, from land to land" and "has strange power over speech." The great empires of the Egyptians, of the Greeks and Romans, favored the universality of one god to whom other local deities were subordinated or with whom they were easily merged. Yahweh was, at the time of Moses, the God of Israel and they were His people as Marduk was the God of the Babylonians. The religion of the early Israelites was henotheism, not monotheism. The famous credo, "Hear, O Israel, the Lord, our God is one God," originates in a later phase.

The significance of Moses' liberating deed and religious innovation cannot be in the foundation of monotheism as Freud conceived it. The idea to which Schönberg gave an artistic shape, namely, the concept of an *invisible* god, of an *imageless* divinity, comes certainly nearer to the character of Moses' religious revolution. A later chapter in this book will be reserved for a consideration of the incalculable influence of Moses' achievement on the cultural evolution of mankind.

Who was Moses? The biblical story tells of Moses' birth, of his abandonment on the Nile river, and of his adoption by the royal family. Also a few ancient writers tell the story of Moses. Philo of Alexandria, who lived about the time of Jesus—Philo was born about 20–10 B.C.—asserts that Moses received at the Egyptian court all the attention "due to a king" and was considered as a successor to the throne and regularly called the "young king."[4] The Jewish historian, Flavius Josephus (A.D. 37–100), whose *Antiquities*[5] were based on Hebrew records, also considered Moses as heir to the throne of Egypt. This author of the first century of the Christian era declares that Moses was a general commanding the Egyptian armies which defeated Ethiopia. Moses is reported to have taken an Ethiopian wife at the end of the campaign. This tale would be in accordance with the biblical story in which Miriam and Aaron complain against Moses "because of the Cushite [Ethiopian] woman whom he had married" (Num. 12:1). Also the early fathers of the church, for instance Eusebius of Caesarea (who died about A.D. 340) who quotes ancient authors, assert that Moses commanded an Egyptian army which was victorious over the Ethiopians.[6]

4.

The Birth of a Hero

The famous Orientalist, James Henry Breasted, tells us that in all his wandering through the ancient lands of the Near East he never failed to be impressed by the outstanding fact that the monuments now surviving have been primarily expression of man's power. Entering one of the lonely valleys of Sinai, one is suddenly confronted by the tall figure of an Egyptian Pharaoh carved in relief upon the face of the rock wall. This monument has been standing there since the thirty-fourth century before the Saviour's birth. The Pharaoh is portrayed with uplifted weapon with which he is about to crush the skull of an Asiatic captive who is upon his knees before him. This monument is, according to Breasted, "a declaration of possession by right of conquest, serving imperious notice on the Asiatics that the king of Egypt had crossed from Africa into Asia and had taken possession of the surrounding copper and turquoise mines."[1]

Moses, "the man of granite," as he was called, gives the same impression of power and brutal force. His figure seems to be chiseled from a rock as though it were one of the colossal statues of a Pharaoh.

Freud's hypotheses have met vigorous contradiction. The arguments against them have sometimes been more emotional than is usual in the treatment of even the most controversial biblical subjects. A few instances of the opinions will suffice: The outstanding archaeologist, William Foxwell Albright, thinks that Freud's book is "totally devoid of serious historical method."[2] The psychoanalyst, A. Fodor, does not consider Freud's conclusions conclusive and sees Moses as a Hebrew who made himself the leader of "his desperate people."[3] The noted philosopher and scholar, Morris R. Cohen, felt that Freud's deductions are "far fetched and fantastic."[4] The student of Jewish faith, Trude Weiss-Rosmarin, expressed the hope that Freud would have the courage "to take the only possible, the only right and the only decent step,"[5] namely, to retract his hypothesis. She sees in Freud's theory a typical expression of Jewish self-hatred.

The present book does not propose to rehearse these arguments nor to offer apologies for Freud. Here it suffices to consider the two main arguments Freud introduces in favor of his conjecture that Moses was an Egyptian. The first is the name of the lawgiver. Moses, in Egyptian, means a child. The name is in general connected with a god. "Amon-mose" means, for instance, "Amon has given a child." Many men of the Levite tribe bear Egyptian names: Phinehas, Hur, Hophmi, Pashur, Putiel, Merari, Assir. Here a confusion has occurred. Freud has concluded too much from a single innocent fact. The bearer of an Egyptian name need not be an Egyptian.

It is very likely that many Hebrew fathers and mothers, dwelling in Egypt, gave their children Egyptian names. This would especially occur in the case of families which had lived long in Egypt. It is to be remembered that some Hebrew tribes lived at least a few centuries in the land of the Pharaohs. Later in their history, the Jews—especially the classes inclined to assimilation—gave their children Greek and Spanish names. Among the Austrian and German Jews of the nineteenth century it became fashionable to give the children Teutonic names. It is amusing to imagine that a historian, three thousand years from now, might publish a hypothesis according to which Freud would be identified as a pure representative of Teutonic civilization because Sigmund is a name which goes back to earliest German sources, or that Einstein might be cited as an exemplar of genuine Aryan culture because Albert or Adalbert is an ancient name to be found in German folklore and borne by many dukes and bishops. Theodor Herzl would, if such arguments were conclusive, have been of Greek descent.

The conclusion that can fairly be drawn from Moses' name is that his parents were assimilated to a certain extent into the civilization in which they lived. If Moses was a Hebrew, perhaps a Levite, his name would, in this context, be the natural result of his milieu and upbringing. It is likely that he reached a respected position within the royal family whether he was adopted by it or not. We know that the Hyksos or Desert Kings who ruled Egypt welcomed the Israelites who were related to them in the Nile delta. It is possible that Moses was elevated to a position similar to that held by Joseph in biblical tradition under the Hyksos regime. (We think that there is some historical truth in the Joseph story in spite of its analogy with an Egyptian tale.) According to Philo, Moses was learned in all the wisdom of the Egyptians. He was mighty in words and deeds (Acts 7:22). Since in ancient Egypt sacred and mundane science was one, we can with great probability assume that Moses was instructed in all wisdom and knowledge offered by the Egyptian priests. Some writers are even of the opinion that he was initiated into the mysteries in which Anubis conducted the candidate "across the threshold of the unseen world, in the presence of terrifying apparitions."[7]

Whatever were the vicissitudes of Moses during his early youth, he was alienated from his people and came back to them on a detour that led him to Midian. It was there that he had the vision of the Burning Bush. His religious conversion was, as in most cases of this kind, preceded by a rejection of the traditional religion. Only a great inner experience, in which he deeply felt the misery of his people, was powerful enough to make him aware of their destiny and to make him decide to share it with them.

The other main argument of Freud rests upon an observation of applied psychoanalysis, namely the interpretation of the typical myth of the Birth of the Hero. The essential features of this myth are the following: The hero is the son of a parent of high station, frequently the son of a king. The father, warned of the child's birth as constituting a threat to him, orders the new-born baby to be killed or placed in a basket and delivered to a river. The babe is saved and suckled by a woman of humble birth. The hero discovers, when he grows up, who his parents are. He takes vengeance on his father and obtains fame and greatness.[8]

This typical myth, which attaches itself to many historical persons, is, so to speak, a collective "family romance"—a fantasy which can be followed from the Babylonian King of Agade (about 2800 B.C.) to Moses, Cyrus, Romulus, Oedipus, and others. The exposure in the basket is a symbolical representation of birth: the stream represents the water at birth. Freud points out that in one essential regard the myth and the exposure of the Moses child shows a significant difference from the others. In contrast with the other myths, the first family which is conceived as royal is that of Jewish Levites. The second family in which the child grows up and which is generally supposed to be a humble one, is here that of the Pharaoh. The princess of Egypt brings Moses up. This divergence from the usual birth myth presents itself to Freud as a fresh argument for his thesis that Moses was a noble Egyptian. The myth tried to transform him into a Jew. Freud does not conceal the fact that this argument is debatable and cannot claim to be called a persuasive proof for his suggestion that Moses was an Egyptian of noble birth. The analytic interpretation in the case of Moses' birth myth has been criticized several times. A. Fodor, for instance, pointed out that the legend could be the result of a "secondary elaboration" which reversed the original tradition.[9]

There is another possibility which to my knowledge has not previously been discussed, namely that the "legend" enshrines some reality or historic truth. This sounds strange, but numerous and reliable records show that many Jewish mothers in Poland, Austria, and Holland who were afraid that their babies would be killed by the Nazis left their children in the care of gentile women who brought them up. John Bartlow Martin and S. I. Schneiderman reported recently the case of a Lithuanian mother who lived in a Jewish ghetto when the Nazis occupied her little town.[10] The Gestapo decreed on June 15, 1942 that all pregnant women in the ghetto must submit to abortion. (The Germans shipped all children of the ghetto—about 630—to the gas chambers at Auschwitz). Mrs. Goetz found herself pregnant shortly afterwards. The delivery was secret and the baby, a few months old, was brought furtively to a gentile woman to whom a Catholic priest gave a false birth certificate. Packed into a suitcase into which holes were bored, the baby was smuggled out of the ghetto during the night. In 1957, fourteen years later, the boy saw his mother for the first time again in Brooklyn. He is now in a New York school where the boys compare him with Moses. Hundreds of similar cases prove that even in our time life is stranger than myth—and greater miracles take place than the redemption of a baby boy in Egypt three thousand years ago.

The leader and lawgiver, young Moses, would certainly be the appropriate protagonist of a play. *But who would be his antagonist?* It could not be the Pharaoh Rameses or Meneptah because that would restrict the drama to the problem of the Exodus ("Let my people go") and place the theophany outside the frame of the drama. The play would have to end with the liberation from Egypt and would not include the revelation on Mount Sinai, the core of the dramatic action. The instance of Schönberg's unfinished composition should caution a playwright against casting Aaron as antagonist to the figure of Moses. The profound text of Schönberg's opera points in the direction of a drama of abstract ideas and sublime concepts. The only possible and appropriate antagonist of Moses in a drama would, therefore, be not Aaron, *but the Jewish people,* who rebel against the new religious concept.

With this insight we arrive at a further decision regarding the steps in our narrative. In order to get new clues to the events of Exodus and Sinai we must now pass on to the stories of the Jewish people in Egypt and in the desert. We want to examine what took place before the Exodus in Egypt and what the wandering in the desert and the revelation on that mountain mean. Is there a secret here? *Is anything concealed behind the revelation?*

To return again to our comparison of Exodus and Sinai with a play: It is vital to know the plot of the play before we think of the characters within it. It is imperative to understand the essential content of the drama. This is more important than the characterization of the individual parts presented by the actors. We hasten, thus, to ascertain the outline of the action. We want to find first what the events were that took place between the Exodus and the entry into Canaan—and especially what happened on and around Mount Sinai. In the words of the young Prince of Denmark: "The play's the thing."

5.

The Forming of the Tradition

The biblical information about the events of the Exodus and at Sinai may be compared to a much-edited anthology of sagas composed at various times by various writers. Different compilers and scribes viewed the traditions handed down to them with different eyes. The sources composing the Pentateuch come, so to speak, from different age groups of the Jewish people and are as far separated from each other as the ninth and fourth centuries B.C.

The result of the work of the various editors and compilators is a narrative that often gives the impression of a cohesive and consequent tale and at other times that of a scatterbrained account in which the essential is mixed with the unimportant. The editors and authors are, it seems, not aware of certain divergencies and contradictions and let them pass unnoticed into the sacred text. This is bad. But when they become aware of them, they often try to harmonize the different sources, and that is worse. The bridges they sometimes build are flimsy and their attempt at rationalization leads occasionally to irrational passages in the text. Yet besides and beyond many changes and modifications, distortions, and elaborations by writers, scribes, and priests, a core of historical tradition is preserved intact. It is sometimes necessary to dig it out from the superimposed deposit of centuries. As a matter of fact it is astonishing how much of the original saga-material has withstood the attempt to change, transform, and rationalize it.

We do not forget that a long oral tradition of tribal history preceded the written text. The characteristics of oral tradition, of stories told around campfires and in tents, have been well presented by professor W. F. Albright in a book in which he follows the development of religious beliefs in the ancient Near East.[1] Historical narratives are usually transmitted orally in the form of poetic sagas, more often

19

told in verses than in prose. The form of those tales plays a great role and has a bearing on the question of historicity of oral tradition especially in the people of Israel who have strong tribal and familial ties. Stories of what befell the Hebrews in Egypt, in the Sinai Peninsula and Canaan were told by word of mouth long before a written tradition developed. It seems to me that Albright's excellent characterization of early verse tradition does not consider an even earlier phase in which the tribal stories were preserved in the form of songs. The song of Deborah is, for instance, perhaps a remnant of this pattern. The archaic traditions of the Semites were song-cycles, accompanied by dances or pantomimes similar to those of the Australian natives. I am inclined to go in this direction beyond the position of Robert H. Pfeiffer who only considers it probable that "considerable portions of the stories of Genesis were sung in verse by minstrels before they were retold in prose. . . ."[2]

The conventional methods of historical and literary criticism of the Bible have stressed the tendencies of later text editors to omit words and sentences that were in conflict with the advanced views of their time. Modern investigators emphasize the tendency of ancient Oriental scribes and compilers to add to rather than to subtract from the text. The result of such trends on the part of the ancient scholars to whom we owe the Pentateuch was a swelling of the text by accretion. Since they did not always try to bring the divergent traditions they found into harmony, some striking variations are to be found.

Everybody now knows that throughout the Pentateuch God is sometimes called "Elohim," sometimes "Yahweh." The alteration of the Lord's names are traced by scholars to two main sources known as J (Jahwist) and E (Elohist). Besides those sources there are others; best known of them are D (Deuteronomic) and P (Priestly). Differences of language and style as well as other peculiarities differentiate the one source from the other. There are several sub-sources, some of which secured material even from outside tradition.

A full discussion of text criticism is beyond the scope of this inquiry. It should only be mentioned that the source J is perhaps closest to folklore tradition and is dated about 850 B.C. or earlier. The source E is considered younger and perhaps dated 750 B.C. An editor combined J and E about 650 B.C. Together with additional material a compilation of J, E, and D was produced during the exile in Babylon. The Priestly Code P was added to the previous parts so that about 400 B.C. the Pentateuch had almost the form known to the modern reader.

We return to the discussion of conspicuous contradictions determined by the composite character of the Pentateuch. We choose one
of the simplest examples and one that concerns the problems of the
Exodus-Sinai narrative with which we are dealing. As the book of
Exodus (6:2–3) reports, the Lord says to Moses: "I am Yahweh:
And I appeared unto Abraham, unto Isaac, and unto Jacob, by the
name of El Shaddai, but by my name Yahweh was not known to
them." It is thus indicated that Yahweh introduces Himself by this
name for the first time. Yet that name had appeared quite often in
the Pentateuch before. We already read in the first chapter of Genesis
that at the time of Adam's sons and grandsons: "Then began men
to call upon the name of Yahweh." Not only that; the Lord said to
Abraham: "I am Yahweh that brought thee out of Ur of the Chaldees' (Gen. 15:7). To Jacob He said: "I am Yahweh, the God of
Abraham thy father, and the God of Isaac" (Gen. 28:13). Since it
would be irreverent to assume that the Lord shows a weakness of
memory, we have to suspect that the discrepancy is due to two different sources without rewriting the copy. The editors of the Pentateuch
saw no necessity to bring the two reports into harmony.

Does this hypothesis explain the contradiction? We rejected the
fantastic possibility of a divine amnesia, but is the problem solved by
the assumption of forgetfulness on the part of an editor or a group
of editors? For psychologists another question emerges at this place:
Why was it forgotten that the Genesis account, which was known to
later editors, mentioned the name of Yahweh? We cannot remain
content with the explanation of the commentators who agree that the
discrepancy becomes comprehensible by the different text of two editors.

Did one group of writers or scribes simply forget that the Lord
used His name in introducing Himself to the Patriarchs, or did they
disavow or deny it? And if so, which tendencies were operating, what
motives or forces destined the disavowal? It seems that there are invisible strings attached to the newly introduced name of the Lord.
We postpone the search for them and the research into their character. For the time being we leave, so to speak, those strings unpulled.

Some of the changes produced by the editors within the text are
obviously influenced by the tendency to adjust the tradition to the
views of their times. Take, for instance, the elaborate discussion of
the Pentateuch about tabernacles, sacrifices, and altars. The prophet
Amos, who lived in the eighth century B.C., reveals, without planning
to do so, that that material cannot belong to the Mosaic period and

must have originated at a much later phase. This means that it is fictitious; that it is fancy, disguised as historical fact. Amos, who was passionately opposed to sacrifice, asked (5:25): "Have ye offered unto me sacrifices and offerings in the wilderness forty years, O house of Israel?" Since there was, of course, no sacrifice in the desert, it is a rhetorical question intended to prove that those regulations about sacrifice were inserted later. It is important that the question invalidates the assumption that those ordinances could belong to the time of the Sinai revelation. The fact that Amos was opposed to sacrifice as part of the worship of Yahweh is important only with regard to the formulation of the question.

We are not sufficiently aware for our present purpose of the manner in which the Pentateuch came into being. We have telescoped the history of the Sacred Book and we know its main sources. Although we clearly recognize the many contradictions and inconsistencies of the text, we have to make an effort to shake off the suggestive power of that familiar prose and to resist its influence.

Such a word of warning has its place before we discuss what is fact and what is fiction in the biblical report of the revelation. Many modern readers of the Exodus-Sinai account, with the exception of the fundamentalists, will assume that here is a conglomerate of historical truths and legends, a mixture of fact and fable. Here are names of places and cities whose ruins have been excavated by archaeologists, and of mountains which appear on any good map and which have been visited by modern travelers. Along with such precise data are narratives of a fantastic character which suggest the atmosphere of fairy tales. Here are minutiae mingled with mirages in such a manner that their separation makes great difficulties for biblical scholars. Similarly, historical events are sometimes fused with legend.

Yet even the most incredible tales occasionally conceal a grain of historic reality. A comparison may best clarify the matter: Imagine that one reads in the New York *Times* that Little Red Riding Hood was chased by a wolf yesterday at three o'clock in the afternoon at 60th Street between Madison and Park Avenues. If one does not think of the connotation of the word "wolf" in American slang and does not assume that Little Red Riding Hood is a nickname for a pretty typist, the report sounds incredible, although the time and place of the event are precisely stated. What would one think if one heard that Cinderella had gotten into an argument at Sak's Fifth Avenue store about the size of her shoes?

Before proceeding with our exploration, we remind ourselves again

of the many transformations to which the original tradition was subjected. When we tentatively accept the conventional chronology dating the Exodus around 1280 B.C., the first attempt to set down in
written form earlier oral reports of those events has to be dated more
than four hundred years later. How many distortions, omissions, and
accretions have changed the original tradition in those four centuries,
we can only guess. We will never know.

6.

The Birth of a Nation

According to biblical tradition, the
people of Israel has its origin in the land between the Tigris and
Euphrates, in Mesopotamia. They appeared on the stage of world
history at a phase when the civilizations of Mesopotamia and Egypt
had a past of more than two thousand years of advanced cultural life.
As a matter of historical fact, the Hebrews appear first in the lime-
light of history when those older civilizations have already begun to
disintegrate slowly.

The patriarchs are to be considered not only as heads of families,
but as leaders of clans or tribes. The first migration of the Israelites
as a group of a greater Hebrew-Aramaic movement into Canaan
probably took place before the middle of the second millennium B.C.
The Habiru, who are mentioned in the cuneiform text of the beginning of the second millennium, also perhaps comprise Hebrew
groups. The Habiru often appear as raiders and rebels against Canaanite and Egyptian authorities. They seem to have been landless mer-
cenaries, day laborers, and servants—a socially and economically
dependent people. Also, from patriarchal times on, the Hebrews were
only accepted or tolerated strangers. They were often compelled to
leave their homes and search for new ones. Jacob, who is called the
lost Aramaean (Deut. 25:5), was compelled to toil for years as a

bonded servant of Laban. Already the first part of Hebrew history is full of complex migrations and extraordinary vicissitudes. From Terah's migration from Ur to Haaran (perhaps around the third quarter of the twentieth century B.C.) to the present, the history of the Jews is an uninterrupted story of migrations. They were wanderers, roaming the earth. They were, and are, strangers everywhere. It is generally assumed that some Hebrew tribes came to Egypt when the Hyksos conquered this country about 1730 B.C. During the two hundred years in which the Hyksos governed Egypt, the new masters who were of northwest Semitic stock and akin to Hebrew groups favored the Israelites. The Hyksos were expelled by the Egyptians under the Pharaoh Amosis I about 1560 B.C. It is probable that some Hebrew tribes also left with them.

The traditional version is that those remaining were later pressed into forced labor by Rameses II, who reigned from 1301 to 1234 B.C. The Israelites were forced to build the treasure cities of Pithom and Rameses, whose locations have been established by archaeologists at modern Quantir in the Nile delta.[1] According to tradition the Exodus took place during the reign of Rameses' successor Meneptah, perhaps about 1230. In the new edition of his book *From the Stone Age to Christianity,*[2] Professor Albright assumes that the Exodus is to be dated about 1280 B.C.

The time of the Exodus can be determined only inferentially and the conclusions which the historians and archaeologists have drawn do not coincide. The data reach from 1445 to 1280 B.C. A little help in fixing the chronology is provided by the stele of Meneptah (1225–1215 B.C.), which boasts of victory over Israel and the destruction of her seed. Eduard Meyer takes the stele as evidence that Meneptah could not have been the Pharaoh of the Exodus.[3] Freud assumes that the Exodus from Egypt falls into the time after the Eighteenth Dynasty, about 1350 B.C. Also other scholars[4] consider this period or a little later very likely, and support the thesis by considerations about the political and religious situation in Egypt and in Palestine. The period of the fourteenth century was a time of an interregnum, ended by Pharaoh Haremhab, who restored order and reigned until 1315 B.C. In this stormy and confused phase of Egyptian history, many Hebrews undoubtedly escaped into Canaan. But are these groups of refugees identical with those led out of Egypt by Moses?

It is difficult to express an opinion in the chronological discussion in which so many scholars take different sides. As far as it is possible to do so, I am inclined to date the Exodus about 1350 B.C. It seems to me possible that there was not one Exodus, but several departures perhaps separated from each other by decades, and that the one to which we give that name is only the last one—or the one to which we attribute the greatest religious and historical significance.

The controversy about the date of the Exodus is related to others whose impact reaches far beyond chronology. If, some centuries before the Exodus, Hebrew groups were safely settled in Canaan, as most modern scholars assert, what was their religious situation and what were their relations with the Canaanites? What was their attitude toward their kin coming from outside? We can conclude from Genesis (38) that the tribe of Judah, a couple of centuries before the time of Moses, was settled in Canaan and many Israelites were married to native women. Those Hebrew groups lived with or near Canaanite communities and doubtlessly adopted many of their ways and views.

In all likelihood the Israelite tribes that had been for perhaps two centuries in Palestine while their brethren were in Egypt, absorbed the Canaanite civilization and became an agricultural people, while the groups in Goshen remained nomads and shepherds. The Hebrews in Palestine began to worship Canaanite gods and goddesses and followed the fertility cults of the country. Several Hebrew names of gods appear as appellations in Canaanite sources. Not only the figures of Baal, Astarte, and Anath were worshipped, but there were also conspicuous parallels between Canaanite and Israelite rituals, as we know from important texts such as the Marseilles Tariff and the inscriptions from Ugarit. Superficially observed, the Israelites in Canaan were safely settled and to a great extent assimilated to the superior Canaanite civilization. They were prosperous and self-confident in contrast to their poor relatives on the Nile delta who had become slaves to the Pharaoh and had led a half-nomadic existence. This had not always been so, and was perhaps not so for all levels of the Hebrew people who had lived in Egypt since the time when the Hyksos reigned. While these Desert Kings ruled Egypt, they were friendly to the Israelite tribesmen on the Nile delta. The story of Joseph, which is to a great extent mythical, reflects at least that Hebrews could reach a high position at the court of the Pharaoh. If we can believe the Pentateuch, all this was changed when a Pharaoh "who knew not Joseph" (Exod. 1:8) became ruler of Egypt. We can guess that this Pharaoh was Amosis I, who expelled the Hyksos about 1560 B.C. Perhaps the change did not come suddenly, and the Hebrews who did not leave with the Hyksos remained for some time peaceful shepherds on the northeast delta. They became serfs and slaves under the successors of that victorious Pharaoh.

But what was the religion and the civilization of those tribes in Egypt? We can imagine that a part of them became assimilated to Egyptian civilization. No doubt Moses was a very educated man and his loyal Levites had perhaps learned much from Egyptian teachers. It is likely that many Hebrews, disappointed and deeply hurt by the change of destiny, turned away from the civilization of the Nile. Yet they could not eradicate in themselves the traces of the culture pattern into which they had been born and bred. I have know German and Austrian refugees from Hitler's Nazi regime who developed a passionate hatred against German civilization and even refused to speak German. Yet they could not disavow or obliterate the deep imprint their German education had made upon their development.

This last comparison awakens the thought that there are at least some analogies between the situation of the Israelites in the Egypt of the Eighteenth or Nineteenth Dynasty and their remote descendents, the Jews in Germany three thousand years later. For two centuries the German Jews had taken an active part in the civilization of the country and many of them had made valuable contributions to it. They had absorbed essential aspects of the German mentality and were to a great extent assimilated. Then they were pressed into servitude and had to do forced labor. Compared with Hitler, Goering, and Goebbels, the Pharaohs of Egypt were, it is true, amateur dictators. The Egyptian sovereigns were less cruel and methodical and did not dispose of thousands of men and women in gas chambers and concentration camps.

The comparison of the Egyptian situation with that in Nazi Germany can be followed up in other ways. Many German Jews escaped in groups from the Nazi terror. In the beginning there was even an organized emigration along with unorganized and hurried flight. Even the homesickness and the longings of the Hebrews for Egypt and her fleshpots during their flight had its parallel in the emotional life of many refugees from Germany. The French used to call them *"les 'chez nous'"* ("at homes") because many Jewish emigrants looked critically at French institutions and compared them unfavorably with those "at home" (*"chez nous"*). Even the biblical tales of pursuit and slaughter of fugitives find their analogies in the records of the Storm troopers and examples of miraculous escapes and fantastic redemptions were told by German and Austrian Jews. In the first years of Nazi persecution some negotiations between the German government and Jewish groups took place in order to accomplish some ransom.

What was the attitude of the Canaanite Hebrews toward their kin coming from outside? Again the comparison with the situation at the outbreak of the Nazi catastrophe occurs to us. The Hebrew tribes, settled in Canaan, had certainly many relatives amongst the groups on the Nile delta and it is very likely that there was a kind of news communication between them. The late Bronze Age in the Near East was a period characterized by a vivid exchange of cultural and material elements and was justifiably called the "First Internationalism" by J. H. Breasted.[5]

The American and British Jews were prosperous, safely settled, and shared the cultural and material life of Gentile communities when the Nazi terror struck Germany. The refugees who succeeded in reaching England, France, and America were penniless, insecure, and badly shaken by the traumatic experiences endured "at home." In spite of the differences in culture and social habits, as well as those of language, the refugees were well received and welcomed. The American and British Jews saw in them brothers in distress and dire need. The solidarity of the Jewish people, dispersed all over the world, but united by the ties and memories of a common past has its precedent in the acceptance of the Hebrew tribes, coming from Egypt. There was perhaps a long process of mutual adaptation, many years of conflicting views and clashing of wills. This lasted some centuries before the Israelites who had worshipped the Baalim, Asherah and Ashtaroth, in Canaan were converted to the religon of Yahweh which was brought to them by the refugees from Egypt. But also the immigrants had to be "depatternized" and had to forget much before they could adjust themselves to the new form of existence and to a new religion. They had already rebelled against Moses in the desert and had been deeply dissatisfied with their lot. They complained: "Wherefore hast thou dealt with us, to carry us forth out of Egypt?" Did they not tell him: "Let us alone that we may serve the Egyptians. For it had been better for us to serve the Egyptians, than we should die in the wilderness"?

Yet there followed a period in which a kind of confederation of Hebrews was created. It was not restricted to the refugees from Egypt, but joined by groups of Canaanite Israelites. There was a covenant near the Mount Garizim in which a code of laws was promulgated.

The picture that now presents itself is very different from that painted by the biblical narrative. At least a century and a half before some Hebrew tribes left Egypt other Israelites had invaded Canaan. Schechem and the hill country were in the hands of Hebrew settlers. What was called Israel, the northern area, was taken by Hebrew groups that had never been in Egypt, while the southern part, later known as Judah, had been gradually subdued by Israelites who had come from Egypt and later on had infiltrated the country. We have to face the fact that the Hebrews of the ancient Near East were already composed of two parts. There was the one that had been in Canaan a long time and had never eaten the bitter bread of slavery in Egypt. Then there was the other that had gone through a long phase of oppression and misery and in whose tradition the liberation from Egypt was commemorated as Yahweh's great deed of deliverance.

The more you penetrate the realm of the Exodus-Sinai tradition, the more clearly you realize that here is a great complex of problems and uncertainties not only concerning date and place, but also the backgrounds of those two Hebrew groups. You encounter elsewhere in the biblical narratives the traces of later elaboration, signs of secondary transformations of an old tradition that had been changed by omissions and accretions. It should not be forgotten that the oral transmission of the events of the Exodus and of the Sinai covenant was put into written form about fifteen centuries later by editors and scribes. It was seen through the eyes of the authors in an age in which the Hebrews had kings and priests and a strictly formalized, institutional religion. All the conscious and unconscious efforts of those late compilers and scribes to change the tradition cannot efface the impression we have that the tribes of Hebrews that arrived in Canaan, and who mixed with other non-Israelite groups, were poor, nomadic Bedouins who had experienced terrible privations and miseries. They were not likely to be really happy for quite a while to come.

The historian has often been called a prophet in reverse. How could he have predicted in his original position that this rabble of illiterate Syrians would found a new religion of high ethical character and give the world a moral code that would be valid for the future civilization of the West? Amongst all the nations of the ancient Near East those poor and miserable refugees from the powerful Egyptian Empire would have seemed the most unlikely to succeed.

7.

Exodus as Genesis

But why is it so important to explore the history of Israel, to date the exact period during which the Hebrew tribes were in Egypt, to determine when the Exodus took place—when and where they entered the Sinai Peninsula and so forth? Such an undertaking is certainly not necessary for the theologian who identifies revelation with the communication of timeless truths. It is only demanded from the historian who inquires into the course of events of the Exodus and on Sinai.

Systematic theology and comparative history of religion are separate fields and should be kept strictly apart. The historian and the psychologist who explore the origin and growth of religion—or rather of religions—have to study the beliefs in God and in His purposes for men as they were conceived at different times. They have to explore their premises and interrelationships. To answer the question of truth of revelation is not their task. They are not required to have an opinion—or to express one—on the claims that faith makes. There is a gulf between science and religious belief, a gulf which can only be crossed by the "leap of faith."

A recent work by H. Wheeler Robinson discusses the relationship of revelation and history in an interesting manner.[1] Defining revelation as the making known of God's will which is to be performed in the particular and concrete situation, Robinson states that God revealed Himself to Israel in a certain series of events which were interpreted to the people by Moses. Their knowledge of God was thus "through the concrete experience of living, rather than by any intellectualistic construction." If God reveals Himself in Israel's history, it is necessary to study this history as well as the history of ideas which the Israelites entertained. Old difficulties are thus removed, but only—as Wheeler Robinson points out—to create new ones. He

gathers them up by saying that "the very phrase" of a "historical
revelation" is a paradox according to conventional ideas of revelation. Robinson goes on, saying that history implies movement of
some kind while revelation implies static and permanent truth. "How
can absolute truth be relative to each series of generations? How can
human transiency express divine eternity? How can free human activity be made to serve fixed divine purpose?" But all these questions
belong to the realm of philosophy and of history. They extend beyond
our scope.

We are more interested in what Wheeler Robinson calls the
"media of revelation." The Lord who discloses Himself to man,
uses as mediation the moral consciousness of man so that His revelations present an inseparable union of the divine and the mundane.
Revelation came to Israel not through a communication of doctrine,
but through the interpretation of historic events. Revelation does not
consist in a series of propositions about God, but in a disclosure of
God Himself as far as the events can disclose Him.[2]

The meaning of history within Judaism, Christianity, and Moham-
medanism is intimately connected with revelation. Within a blessed
circle, revelation is, in a theological sense, a historic event that illu-
minates history. The most crucial event of Hebrew history is the
revelation at Sinai, and this revelation provides meaning to all events
of Hebrew history. In Jewish thought it is through this event that
"we understand what we remember, remember what we have forgotten and appropriate as our own past much that seemed alien to
us."[3] The Sinai event thus makes all other events intelligible.

A well-known scholar has stated: "In Israel, all religion is history." He could have added that all history has its center in Exodus-
Sinai—in that encounter between the Lord and the people He has
chosen. "I am the Lord thy God, which have brought thee out of
the land of Egypt" (Exod. 20:2; Deut. 5:6) is the key formula in
which God reveals His premises. Exodus-Sinai signifies not only the
covenant between Yahweh and the people, but the creation of Israel
as a people. As such it is the central crisis by which the people were
created. Whether the great confederation of Hebrew tribes was made
at Mount Sinai or Mount Garizim, is unessential. It is important that
it is the birthday of the Israelites. The tradition shows that those
events which we call Exodus-Sinai made the Jews the covenant-folk.
Here they started on their road through the world as a "gathered
community." Whoever wants to understand the religion of Israel,
and whoever wants to inquire into the mystery of Jewish destiny and

the particular features of the Jewish character, has to take the Exodus and Sinai as ultimate points of departure.

Israel was born in the Exodus. "When Israel was a child, I loved him and from Egypt I called my son" (Hos. 11:1) says the Lord. As it is impossible for a psychologist to understand a person's character and vicissitudes without exploring his childhood, thus it is unfeasible to comprehend the nature and destiny of the Jewish people without exploring the early phases of their history, of their emergence on the scene, and of their formative years "when Israel was a child." He was, no doubt a problem-child—and remained one when he grew up.

The impact of the historical aspect expands beyond the theological and genetic realm. Without understanding the significance of the Exodus-Sinai as the most important event, the solidarity of the Jews will always remain a puzzle. "The Exodus was basic in the consciousness of Israel," writes J. Coert Rylaarsdam,[4] "for Israel, reality was laid bare in that bit of history." It became the formative and guiding event in Israel's tradition, its central and focal point.

A prominent biblical scholar, Millar Burrows, once declared that chronology is of no moment. His colleague and disciple, H. H. Rowley, who quotes that statement[5] excuses it as made "in an unguarded moment." History cannot be written without an attempt at determination of at least approximate data, of informed guesses or inferential evidence about the phase in which important events or changes took place. It makes a great difference whether the flight of the Hebrew tribes occurred in the fifteenth or thirteenth century. Precise chronology of those events will be highly important to the scholar. But they will also have great meaning to us students who are eager to understand how the great monotheistic religions of the Near East came into being.

Yet the impact of those crucial events reaches beyond the historical interest. It touches the core of Judaism as a religion because every Israelite is called upon to re-enact in his own life the redemptive history of Israel and must experience again the encounter between Israel and Yahweh. Will Herberg has justly pointed out that in the Passover ritual every Jew becomes a contemporary of Moses whom Yahweh is drawing out of Egypt to bring him to the foot of Sinai to receive the law.[6] The Passover service says: "All of this I do because of what God did for me in bringing me forth from Egypt." "For me, not for my ancestors or for someone else but for me in exactly the same way as He did for Moses and the Israelite slaves of the time."[7] It is thus not past history, but the past become alive. It has the character of contemporaneity. The Jew who reads in Scripture (Exod. 19:1): "The same day came they into the wilderness of Sinai" repeats thus the events which occurred there. He should feel that he stands at the foot of Sinai and receives the Torah now, not then. "Why on this day rather than on that day?" asked the rabbis discussing that biblical passage—and answered: "So you may regard as though the Torah were given on this day." Solomon Schechter declares that to the believers "the revelation at Sinai and all that it implies was not a mere reminiscence or tradition, but they rewitnessed it in their own souls so that it became to them a personal experience."[8]

Such intense reliving that changes past time into contemporaneity occurs in many individual lives where persons seem to repeat the same experiences again and again as if they acted and reenacted under a "compulsion repetition." That collective acting-out in Judaism adds only a new riddle to the mystery of Israel. Can we hope to find the key to the riddle? Can we resolve the enigma?

8.

The Setting of the Stage—The Wanderings and the Mountain

We are certainly not alone in comparing the Exodus-Sinai events with a play. In a perceptive foreword to Solomon Goldman's stimulating book, Maurice Samuel remarks that the early story of the Hebrews "may without impropriety be looked at from the artistic side":[1] the preparation of the children of Israel for the unique event, the theophany and the psychological aftermath. We have thus, he says, "a prologue, then a one-act drama which is a monologue by the Divinity and then an epilogue; the one-act drama was the greatest in the history of mankind."

What is the stage? What are the attendant circumstances of the setting of the stage? The stage is the top and the foot of a high mountain. W. Robertson Smith notes that in the history of Jacob's vision the idea is not that Jehovah came to Jacob, but that Jacob was unconsciously guided to the place where there already was a ladder set between heaven and earth and where therefore the godhead was peculiarly accessible.[2]

There are different stairways to Heaven. When Alexandre Davy de la Pailleterie Dumas, Napoleon's brave general, died in 1806, his son Alexandre, who became a famous writer much later, was three years old. He was told that he would not see his father any more because God had taken him away. "Where does God live?" asked the boy. "In Heaven." The child took his father's gun and went upstairs. On the landing he met his mother who, dissolved in tears, came from the room where the body was laid out. "Where are you going?" she asked. "To Heaven." "And what are you going to do in Heaven, my poor child?" "Kill God," said the boy, "because he has killed Papa." *"J'y vais tuer le Bon Dieu qui a tué Papa."*[3]

It was not difficult for the little Alexandre to imagine that he could go to Heaven. The people of the ancient Near East did likewise not doubt that they could approch the gods whom they conceived as living in Heaven. The Babylonians built high towers to reach to Heaven. There are still ruins of such temple towers preserved, for instance at Uru—the Ur of the Chaldees from which Abraham is said to have immigrated to Canaan.

Another way to reach the neighborhood of Heaven was for the people of the ancient Orient to visit the mountain peaks. The worship of high places is especially widespread among the Semites. Christianity has inherited the custom from the Jews. The village church is usually, even today, located on a hill—as if you were there "nearer to thee, my God."

The heights of mountain summits near the sky, often surrounded by remote and mysterious clouds, impress people as the dwellings of the gods or as gods themselves.[4] To the Huichof Indians every hill and rock is a deity and some tribal gods of the Thompson Indians are hills. The Incas worshipped the Hill Huanacauei. Mount Kanchinjunga was considered a god in Tibet. To the ancient Semites, mountains and hills were personified and gods were associated, if not identified, with them. Cybele was the Mountain-Mother. Some Babylonian gods were called "ruler of the mountain" and Enlil, who was one of them, is called "the Great Earth Mountain." Later on mountains were seen as the abode of ghosts and spirits.

Yahweh was commonly worshipped on high places and was supposed to dwell there. Israel as well as the Canaanites offered sacrifice and incense to the Baalim of the hills (Hos. 4:13; Jer. 2:30; Ezek. 2:28; I Kings 3:14, 23, II Kings 16:4, 17:10). In the Old Testament references to the cult of Yahweh on high places are frequent (I Sam. 7:1–17; 19:12, II Sam. 15:32, I Kings 3:4, 18:20, Judg. 6:26, Deut. 27:4). Especially the Mount Sinai was called the mountain of God (Exod. 3:1, 24:13, I Kings 19:8) and perhaps considered as sacred before Israel received the law upon it.

The destination of the Hebrew tribes coming from Egypt was Mount Sinai (or Mount Horeb). It was there that the Lord identified Himself to the Children of Israel. It was there that He gave them the Code and where He and the people made their covenant. It is there, if at all, that we have to search for the solution of the problem of revelation.

As far as I know, none of the biblical scholars has stated that the Exodus-Sinai narrative is purely fictitious and none of the modern theologians has claimed that it presents unadulterated truth. There are transitions and transgressions in both directions. The attempts to present some biblical legends as historical truth did not remove the miraculous. They shifted only its scene to open doors and to the inventiveness of the inquirer. Not long ago, a German scholar tried to prove that the Hebrews walked dry-footed through the Red Sea while the pursuing Egyptians drowned, and that the biblical food of manna was an edible plant.[5] Some theologians have tried to use the fact that there is a Mount Sinai in order to establish the truth of Yahweh's appearance there. This brings us to the place where the great theophany occurred.

But before we discuss the locations, another question has to be settled. How large was the group that was led by Moses from Egypt? It must have been small indeed since the Bible tells us that only two midwives looked after the colony. T. J. Meek thinks with many scholars that all the evidences quite definitely indicate "that there were Hebrews in Palestine—particularly in northern Palestine—during the time when there were Hebrews in Egypt, and that only a comparatively small group ever went to Egypt."[6] Did the "Hebrew people" move from Egypt to the Sinai Peninsula?

The Bible asserts that they did, and the prophets and psalmists refer again and again to that great event of deliverance of their people. But it is very likely that not the Hebrew people, but only a few tribes, were in Egypt and left this country and the oppression to which they were subjected for so long by the Pharaoh. The most likely assumption is that there were only two or three tribes—perhaps only the Levites—that left Egypt and journeyed to Mount Sinai (or Horeb) where they formed a covenant with other Hebrew—and perhaps also non-Hebrew—tribes as well as with God.

But what about the number of the emigrant Hebrews mentioned by the Pentateuch? The six hundred thousand people appearing there are perhaps the result of a misplaced census, possibly that of King David, to whose period they could reasonably belong. The motivations behind such choices of numbers in pre-modern sources need not be discussed here. They have been similar to those to which Abraham Lincoln smilingly alluded. During the Civil War the President was asked what was the number of the enemy of the Confederate Army. He said: "They must be at least one million men, for ten of my generals have reported to me that they have defeated forces of at least one hundred thousand." One may be safe in estimating that not more than six thousand Hebrews left Egypt. A higher number is not likely even if we grant that the Hebrew tribes after the flight from Egypt had been joined by other groups—for instance, by the Kenites.

The topography of the mountain that was considered the abode of Yahweh was less important to the ancient Israelites than it is to the modern theologians. Yahweh may have come down to Mount Seir, Mount Paran, or Mount Sinai. As a matter of geographical fact, it is rather unlikely that He chose that latter mount as the locale of His revelation. The oasis at the Sinai Mountain is such that it could not support a large company. It is perhaps not the Sinai which is meant by the Holy Scripture (which sometimes calls the mountain by the name of Horeb). It is possible that the peak meant was near the northern end of the Gulf of Akaba in the region known as Midian. Some biblical scholars present various reasons for the hypothesis that the covenant and the confederation of Hebrew tribes had their origin neither at Mount Sinai nor at Mount Horeb, but at Shechem which had been an old Semitic center. The scholars have enumerated, moreover, quite a few possible and some impossible locations at which the revelation and the covenant are claimed to have taken place.

T. Erich Peet once called the route of the Exodus a happy playing-field for the amateur.[7] It is still a subject of lively debate among the experts. It seems that the "southern" route across Suez was impossible. Recent finds make it very likely that the route led from Rameses to Pithom and then back to the coast and across the Papyrus Lake (the Hebrew Red Sea) into the Sinai Peninsula. In his recent book, *Rivers in the Desert,*[8] Nelson Glueck, who based his finding on six years of archaeological work in the Negeb, has identified part of the route taken by the Jews in their great Exodus. The question of the route of the Exodus is somewhere connected with its date. The Bible tells us that the Israelites on the march to Canaan asked the King of Edom and Moab to use the "King's Highway"—the best and most frequented route leading to Sinai. This permission was not given and the Hebrews had to take a long detour, the circuitous route around Moab. If we accept the thesis that the Exodus occurred in the thirteenth century, we can easily believe that Edom and Moab, then formidable kingdoms, refused to give permission to cross their countries. Yet some biblical authorities (with whom Freud agreed) assumed that the flight of the Hebrews should be dated at the fourteenth century—a hundred years earlier. It was at this time, as archaeological evidence shows, that Jericho was taken by the Hebrews. The same evidence proves that at this period Edom and Moab did not exist. The area was sparsely populated and the Hebrew tribes would not have encountered any resistance.

It goes beyond the scope of our inquiry to examine the biblical reports about the wanderings of the Hebrew tribes from Mount Sinai until they reached the Jordan, crossed it, and penetrated the Promised Land. It is very likely that this happened at first in the form of raids and sudden attacks by small forces which invaded certain territories and finally seized them. For a long time after the original invasion many Canaanite fortresses remained unsubdued. The primitive Israelites, who were cruel, fierce, and barbarous, felt that they were justified in destroying the cities of the Canaanites and also their inhabitants. Newer careful analyses by Albrecht Alt and his pupils have shown that the role attributed to Joshua by tradition as leader of the Hebrews in the conquest of Judah and Galilee is exaggerated. These scholars deny the historicity of certain Israelite traditions of the conquest. Certainly some of the stories in the book of Joshua handed down as triumphal poems contain legendary material—for instance the account of the battle of Gibeon (Josh. 10). It is likely that this report would have surprised Joshua, the son of Nun, himself. During the First World War Anatole France once maliciously remarked that General Joffre had learned from the Parisian newspapers that he had won a victory on the Marne.[9]

It was a long way from Mount Sinai or Horeb to the Jordan. The peak of that Sacred Mountain is covered with clouds and is veiled with Yahweh's mystery. The Hebrew tribes, led by Moses, fled from the Egyptians to that rock in the southern part of the peninsula. Will Yahweh's mount reveal its secret to our inquiring research? We hope so because mountains, like human beings, cannot keep secrets forever. The old Negro spiritual song says:

> De rock cried out, "No hidin' place,
> Dere's no hidin' place down dere."

9.

Passover and the Redemption of Israel

The crucial event in the redemptive history of Israel, the event re-enacted by every believing Jew, is the Exodus. Here is the entrance into a shaft at whose depths we assume hidden treasures of prehistory are to be discovered. But before we go too far down, it is necessary to recall several notions. Our aim is to find the meaning of the event called "revelation" by theology. In other words, we would like to reconstruct what happened on Mount Sinai, or Mount Horeb, to find out what really occurred and what was later, after centuries of oral tradition, written down as the most important event in Israel's past.

In trying to present the "inside story" of that tradition, we are aware that in this respect, at least, we share one premise with the theologians. We believe, namely, in the historicity of a series of events, however distorted and elaborated by later tradition, which led to a covenant of some Hebrew tribes and to the birth of a nation. Those events formed the foundation of a new religion or of the renewal of an old faith that was certainly different at that time from the spiritual, monotheistic religion of Israel, yet contained the germ from which it evolved. In reconstructing the inside story of the biblical account, we thus admit that there must be a core of historical truth in it—a core which we would like to penetrate. In a certain limited sense we thus confirm the biblical tradition, however much we differ from the details of its account. Tradition, a well-known Orientalist reminds us, "is often incorrect in detail, its chronology is generally poor, it telescopes and duplicates, and its geography is rarely consistent. But in most cases, in which archaeology has permitted a test, the central facts of tradition are found to contain some kernel of truth."[1]

The boundary lines for our inquiry are determined by our objective, which is to discover the concealed quintessence of the revelation. The Exodus of Hebrew tribes from Egypt is the point of departure for our exploration and the theophany and lawgiving marks its end. All that went on before is, so to speak, a prologue, and all that follows it has the character of an epilogue. The prologue is presented in the story of the refusal of the Pharaoh to allow the Israelites to go on a three-day journey into the wilderness to observe a special festival for Yahweh. In this way the Scripture introduces the celebration of the Passover festival, which was certainly a pre-Mosaic tradition and which bears the marks of extreme antiquity. Whoever wants to find what is at the core of the Exodus-Sinai narrative has to establish what the connection is between the Passover festival and the events on the Sacred Mountain. Rare is the scholar who has contributed to our understanding of this ancient tradition.

It is obvious that the Passover in Egypt differed from that of subsequent generations who observed it as a memorial and as a thanksgiving for the deliverance from the Egyptian bondage. Like many of the religious holidays we celebrate today, Passover has absorbed much older and more primitive festivals and was given a new meaning. Apart from the mention in Exodus we find the Passover in the Scripture connected with reaching the Promised Land. From Num. 9:1–4 we would conclude that a year had gone by since the Hebrews emigrated from Egypt. The Israelites kept Passover according to the Lord's commandments on the fourteenth day of the first month even in the wilderness of Sinai. The Israelites held another Passover at Gilgal (Josh. 5: 2–11) after they had crossed the Jordan. This first Passover, or rather the first on Palestinian soil, was preceded by a mass circumcision, because "all the people that were born in the wilderness by the way as they came forth out of Egypt, them they had not circumcised" (Josh. 5:5).

What originally was the reason for, or the character of, the Passover festival? In the biblical tradition it is to provide protection from the Lord who "smote all firstborn in the land of Egypt" (Exod.

12:29). The essential feature of the Passover proper was the sacrificial feast of the paschal lamb. There was an old tradition that the firstlings and first fruits belonged by right to Yahweh (Exod. 13:13, 23: 19, 34: 11–20). Passover is perhaps the most primitive of all religious festivals of the Hebrews and its origin has to be traced back to the time when the ancestors of the Hebrews were nomadic shepherds.[2] The lamb, a male in the first year, was sacrificed by the head of the house. The entire lamb had to be roasted, not boiled as other sacrificial animals were, and had to be eaten in haste so that nothing of it was left. The blood of the animal had to be smeared on the doorposts and lintels of the house.

The Passover traditionally commemorates the last of the Egyptian plagues when the first-born sons of families were smitten except in those houses on which the paschal blood was smeared. The original meaning of the celebration is, of course, much older than the connection with the Exodus events which were secondarily connected with the festival. Already Wellhausen[3] and J. Mueller[4] saw in the Passover sacrifice a survival of an ancient pastoral feast. The traditional details such as the rapid devouring of the animal and the smearing of the doorway with its blood reminds us of the famous Arab Camel-sacrifice described by Nilus, to which W. Robertson Smith alludes.[5]

Passover was an established institution when the Israelites left Egypt. The Bible tells us how it was preserved, not how it began. The Hebrew Passover is undoubtedly in its origin a rite of transition a *"rite de passage"* in the sense of Gennep's characterization, as already the name not visiting = forbear shows.[6] The word *"Pesach"* is explained by the story that Yahweh abstained from crossing the threshold of the houses that were marked by the blood of the sacrificial lamb. That sacrifice was presumably a substitute for the first-born son who was slaughtered by Yahweh in the Egyptian families. Sir James Frazer has shown that there is good reason for regarding the lamb as a redemption for the first-born.[7] Among the Semites of Western Asia the king in a time of national danger sometimes gave his own son to die as a sacrifice for the people. We remember the story of Abraham's sacrifice of Isaac in Gen. 22 where, at the last minute when he is about to slay his son, the Angel of the Lord stays him and a ram is substituted for Isaac as sacrifice.

Recently a different view has been expressed by many scholars. It also starts from the Hebrew name of the festival. "Pesach" can also be traced back to a word meaning "to limp." A limping dance is a

well-attested feature of religious ritual of mourning in Syria and Canaan. In a Babylonian document the word "hopper" or "skipper"
denotes professional mourner. A Canaanite poem of the fourteenth
century B.C. uses the word "hoppings" or "skippings" in the sense of
mourning exercises.[8] Limping in this view has thus the character of
a ritual dance or of a mourning ceremonial.

Ancient Passover, was originally a seasonal festival of the beginning of the year. Now the ancient people of the Near East connect
the cycle of seasons with the idea of the dying and resurrected god.
During certain months the Egyptian Osiris, the Babylonian Tammuz,
the Syrian Adonis, the Phrygian Attis are supposed to vanish or to
have descended into the netherworld. Resurrection (at the first approach of spring) is celebrated with great rejoicing. The death
of the young god was solemnly bewailed as well as his fate. The limping dance, and with it the original Passover, would thus be a part of
that ceremonial mourning.

We can take it for granted that the form of celebration of the
Pesach feast underwent several changes. It has been suggested that
the Passover presents an instance of the transformation of earlier
forms of ritual under the influence of later Yahwism. It was originally a festival of the Hebrew New Year and its ritual resembled
the one practiced in Mesopotamia and Canaan. Those celebrations
as well as that of Israel represent an independent development of a
common central ritual, of which the Tammuz ritual may have been
the earliest form.[9] The transforming influence of later Yahwism
almost succeeded in obliterating the central elements of the dying
and rising god.

The discussion stimulated by different scholars concerning the original meaning of the Pesach festival has not yet led to a definitive
solution. The facts are undeniable, but the evidence cannot be clearly
integrated in a single explanation. Not the facts, but their interde-
pendent meaning is in question. Intensive research remains to be
done before we will be able to see clearly if and when the idea of a
dying and rising god became connected with the Pesach celebration.
At present, one has the impression the idea was chronologically as
well as theologically secondary and did not play a leading role in the
phase of the Exodus and Sinai events.

It can definitely be stated that, according to the biblical tradition,
the Exodus of the Hebrew tribes from Egypt was, in the last analysis,
decided by the Pharaoh's refusal to let them go and to celebrate the
festival of Passover in honor of their God. Every explanation and in-

terpretation of the Exodus-Sinai tradition which neglects this point of departure misses the mark and cannot be accepted as valid. Each interpretation must make us understand that the Passover celebration has to do not only with the Hebrew emigration, but also with the covenant and the confederation of the Israelitic tribes, with the giving of the Law, and with the mass circumcision. Whatever are the origins of the Passover feast, it cannot be accidental that it is in tradition always and intimately linked to the story of the Exodus. William Arthur Heidel, to whom we owe a detailed study of the sacred days and ritual forms in the ancient Near East, considers Passover the heart of the cultus of Israel. He calls the Hebrews "Passover-people" and their national deity a "Passover-god."[10] The same scholar emphatically declares that to consider Passover without regarding the fact that it relates to the deliverance or salvation of Israel is "to omit Hamlet from *Hamlet*."

PART TWO

Revelation as Initiation

10.

Toward a New Beginning: Beyond Higher Criticism and the New Archaeology

Some utterly unexpected discoveries in the field of archaeology within the past decades have led to profound reinterpretations of the history of ancient Israel. Our knowledge of the culture of Southwest Asia has been greatly advanced by the uncovering of the tablets of Mari in Syria, the publication of the new Execration Texts from the nineteenth century B.C., and the discovery of lists of Asiatic slaves in Egypt of the following century.

Higher culture, literature, and religion, we have long known, flowed between Mesopotamia and Egypt, between the empire of the Hittites to the north and the Aegean lands. Canaan was at the crossroads of the interchange of ideas and of material goods. The more our knowledge of the evolution of Mesopotamian and Egyptian civilizations increases, the more we can understand how much of the religious and social development of ancient Israel was influenced by the higher culture of her powerful neighbors. Albright[1] points to Babylonian passages, Hittite hymns, and Egyptian addresses to the god Amun Re in order to prove that the period between 1350 and 1250 B.C. "was ideally suited to give birth to monotheism." Recently discovered data, especially inscriptions discovered in Syria and Palestine, give a better picture of the dependence of the Mosaic law on earlier sources. Law codes dating from the second millennium, such as the Code of Eshmuna and the Sumerian Codes of Lipit-Ishtar and Zur-Ishtar and Zur-Nammu, show the same basic structure as the biblical Book of the Covenant.

Contemporary archaeology has brought about a great change in the study of Hebrew religion. The collation of so much new material reveals the outlines of an original stock of Semitic law and religious concepts of which the early Hebrew civilization presents a special offshoot. The nature of the older sources which underlie many Hebrew religious and social concepts became known to us in a fresh way as a result of the light which archaeology has thrown on the various civilizations of the Near East.

It is very interesting to observe the result to which those new findings of archaeology and of higher criticism of the Pentateuch have led. The first result has been a concerted attack on the concept of the unilateral theory of the evolution of Hebrew religion as it was originally formulated by Julius Wellhausen in his famous book, *Prolegomena zur Geschichte Israels*.[2] Wellhausen and his school, to which every Protestant and Jewish biblical scholar of good standing subscribed in the last decade before the First World War, had defined a coherent scheme of the religious evolution of Israel. Under the strong influence of Hegel, the religion of the Hebrews was conceived as having three sharply distinguished phases: the *animistic* (or polytheistic) phase, the *henotheistic* phase (represented by the prophets), and the *nomistic* or *monotheistic* phase. According to this strictly evolutionary conception, the religion of Israel revealed a gradual unfolding from a primitive naturalism to the lofty heights of an ethical monotheism.

The progress of religion from lowly origins to its peak in Western Europe was believed to have evolved in clear, unbroken lines. In accordance with this often arbitrary and indiscriminate application of an evolutionary concept to history, Hebrew literature was chronologically arranged into early poetry, prophetic writings, and legal codes. The history and religious development from the time "when Israel was a child" (Hos. 11:1) until the time when she reached adulthood, was presented in a clear light. The students of the famous German scholar felt well sheltered—if one may be allowed a pun, *wellhausened*—in this theory; they were rarely in doubt as to which phase every single tradition and every biblical phrase belonged.

In the opinion of contemporary critics, the picture of the development of Israel's religion from the primitive stage through the prophetic movement and on to the monotheism of the post-exilic period is gravely distorted. The history of ancient Israel simply does not lend itself to such a ready-made scheme.

To my way of thinking, the contributions of Wellhausen and of his school are not to be forgotten. Here for the first time an attempt was made to see the history and religion of Israel in the light of the evolution of culture. The justified arguments against some evident inadequacies of that concept do not impair the validity of the basic idea of a gradual development of Hebrew religion. The attack against Wellhausen and his school has recently gone to an extreme and threatens to imperil the bases of established criticism. The revolt against Wellhausen and his school has been directed not only against its literary analysis, but also against its ingenious and often helpful historical reconstructions.

The new materials brought to light especially by archaeological studies clearly show the relation of early Hebrew religion to its environment, the mythology and cult of the ancient Near East. Yet the new findings have also made clear that the Hebrew religion differed decisively from that of neighboring peoples. The characteristics of that religion have had to be newly defined and the extent and peculiarity of the differences have had to be clearly depicted—a task that has not yet been completed. The peculiarity or property of the Hebrew cult and ethics may not be denied, but scholars have not yet succeeded in explaining them in a way at a level of depth we have come to expect from anthropological accounts of the distinctive patterns of particular peoples.

The initial stage of the belief in God has, of course, stood in the center of the new discussions, especially of the Hebrew monotheistic faith. Under the influence of scholars such as Andrew Lang, Archbishop Nathan Söderblom, Father Wilhelm Schmidt, and Gustav Widengren the concept of a high god as deity of the ancestors of the Hebrew has been put into the foreground. An original monotheism in primitive religion appears to many Scandinavian scholars, especially to those of the University of Uppsala, as an ultimate fact and point of departure from which the later religious development can be understood.

We cannot here elaborate the specific evidences of this theory nor the controversy to which it has led. We must restrict ourselves to the question of how to characterize the work of Moses in his religious renovation and how to understand the essential character of the Exodus-Sinai events in the light of the new materials. According to a representative scholar associated with the Uppsala University, I. Engnell,[3] Yahweh presents one form of the high god, who was certainly otiose, but was activated by the work of Moses. This religion is founded on primitive monotheism. W. F. Albright also rejects the concept of a straight-line evolutionary development in Wellhausen's sense, yet maintains that the chief god of the early Hebrews was a mountain god while the God of the revelation was a creator God, unrelated to any other deity. H. H. Rowley sees in the Mosaic religion an incipient monotheism.[4]

The core of the question is not the origin of the idea of monotheism, but the distinctive character of the Mosaic religion. The problem of monotheism has became a subject of controversy that threatens to obscure the central issues. G. W. Anderson has rightly reminded scholars that the debate approaches the character of a mere logomachy and that the label matters less than the content of the packet.[5]

Indeed, the search for the special characteristics (*Eigenart*) of the early Hebrew religion assumes added urgency now that so many notable scholars have questioned the simple structure of Wellhausen's concept of linear evolution. Those scholars who assume that there was an original high god, a sole deity from whom, much later, the polytheistic pantheons arose, have not been able to define that distinctive character of the Mosaic religion.

One is, therefore, obliged to conclude that the sensational archaeological finds of recent years have enriched but not fundamentally altered our insight into the specific character of the Hebrew people and their religion. The archaeological material as well as the progress in the field of higher criticism have made us understand much better how much of the tradition connects the ancient Hebrew tribes, their customs, religion, and morals with other people of the ancient Orient, especially with the Canaanite civilization. Israel's life and thought now seems, in the opinion of some scholars, so intimately associated with the Baalim-cult of Canaan that there is often a difficulty in differentiating Yahwism from it.

In addition to the new archaeology, we must take note of innovations in interpretation of older sources. Improvements in the methods of literary analysis have revealed traces of oral sources which hitherto went unnoticed. S. Mowinckel's studies of the Psalms,[6] the researches of S. H. Hooke[7] and others have emphasized the fact that behind the rituals of the Hebrews a pattern becomes recognizable whose elements are common to the most important cults of Egypt and Babylon. But when all is said about the resemblances between the Babylonian, Egyptian, and especially Canaanite religion and that of ancient Israel, and when all is done to refute the view that the Hebrew concept is, so to speak, born from nothing, the question of the distinctive characteristic of the Old Testament remains unanswered.

G. W. Anderson has recently pointed out that at no time was it harder to describe and assess the contemporary position in the study

of Hebrew religion than now.[8] A large measure of agreement will
not be found today among scholars, comparable to the earlier synthesis of literary and historical reconstruction. It is, indeed, apparent
to all today that Hebrew religion cannot be conceived in terms of
symmetrical patterns of a simple development. As George Ernst has
insisted, the idea of progress had taken such a powerful hold upon
the minds of the scholars of the last two generations that it was
almost impossible for them to think of biblical faith in any other
than in developmental terms. The way to a fresh reconstruction is
thorny.

A number of modern scholars insist that the central elements of
biblical faith are unique; that they cannot have developed by any
natural evolutionary process from the pagan world in which they
appeared. They cannot therefore be explained by environmental or
geographical conditioning. According to E. Wright, who is a noted
representative of those scholars, the faith of Israel in its earliest and
basic form is so utterly different from that of the contemporary polytheism that one cannot explain it by evolutionary categories.[9] It is
no longer possible to see in the Hebrew tradition the record of a
gradual evolution, of "a development from seed to plant, to fruit,
or from babe to youth, to full-grown maturity. . . . The question
that the study of environment and development was unable to answer is: What is the Israelite mutation which made the particular and
peculiar evolution possible?"[10] Even Wellhausen, the great nineteenth-
century protagonist of the evolutionary theory in biblical study, used
to admit: "Why Chemosh of Moab never became the God of righteousness and the Creator of heaven and earth, is a question to which
one can give no satisfactory answer."

The accumulation of a vast number of facts and information have
proved that the Hebrews are greatly indebted to other peoples. The
uniqueness of their contribution consisted in the way and extent to
which they enriched this legacy. W. F. Albright, W. Eichrodt, E.
Wright and many other scholars are correct in observing that the
source of the difficulty lies in the inability of the developmental
hypothesis to take the story of the revelation and of the covenant at
Mount Sinai seriously. No fixed starting point for the unfolding of
Israel's religion was thus provided.

The religion of Israel appears in history with a startling sudden-
ness and seems to be a new creation. There is no doubt that the
fundamental elements of Israel's religion were established early in
her history, "which means that we are led to Sinai and to the work of

Moses."[11] These distinctive elements are the primary data of the Old Testament and point to something in early Israel which predisposed and predetermined the course of biblical history.

The arguments brought forward against the straight-line and streamlined evolutionary hypothesis are true enough. However, the critics themselves have been unable to provide a satisfactory thesis in the place of the one they have so effectively criticized. What was the mysterious "something"? What were those "distinctive elements" which made the uniqueness of Israel possible?

With good reason, almost all modern experts of history have pointed to the Exodus-Sinai events as the central or focal point in Israelite history and religion. We will not pretend to achieve a reconstruction of the past "as it actually was," in Ranke's famous phrase, *"wie es eigentlich gewesen."* The oral and written traditions have changed so often and become so distorted in the course of events that modern study remains unable to reconstruct the events despite the profusion of new data and hypotheses. A new approach to the unsolved problem and a new interpretation continue to be needed.

The following chapters present a new attempt at penetration of the core of the Exodus-Sinai tradition. In undertaking this venture this writer, as the introductory remarks indicate, returns to problems that preoccupied him almost forty-five years ago. In this late regression to the interests of the young man, the inner truth of the line with which the aged Goethe prefaced the collection of his poems in 1815 is confirmed: "Late resounds what early sounded."

11.

The Meanings of Initiation

As we have said again and again in the preceding pages, the mystery of the revelation on Mount Sinai remains unsolved by historical science. The archaeological and philological discoveries of the last decade have not established what happened on that mountain. Little light has been cast on those mysterious events by the science of comparative religion and by psychology whose efforts are directed to the exploration of the phenomena of religious evolution. It is as though we had here a unique event that does not allow any rational explanation or interpretation. Spade and pen are yet unable to make those events transparent. The main reason why the problem is not accessible is that there is scarcely any historical material that can serve as object of comparison. Science can be very efficient if it succeeds in tracing the uncomprehended or surprising back to modifications or transformations of well-known familiar elements.

While I am writing this, my glance lights on the picture hanging on the wall across from my desk. It is a reproduction of Ingres' "Oedipus and the Sphinx" whose original is to be found in the Louvre. The image of the sphinx is composed of a body—part lion and part woman. The parts of the figure can easily be recognized and that allows an approach to its identification and interpretation. Other mythological figures of the Egyptian or Indian civilization are more difficult to identify, but scholars almost always succeeded in this task with the help of comparative material. Where such is lacking, for instance in the deciphering of unknown ancient writing, research is sometimes arrested for many years.

Where do we find a phenomenon in the history of religion like the revelation on Mount Sinai? There are, of course, many cases of revelation, of self-disclosure of the deity in monotheistic and polytheistic civilizations. We encounter them in the form of appearances and miracles, inspirations of prophets and religious heroes who gave testimony to the words, visions, and signs of the god who spoke to them. There are many cases of theophany in which the deity appeared to saints and sinners; among them quite a few—like those of Zoroaster and Mohammed—which were destined to become the cornerstone of a new religion. But those cases concern apparitions and voices perceived by individuals, called by the god. At Sinai the Lord appeared and spoke to a whole people and made a covenant with them, gave them the Law and instructed them as to how they should live. Those events at the Sacred Mountain did not only introduce a new religion and new morals, but also marked the birth of a new nation. A modern writer puts the point with extraordinary force: "If there is any special character in the account of Israel's emergence into nationhood, if it is of a totally different species from the accounts of the births of other people—it is because of the auspices under which the emergence came about. We are dealing for the first and only time with a purposive or programmatic creation of people-hood."[1] The same is true with regard to the emergence of a new religion and of the purpose and significance of the moral code revealed at Sinai. There is nothing comparable in the realm of ancient religions. The Orientalists, eager to find similar experiences in the Near East of antiquity, have had to admit that here is a unique phenomenon. Must we abandon the field to fundamentalist theologians who equate the literal acceptance of the biblical account with proper faith in God?

The author will not pretend that he can untangle the many religious, historical, and sociological puzzles that have baffled the sagacity and the patience of biblical scholars for so many years. His knowledge is too fragmentary and his lack of scientific training in specialized fields of philological and archaeological research too evident to allow him to carry the attempts at explanation beyond a certain point. Yet it is the author's conviction that the novel hypothesis he proposes goes a long way towards uncovering the hitherto concealed significance of the events described in the biblical Exodus-Sinai narrative. I would be satisfied if this essay should be felt to succeed in ranging the Sinai revelation among phenomena familar to us through other sources. If this objective be approximated, we cannot be far from an explanation and interpretation of those puzzling phenomena and from an understanding of their significance in the evolution of our civilization.

It is only fair to the reader to anticipate the essential results of the inquiry that follows in the form of short statements:

1. The Biblical account of the revelation is a distorted and modified report of a prehistoric great initiation or puberty festival of some Hebrew tribes. This account is fused with a tale of the Exodus from Egypt.

2. The biblical narrative is the central part of the national history whose quintessence is the description of a puberty ritual with the following features: seclusion of the young people, their introduction into the tribal customs and beliefs, the appearance of the tribal god who terrifies them, their alleged death and resurrection preceded by circumcision and followed by incursion into Canaan.

3. The great innovation which was introduced by Moses and the Hebrew leaders is in its essential character a regression to a primitive belief that had long been relinquished in favor of Egyptian and Canaanite religious cults and customs. The new cult of Yahweh is a

return to the faith of the forefathers. It is at the same time an energetic rejection of the cults and religious concepts of the nations in whose midst the Hebrew tribes had lived—cults which, before the Exodus, had been to a great extent accepted.

The striking character of these assertions must, at first, make a bewildering impression. The lonely road I have been following may seem to lead nowhere; or better still, to lead from the wilderness in the Sinai Peninsula to another in Central Australia. Is it scientifically permissible to offer as evidence for the comparison we are attempting the reports of anthropologists, ethnologists, and missionaries concerning the aborigines of Australia?

The arguments against the procedures I shall adopt are sometimes so vehement that we had better grant them a hearing before venturing too far on the road. Some of the criticisms are of a religious nature and reject such comparisons on principle. The revelation that disclosed His name and will to the faithful may not, to a believer, be compared with the ritual of the most backward and miserable savages. The divine voice proclaiming statements of eternal validity and value appear to be an infinity removed from the raucous and rancorous articulations of Australian totemistic monsters. It is easy enough to counter this argument—even from a theological point of view. Theology does not deny that the revelation was given to man in different ways and languages, appropriate to the phase of his cultural evolution. It would certainly be nonsensical to give a lecture on subtle ethical questions to a child of kindergarten age or to discuss abstract problems of morality with a boy in grammar school. The Lord chose to speak with His worshippers in a language they could understand. The outstanding Catholic anthropologist, Father Wilhelm Schmidt, in the many volumes of his work *Der Ursprung der Gottesidee,*[2] collected a vast body of pertinent data and tried to demonstrate that among savage people all-powerful, high gods are worshipped and that these supreme beings are remnants of a primitive monotheism. He and his students, among whom R. Pettazzoni and N. Söderblom published many contributions to his theoretical system, speak even of a primitive revelation which evolved into various patterns found in savage and semi-cultured tribes.[3]

If we have thus offered an answer to an important argument, which rarely fails to be raised from the theological side, we still have to face a possible objection to our method in the name of scientific principles. Scholars consider it, of course, necessary to compare the Hebrew religion and social organization with the civilizations of the ancient

Near East, especially with the Babylonian, Egyptian, and Canaanite culture patterns. Many features of the Hebrew tradition have been traced back to a common stock of early Semitic sagas, and it has been shown that many rituals and religious concepts have their origin in the prehistoric heritage of the Mediterranean people and their neighbors. But what ground is there to expect to find comparable material in the life and customs of savages in a very distant continent and in the customs and ideas of Australian aborigines who are neither physically nor psychologically akin to the ancient Israelites? The argument is, indeed, cogent, but we do not intend to claim historical connections between the Hebrews of the Mosaic age and those black men of the Australian continent. We want only to point out certain likenesses between the features of the revelation tradition and the characteristic traits of the puberty rites of those aborigines. We do not intend to claim that people so remote from each other have identical or parallel religious structures, but to refer to similarities that have their psychological and sociological premises in a certain phase of religious and tribal development. If my presupposition that the revelation tradition is an often-modified account of puberty or initial rituals of Israelite tribes be correct, it is to be expected that such a likeness would be found because the puberty rites of all people have certain features in common in spite of great differences of civilization. We want to deal with those features and, only with those features, which lend themselves to comparison.[4]

The Australian tribes about whose customs and rites we have reliable information through the work of anthropologists and missionaries are, of course, on a much lower stage of civilization than the Hebrews of the fourteenth or thirteenth century before Christ. Some of those tribes in Australia and New Guinea do not build houses or cultivate the soil; many do not even know the art of pottery. They keep no domesticated animals except the dog.[5] The Hebrews of the late Bronze Age in which we have to date the Exodus and the revelation were nomads or half-nomads who had seen better days. We have to conclude that under the regime of the Hyksos who were of Semitic stock, some Hebrews had even attained official positions at the court of the Pharaohs. The Hyksos were defeated and their capital Avaris (later called Tanis) captured by Amosis I about 1560 B.C. The Hebrew tribes who lived in the northwest delta of the Nile were oppressed after the expulsion of the Hyksos, and had to work as slaves in the immense building projects of the Egyptian kings. They lived in the late Bronze and early Iron Age, which means they had progressed considerably in their evolution as compared with the Australian aborigines who are still living in a Stone Age phase. Even the early ancestors of the Hebrew tribes, the contemporaries of Hammurabi, Abraham, and the Patriarchs, were witnesses of the high Mesopotamian culture which must have affected them. They were shepherds, had domesticated animals like goats, lambs, and asses; they lived in tents and were in their customs and organization close to Arabian nomads. We know little about their religions and their rites, but it is likely that they were also in this direction akin to the Canaanites and Amorites. The Israelites themselves asserted that they descended from a fugitive Aramaean (Deut. 26:5), but there is the possibility that they were more akin to North and South Arabian tribes. At all events, at the time of the Exodus a great part of the Hebrews had been very remote from the evolutionary phase of their early ancestors for a long time. They had adopted many of the religious concepts and mores of the Egyptians while other tribes camping in Canaan had been assimilated to the worship of the Baalim and shared the fertility cult of the agricultural Canaanites.

The thesis of this book is that the religious reform introduced by Moses and reaching its climax in the Sinai revelation, signifies a turning away from this trend and presents a return to the primitive phase of religious evolution. It is possible that the last and perhaps strongest impulse to this change came to Moses during the many years he spent amongst the Midianites who were akin to the Hebrews and who, relatively unaffected by the Egyptian and Canaanite civilization, maintained the ancient religious beliefs and rituals of their forefathers in greater purity than the Hebrews in Egypt and Canaan. Among those rituals an initiation festival was perhaps the most important ceremony.

The two subjects of our comparison are thus the puberty rites of savage tribes, especially of Central Australia, and an alleged initiation festival of prehistoric Hebrew groups. While we know very much about the religious beliefs and customs of the Australian aborigines, we know very little about the concepts and rituals of the prehistoric Israelites. The data of the biblical tradition are few and far between, interspersed among later stories and sagas. The little we can deduce from the biblical sources is so adulterated and modified by editors and scribes that it is of doubtful value and can be used only after it is subjected to very careful textual criticism and examination. We do not forget that also the primitive Australian tribes have a long past and that their concepts and rituals are transmitted to us in a secondary and often very modified form. Our work is in certain respects similar to that of an archaeologist who excavates remnants of an ancient city and who, digging deeper, discovers stone images of a much older primitive civilization upon whose place the younger culture was superimposed. Our aim is to examine the survivals of prehistoric Hebrew religion with the help of a comparison with contemporary savage rituals. The puberty ritual of savage and half-civilized tribes is thus used here only as a material that can be compared with the unknown rites of prehistoric Semitic religion. Not more than a comparison is intended, but the analogy between certain features of the Sinai tradition and those of primitive puberty rituals has far-reaching consequences and leads to a definite hypothesis about the character of the revelation and of early Semitic religion. There are numerous points of agreement, and it is to be hoped that their psychological interpretation will throw a new light on the mysterious events on the Sacred Mountain.

In spite of the careful reconstruction of the past made possible by the new archaeological discoveries, that focal crisis of ancient Israel is still an enigma. Clemenceau once remarked that war is too important a matter to leave it to the generals. Similarly the reconstruction of the prehistoric past should not be entrusted only to the archaeologists. A great silence still surrounds the center of the Hebrew history: the Sinai revelation, upon whose message Judaism, Christianity and Islam were founded. The lines that the gentle British poet William Cowper wrote more than a hundred and sixty years ago are still valid:

> 'Tis revelation satisfies all doubts
> Explains all mysteries except her own.

12.

Primitive Initiation into Manhood

Initiation rites have the central place in the religious and social life of primitive peoples. More than fifty years ago, a historian of civilization emphasized that they are more impressive and of longer duration than the marriage celebrations.[1] It is easy to understand why these initiation rituals are considered so important by primitive society. They permit the young people to marry, grant them all rights and impose on them all obligations which are valid for the members of the tribe. The puberty rites form the portal to manhood. No other caesura in the individual life of preliterate societies reaches the fundamental significance of that transition from boy to man. The introduction into adulthood is generally accompanied by more or less extended ceremonies whose forms vary from tribe to tribe, but follow the same basic pattern and have certain features in common. These ceremonies that were spread throughout the world and varied due to the long history of the rites, are not rites of transition, *"rites de passage,"* in the sense of A. van Gennep.[2] It is true that they aim to mark the turning of the boy away from childhood so he may enter a new phase of life where he will function as a responsible member of his tribe. But there are other functions of the initiation ceremonies that are no less important in their social and religious aspect. We will find, in societies of every stage of cultural evolution and in all parts of the world, initiation rites uniting young men with the elders of the tribes in social cohesion.

It is perhaps most advantageous to conceive of those rites as primitive attempts at educating boys of the tribe. A story from my own experience will illustrate the point: The little son of the psychiatrist, Dr. Carl Sulzberger, had visited the zoo several times before his parents took him to the Metropolitan Museum of Art. When, the following Sunday, they expressed the intention of going to the Museum again, the boy cried and said: "I don't want to see the picture zoo. I want to see the animal zoo!" Let us now look closely—at the human animals in that phase when the first attempts were made to tame them (which were, we must admit, only moderately successful). The puberty rituals of the savage tribes are nothing but such an attempt at subduing and domesticating the young at their rebellious age.

What are the essential traits of those periodic educational ceremonies? The novices are, in most cases, taken to a secluded place away from the women and children where they have to undergo a more or less protracted period of preparation. The details of the ceremonials are, in general, kept secret from the women and the uninitiated of the tribe. In the initiation proper, the young men have to pass through a series of ordeals which test their courage, endurance, and ability to stand pain. Finally a bodily mutilation is inflicted upon them: frequently it is circumcision—in some Australian tribes, it is the cruel operation of subincision of the penis. The seclusion, the ordeal, and the reappearance of the initiated boys is usually associated with the idea of their death and resurrection. The women of the tribe are told that a monster or terrible spirit has killed their sons. When, some time later, the young men return to the village, they behave as though they were babies. Among most primitive tribes, for instance those of southeastern Australia, the novices are given a new name immediately after their initiation in token of their new existence.[3] During the period of seclusion the novices undergo a primitive kind of education and instruction. They are initiated into the lore and customs of the tribe by its elders. Certain rules and regulations are given them; also some commandments under threats of severe punishments are transmitted to them—among them the special order of secrecy about the rituals. The tribal mysteries, including myths and traditions as well as sacred objects, are unveiled to them. After their having passed the initiation they are considered members of the tribe and warriors. They can now marry, and often they go out to fight with other tribes.

I have said that a systematic exploration of the biblical report of the Exodus-Sinai events would lead us to the astonishing result that it comprises the tale of a puberty festival of the Hebrew tribes—a tale that was interwoven with the tradition of an important phase of their history. The most convincing way to prove this thesis would be a minute comparison of the biblical narrative with all the details of primitive initiation ceremonials, followed by a survey of all archaeological and anthropological evidence of the Mosaic phase. Such a scholarly elaboration is beyond the scope of the present essay. I prefer to adopt a shorter and less conventional procedure. In collating the most characteristic features of the biblical account and of the report of anthropologists (and contrasting them), we shall emphasize what seems to confirm and contradict such a thesis.

But before undertaking that, a remark concerning the term "puberty rites" is indicated. It is characteristic of the so-called uncivilized societies that members of the same sex and age form social groups. Entrance into such a group that has special privileges requires an appropriate preparation, and admission into its ranks is accomplished by rites. It is not always the age which decides that young men are initiated into those rites of puberty. In many tribes initiation ceremonies take place only every four or five years.[4] In others they are postponed on account of a calamity such as war or famine.[5] Sometimes other external circumstances, such as the lack of sufficient food necessary for the ceremonies, make a suspension necessary. In some instances all young men have to wait until the chief's son is old enough.[6] For reasons of convenience or by force of circumstances, rites of puberty are occasionally postponed a long time. A side glance at the biblical story will remind us that Joshua instituted circumcision at Gibeath-ha-araloth (Josh. 5:4), which seems to prove that that ritual was not carried out during the years in the wilderness.

The term "puberty rituals" as object of comparison is chosen here because it denotes the most important and most common of the initiation ceremonies. It is general practice to give this designation, although some anthropologists, like van Gennep, objected to the use of the name and insisted that it can be applied only to certain of those rites. In cases in which initiation is spread over a course of many years, none or only some rituals are connected with puberty. Sometimes a puberty ritual loses its original significance by being merged in a rite of another kind.[7] It would have been perhaps better to chose the more general term, "initiation rite," especially since in many cases the social group of the candidates often approaches the character of secret societies and the ceremonials that of their mysteries.

The organization of the initiation is in almost all cases in the hands of the old men who are the natural guardians of the tribal tradition. "The initiation of adults loses its general character in proportion as the authority of the chief develops and legal institutions become separated from the magico-religious rites of which they were first part and parcel. The age class is thus turned into one or more secret societies, which sometimes recruit their members from various tribes . . ."[8] This sketch of the evolution of puberty rituals, especially of their late ramifications in the form of clubs of men and of secret societies will, I hope, justify the use of the term of "puberty festival." More important than that name is perhaps the fact that this development points to the origin of the covenant of Hebrew tribes in Kadesh or in the desert . . . More will be said about their confederacy later on. It will suffice to remark here that also in primitive tribes in Australia and Africa the puberty ceremonies are sometimes celebrated in association with other tribes and that the members of secret societies often belong to different tribes.

The covenant of the Hebrew clans in the wilderness marks thus a stage of social development whose origins are already recognized on lower levels of society. We ought not forget that according to historical records only two or three Hebrew tribes had been in Egypt and had taken part in the Exodus, while their majority were already living in Canaan. It is possible that some of those tribes joined their kin in the Sinai Peninsula to make that *b'rith* or covenant, but it is more likely that the Hebrew tradition telescoped here a development of a tribal confederacy which extended over several decades and which was realized only much later in the time of the Judges—or even in the age of the Kings.

The puberty rituals of primitive people have the character of long-extended tribal festivals that are celebrated at certain intervals. Is there anything similar in the biblical tradition? My answer will be blunt: Of course! Not only that, but the prohibition of that tribal festival by the Pharaoh is presented there as a last stimulus to the movement of emigration. The traditional story as it is reported in Exodus tells us that the people, convinced by the arguments of Moses and Aaron, are prepared by the elders of Israel to depart. They set forth on a three-day journey into the wilderness to observe a festival of Yahweh. We will endeavor later on to make it apparent that the Passover feast, which is of a very archaic character, is the remnant and survival of an original initiation of patriarchal time. For the moment we only want to emphasize that the point of departure for the Exodus is determined by the observation of that tribal festival. Tradition has it that Moses established a religious and national commonwealth on the Sinai. The historical picture of those events is, of course, obscured through chains of legends that formed themselves around them. Scholars agree that the Sinai events "did not constitute the completion . . . but rather the beginning of the religious devel-

opment of Israel."⁹ At all events, the confederation of the Israelite
tribes, or the Yahweh Amphictyony as modern biblical research calls
it, started there and from then on the periodical national festivals
in the memory of the Exodus and of the union of the Hebrews were
celebrated. The Hebrews later on defied and denied Moses and even
the Lord. An extraordinary pressure and a superhuman power were
needed to transform this unmanageable rabble of slaves and their
hangers-on—called in the Bible "a mixed multitude"—into a people.

13.

Death and Resurrection

The central idea of the puberty
ritual is death and resurrection. In one or another form, the initiation
ceremonies of primitive people re-enact the drama of death and
rebirth of the novices. The concept appears in its crudest form among
the Australian natives who pretend that the Balum monster—the
totemistic tribal deity—eats the young men and vomits them up.

To be initiated means first to die. Sometimes spirits wearing masks
come and carry the neophytes off to some hut or enclosure where
they live in some isolated spot for months or even years. They are,
for all practical purposes, dead and will then be reborn.[1] In the
lower Congo, the initiation ceremonies are called *"Kimbasi,"* which
means "resurrection." During a dance the neophytes fall dead, and
then the sorcerer resuscitates them. Among the Omaha Indians the
neophyte is bound to a plank. A priest pretends to kill him and
another brings him to life. In the initiation ceremonies of the people
of the ancient Orient, the passion of a god or half-god is almost
always represented: the young man is attacked or carried off by
evil or devilish powers, descends to the realm of the netherworld,
and is brought again to life and light. The idea of death and resurrection can be followed as far as the baptism of Christianity in which
the novices are supposed to be reborn after having died with and in
Christ.

Is there any similar situation in the biblical tradition of the Exodus-Sinai age? There is not a trace of that "drama of death and resurrection" which, according to Frazer and most anthropologists, forms the center of the initiation rites. We have heard that the seclusion of the novices of several savage tribes lasts many months—in certain cases, for instance among the Arunta, even several years.[2]

Let us first focus our attention on the length of time the Hebrew tribes spent in the wilderness. It would certainly be legitimate to compare the years of wandering in the desert (which includes the sojourn at Sinai) with that phase of seclusion of the Australian young men. But such a tentative comparison is invalidated by two factors: there is no ritual of death and resurrection in the biblical frame, and the segregation of the Israelites lasted forty years.

Now, forty is a round number frequently encountered in the Holy Scriptures. It seems that the figure of forty years indicated a generation.[3] According to Midrasch[4] the word "forty" was used idiomatically in the sense of "many years." It is not accidental that "the flood was forty days upon the earth" (Gen. 7:17) and that the Hebrews remained forty years in the desert; nor that Elijah travelled forty days to Mount Horeb, that the land had rest forty years after the deliverance wrought by Barak and Deborah. According to Professor Millar Burrows[5] the number was not intended to mean anything more specific than "about a month" or "about a generation," as the case might be. Jesus fasted forty days and nights when he was tempted by the devil. David reigned over Israel forty years. There are cycles of forty years in the biography of Moses. For the case in question the biblical number of forty years would account for a statement that the Israelites were a long time away from other people, in seclusion. The character of this statement is vague and is not changed by the fact that some editors tried occasionally to give precise data. It is all mock precision, many hundreds of years after the original oral tradition has passed. (For instance: "And the Lord spake unto Moses in the wilderness of Sinai, in the first month of the second year after they were come out of the land of Egypt . . ." (Num. 9:1). The old tradition was often changed and its written report edited and re-edited during some centuries.

Perhaps traces of resemblance with the initiation rites of Australian and African aborigines would seem more evident if we could neglect the precise number of forty years. Let us admit tentatively that there is such a link. If it were there, it would be rather weak and certainly not conclusive in its isolation. But are there not other features in the biblical narrative with which it is associated? It would be possible that a vague or unrecognizable outline might become clearer as the rest of the picture comes into shape.

There is another and much more important feature appearing in the biblical record. The Lord decides that none of the people who left Egypt will enter the Promised Land. All of them—according to the Bible, six hundred thousand people—with the exception of Caleb and Joshua, will die before reaching Canaan ("Your carcasses shall fall in this wilderness; and all that were numbered of you . . . Doubtless ye shall not come into the land . . . But your little ones, which ye said should be a prey, them I will bring in and they shall know the land which ye have despised" (Num. 14:29-31). It will be a new generation that will enter the Promised Land while the older one will have perished. Is there not a trace here of a primal tradition of death and resurrection, of a tradition distorted to an almost unrecognizable extent? Do we detect, underneath the later levels, the transformed remnant of an old concept in which men die and are resurrected, transferred from a group of adolescents to a whole generation? In the introduction to this interpretation, we expressed the conjecture that the biblical narrative of Exodus-Sinai presents a distorted report of an initiation festival interwoven into the early Hebrew history and displaced to the whole nation that was about to be formed. We were already facing the possibility that the construction of our hypothesis of a similarity between primitive initiation and the Sinai revelation might collapse. But here, it seems, we have a prop holding it up and perhaps more than a prop.

Let us admit freely that the task into which we have plunged has not gone much beyond the beginning of what is called in research a "conceptual framework" of the secret of the Exodus-Sinai narrative. We encountered formidable obstacles on the road we followed. The darkness surrounding those prehistoric events is not pierced. We saw, in flashes, some similarities: the Passover festival, the Exodus, the long sojourn in the wilderness, the death of the old generation and the growing up of a new one seemed to correspond to some traits of the primitive initiation rituals. But are those resemblances sufficient to justify a comparison of the origin and nature of two phenomena so different in all other respects? We were perhaps too timid or hesitant, too concerned with various divergencies, and did not concentrate on the essential analogies. We will be more daring from now on.

Let us first compare miscellaneous features among which certain taboos and tests of endurance are the most conspicuous. In many tribes the novices are subjected to various food restrictions. In certain cases a particular food is forbidden while in others a special food is prescribed. The adolescent boys of the Andamanese tribes must not eat some important foods for a period of some years. In one tribe, for example, the boys must avoid turtle and porpoise, and then after release from these taboos, must abstain from pork and a series of other foods. At the end of the first period turtle fat is rubbed on the boy's body by an older man and he is finally given some turtle to eat.[6] The initiated of the Arunta and Loritja tribes in Central Australia are forbidden to eat many delicacies and are threatened with being thrown into the fire if they should eat them. The novices in Liberia who spend many months in a "magic" forest are systematically educated to stand hunger and thirst. The Karesau tribes impose certain prohibitions of food on the adolescent boys. The Maskoki Indians in North America submit their adolescent boys to certain times of fasting which are first restricted to privation of a single meal, but are extended later to days without food or drink.[7]

Do we detect remnants of those privations and trials of the primitive initiation in the biblical report according to which the Children of Israel were for a long time short of water, and then of food, becoming thirsty and hungry? Exodus (17:1–3) reports that the Children of Israel did chide Moses in Rephidim and murmured against him, saying: "Wherefore is this thou hast brought us out of Egypt, to kill us and our children and our cattle with thirst?" The parallel account joins the name of Meribah where the Children of Israel strove with the Lord with Massah (= trial, proof) because Yahweh "proved" the people. And is the manna which Yahweh secures as caterer of the Hebrews in the desert not perhaps the remnant of the tradition of "sacred food" to be found also in Australian initiation rites?

The adolescents of the Australian and African tribes are looking forward to their initiation although they are subjected to various and extended tests and tortures, long privations, and finally to a cruel mutilation. The initiation changes them into grown-up men and gives them the rights and privileges of the adult members of the tribe. It makes them warriors and allows them to marry. Is it an echo of such high expectations when the New Testament proclaims: "Blessed is the man that endureth temptation: for when he is tried, he shall receive the crown of life" (James 1:12)?

Before we enter the phase of theophany, we cast a glance backward upon that central rite of death and resurrection and remember that the novices returning from their long seclusion behave as though they were newborn and had to learn to walk and talk. They pretend to be babes coming from the woods. Is there still an echo of that alleged condition in the words: "Except ye be converted and become as little children ye shall not enter into the kingdom of heaven" (Math. 18:3)?

14.

Clues for an Invisible Entrance

The biblical story tells us that immediately after the Children of Israel had rebelled against Moses and Aaron, they encountered the enemies: "Then came Amalek, and fought with Israel in Rephidim" (Exod. 17:8). There follows the memorable scene that describes how Amalek was defeated with the help of Moses' upheld hands. The passage sticks out from the context like a sore thumb and evidently belongs to a later section in the narrative. The insertion here is one of the many examples of the careless work of an inexpert editor or compiler. Many other such lapses and displacements as well as editorial sins of commission and omission have been recognized and examined by higher biblical criticism.

The Pentateuch tells us for instance that Yahweh called Moses to the peak and made him descend to speak to the Hebrews. Moses was directed to warn the people not "to break through unto the Lord" because many of them would die. We find Moses again on the mountain in the twentieth chapter of Exodus. He is depicted here as receiving the Tablets from the Lord. Moses reascends the mountain several times, although we are not told how often he has returned and visited with the Hebrew tribes. The Sinai, it is true, is not a very high mountain—not more than seven thousand feet, but Moses who ascended and descended it several times within a short span, was more than eighty years old. One is tempted to remark that while his incomparable achievements as leader, lawgiver, and prophet are often and eloquently praised, his accomplishments as a mountain climber have not yet been appreciated.

With this expression of bewilderment, we enter the area of the biblical report about the revelation. Moses is the bearer of the divine Law and the representative of his people. He conveys Yahweh's message to the Israelites who are assembled at the foot of the mountain. Yahweh announces that "He will come to him in a thick cloud" and the people will hear His voice. They go through ceremonies of sanctification lasting two days, during which clothes are ritually washed and abstinence from sexual intercourse is ordered. Moses brings the people to the foot of Sinai on the morning of the third day. Then "thunders and lightnings" begin. A thick cloud surrounds the mountain. The voice of the trumpet sounds exceedingly loud and all the people who are in the camp tremble. The trumpet blares still louder. Moses speaks to Yahweh and God answers him by voice. When Moses has ascended the mountain, Yahweh tells him to go down again and warn the people not to try to "break through unto the Lord and gaze, lest many of them perish." The twentieth chapter of Exodus begins with the promulgation of the Ten Commandments. The people tremble at the thunderings and lightnings and plead with Moses that he should speak to them, not God of whom they are terrified.

From that report we turn, to continue our comparison, to the accounts presented by the anthropologists of the center of the primitive initiation. If the initiation rites present a primitive education—and there is agreement among anthropologists that this is their character—the method is one of respressive force and intimidation. Obedience to the rules and the moral code of the tribe is enforced by cruel punishment and threats. One group of those educational measures stresses physical mutilations and punishments inflicted according to the principle that boys will be best reminded of regulations if they remember pain or rough treatment. The second pedagogic method is the visual and verbal demonstration of the terrible fate which awaits the disobedient adolescents. They are threatened with an evil and harm that will maim or kill them if they do not follow the commandments given to them. Since we will restrict our exploration to some representative features of those initiation rites, we will mention only a few instances of those intimidations that are efficient on account of fear and various forms of threats.

In most cases of initiation ceremonies the young people are frightened by the announcement of evil spirits, demons, or gods who
threaten them. The monster Balum of the Yambin tribe in New
Guinea is supposed to eat the novices. From the hut, which represents the belly of the monster, growls are heard from time to time
when the awe-stricken lads approach it. The monster demands its
prey. The boys admitted into the Kakian association remain in the
dark for many days. They hear from time to time the blasts of
trumpets, the shots of muskets, and the clash of swords while they
have to sit in a crouching position without moving. The chief of the
society speaks to each boy and warns him, under pain of death, to
observe the rules of the Kakian society and not to reveal its secrets.
The father-generation of most Australian tribes drag their adolescent
sons to the image of a monster and terrify them by making preparations for their circumcision with deliberate slowness.[1] Schellong
reports, for instance, that during the Balum festival in Kaiser Wilhelm Land the boys who wait for circumcision in the stomach of the
Balum monster are frightened by hideous noises produced by the
men outside who strike their shields, shriek, and whistle "with the
unmistakable intention of thoroughly intimidating the youths." Father
Schmidt describes the secret initiation of the Karesau Islanders in
Papua in which the men pretend to speak with the spirits who want
to devour the boys. Loud flute sounds are interpreted as urgent demands of the spirit whom the men try to keep away. Yet the men
go to the houses in which the boys are waiting; they beat on the
walls and shake them so that the youths are afraid: "On the next
day different spirits appear in the masks of animals and the men
say to the crying boys: 'They will eat you.' Two bird ghosts appear
who have a mask-costume with feathers and wings fastened on their
arms. The two ghosts perform a kind of mock fight, then pass the
boys by in such a way that they touch them with their wings which
frightens the youths again. They disappear then in the ghost house."

We find the element of intimidation in different forms in the
theophany of Mount Sinai again. It is there expressively described
as fear of the Children of Israel to come up the mountain: "Take
care not to ascend the mountain, nor even touch the edge of it! Whoever touches the mountain, must be put to death. But let no hand
touch him. Let him be stoned or shot to death, whether it is beast
or man, it (or he) shall not be allowed to live!" On the morning
of the third day, there was thunder and lightning and a very loud
thunder blast "so that all the people that were in the camp trembled."[2]

Here is a clear analogy to the situation of the initiation rites of Australian natives whose elders speak to the spirits, whose loud flute sounds were heard: "The trumpet blast grew louder and louder— Moses was speaking and God answering him with a loud voice." We read in the second chapter of Exodus that the people perceived the thunder and lightning, the blast of the trumpet and the mountain smoking, and drew back and stood off at a distance. "You speak to us," they said to Moses, "and we will listen, but let not God speak to us, lest we die." Moses encouraged the people and told them not to be afraid, "for it is only for the purpose of testing you that the fear of Him may be present with you so that you do not sin." Yet the people were terror-stricken and stood off at a distance while Moses drew near the thick darkness where God was.

Here again is an analogy to the behavior of the older men of the savage tribes. They who have themselves intimidated the boys, pretend, as all the reports emphasize, to protect them from the monsters of Balum or from the spirits; they often seem to ward off the dangers coming from those attackers. The analogy can be followed up even further. The terrible noises the boys hear while they are inside the stomach of the Balum monster, the menaces to which they have to listen, find their parallels in the biblical story.

The sound and the fury seemed to be a phenomena accompanying the descent of Yahweh on the Sinai. They are, so to speak, elementary effects of His passage down the mountain. The mountain "was altogether enveloped in smoke, because the Lord descended upon it in fire: and the smoke thereof ascended as the smoke of a furnace, and the whole mount quaked greatly" (Exod. 19:18). The Lord has unchained the powers of nature. Do those lines describe a thunderstorm? Or does the sentence "The whole mount quaked greatly" rather point to an earthquake? Alois Musil and Eduard Meyer as well as later historians have expressed the view that the Sinai must have been once a volcano. Yet there is, and there was, no volcano in the Sinai part of the country. Since there are volcanos—and perhaps once active ones—in the neighboring areas of Hauran and Arabia, W. F. Albright considers it possible that the picture of the theophany in Exodus was ultimately influenced by folk "memories of volcano eruptions (preserved in myth or metaphor), combined with more recent recollections of terrific thunderstorms in the mountains of Northwestern Arabia or Syria."[3]

The words "the whole mountain quaked" have often been interpreted as signs of an earthquake. Adolf Lods thinks that the fire, the

clouds, and the thunder are to be conceived as manifestations of the
eruption of a volcano.[4] A search has therefore been made for volcanos
in the realm to the east of the Red Sea, but in vain. The dark cloud,
the thunder and lightning and the smoke are, according to Johannes
Pedersen[5] "meant to express Yahweh's power over the world of
nature." (Numerous similar descriptions comparing Yahweh's approach to an earthquake are present in the Prophets.) There is no
evidence of an old tradition here. Pedersen concludes that the story
has an artificial character also, from the ease "with which the narrator
lets Moses pass up and down the mountain again and again, sometimes quite superfluously, about a matter that has already been arranged."

There are at least two points that cannot be explained as effects of
Yahweh's power upon nature. They have to be considered as produced
by human beings: the blasts of trumpets and the torches.

The appearance of Yahweh, fixed for the third day after the announcement, is in the form of a fire (Exod. 19:18: "And Mount
Sinai was altogether on a smoke because the Lord descended upon
it in fire"). The smoke is said to ascend from the earth as the smoke
of a furnace. In the smoke flickering torches are seen. In discussing
these two factors, we still remain within the frame of our subject
since the trumpet blasts and the torches frightened the people waiting at the foot of the mountain.

The explanation of the tale by commentators is that the scene
presents the picture of a thunderstorm that was considered as a
miraculous revelation of Yahweh. B. D. Eerdmans has shown that
this explanation cannot be correct.[6] A thunderstorm is never concentrated in so small a territory that the people can stay around the part of
the mountain on which the thunderstorm rages. Lightning is seen in
the sky and not on the slopes or on top of a mountain. Since it
appears at various places, now very distant, nearer and again further
away, the phenomenon cannot be compared with fire—fire seen
through ascending smoke on the slope of the mountain. Eerdmans
furthermore points out that in a thunderstorm the flashes of lightning
are the only elements of fire, while in Exodus the fire in which
Yahweh descends comes from the sky and burns on the higher part
of the mountain to be seen by the whole people. Thunderstorms are
accompanied by strong wind, rain, or hail. Nothing of the kind
appears in the narrative.

Through the heavy smoke the people saw the glimmering of
torches. (The word used in Exod. 19:16 is "lappid" which, in all

passages where it occurs, means "torch." The translation "lightnings" is not correct.) The flickering of torches points to the presence of men. So does the thick cloud on the mountain described as smoke caused by a great fire. It was, of course, not a cloud descending from the sky, but a cloud of smoke ascending into the sky like the smoke cloud of a furnace. "This suggests one or more ordinary fires."[7] The sounds that are heard are called *"quoloth,"* a word meaning sounds caused by men, animals, wind, and so on. The translation "thunders" is arbitrary since no thunderstorm is described. The trumpets, the torches, the fire, lead to the suggestion of the human origin of those sounds by hammering on metal plates or gongs. Some auxiliary power was applied in the descent of the Lord.

Eerdmans points to the order of ritual cleanliness of the people on the day of the theophany. The events on Mount Sinai are previously announced since the people must have time for washing their clothes. The signal of the trumpet is given in the morning on the predicted day. Neither a thunderstorm nor a volcanic eruption could have been announced three days before. Those "fireworks" on the sacred mountain are not Yahweh's doing. Our conclusion is clear: the descent of the Lord on Mount Sinai appears in the description of Exodus as a series of human actions.

15.

Human Agencies in the Revelation

Our investigation into the circumstances of the appearance of God on Mount Sinai has led to the conclusion that the theophany was preceded and accompanied by human actions. At this point several questions arise. Let us try to cope with only two of them. The first is certainly neither immodest nor irrelevant: What is the nature of the human agents who produced the effects described in Exodus? In the sense of our comparison that question could also be formulated in another way: Who acts as the stage manager behind the wings? The second question is not as concrete as the first. It transgresses the narrow area of the physical world and touches the vague sphere of metaphysical or theological problems. Does the operation of human agencies invalidate the divine character of the revelation?

The answer to the first question seems simple enough: Who, other than the helpers of Moses, could produce the fires and the resulting clouds on top of the mountain, the "lightning" caused by torches, the "thunder" perhaps effected by hammer blows, the blast of trumpets? If there had been priests at the time of the Sinai revelation, we would not hesitate to assume that they were the natural stagehands who also performed functions similar to those of the electricians in our theaters. Could the loyal Levites, the elders of Moses' clan, perhaps be the people who helped their kinsman prepare the great theophany?

What obtrudes upon our thoughts first, and immediately, is not necessarily the best hypothesis. It is not in this case. It is possible that tribal elders helped in staging the great spectacle, but careful consideration of the details of the theophany leads to another track. We are grateful for the guidance of B. Stade,[1] A. Menes,[2] and especially B. D. Eerdmans who illuminated the concealed road.[3]

Moses, the murderer, escaping from Egypt, found refuge among the Midianites. There was a sanctuary of Yahweh near Mount Sinai, a place which afforded protection to runaway slaves, social outcasts, and even criminals.[4] The Kenites, who lived there, were devotees to Yahweh and wore the sign of their ancestor Cain, who was a murderer like Moses, and to whom the Lord gave a sign to protect him. The Kenites, servants of Yahweh, were not satisfied, however, merely with giving protection to those who came to the sanctuary, but looked upon themselves as the appointed guardians of all oppressed and in particular of strangers. Yahweh is the God of all those who are without the bond of family and tribe.[5]

Moses was married to the daughter of Jethro, who is called a "priest of Midian" (Exod.3:1) and who was of the tribe of the Kenites, kinsmen of the Hebrews. The Kenites were smiths, like their ancestor Cain (the name Cain means "smith"). These desert smiths forged instruments of brass and of iron, which metal was perhaps known to them at the end of the Bronze Age. The Kenites needed fire, which was very probably considered as a divine power. It is probable that they conceived of their deity as a god of fire, thus connecting their profession with religion.

Moses returned to Egypt after he received the oracle of the Burning Bush from the god of the Kenites, as is related in the third chapter of Exodus. Moses, who lived a long time with the Kenites as son-in-law of their priest, became familiar with their religious ideas, many of which he borrowed when he founded a new religion after leading the Hebrew tribes back to Midian and to Mount Sinai in whose neighborhood the Kenites dwelled.

Exodus (35:3) commands the Israelites: "Ye shall kindle no fire throughout your habitations upon the sabbath day," which leads back to an institution of the desert smiths.[6] The Kenites guided the Hebrew tribes on their march. Moses asked his father-in-law: "Leave us not, I pray thee; forasmuch as thou knowest how we are to encamp in the wilderness, and thou mayest be to us instead of eyes" (Num. 10:31). The cloud of Yahweh was over them by day, when they set forward from the camp (Num. 10:34). The Kenites helped the Israelites in their flight from Egypt, showed them where to go in the desert east of the delta and where to camp. Those desert smiths carried fire with them and they could easily have produced that pillar of cloud by day to lead them the way; and by night the pillar of fire to give them light (Exod. 13:21-22).

The role of the Kenites before, during, and after the Sinai theophany cannot easily be exaggerated. They helped Moses wherever they could. Eerdmans has emphasized that it would be a misjudgment if we were to charge them with willful deceit in preparing a theophany since, to them, the human actions were inspired by the deity in the same manner as the words and visions of the prophets. The specific character of those actions is obvious: "The descent of the god of fire, needed for the authority of Moses, was arranged by the Kenites for a fixed day. On this day no one was allowed to go unto the Mountain. They kindled one or more big fires, causing much smoke. They hammered on metal plates, moved torches in the smoke, and gave the signal to bring the people to the nether part of the Mount by blowing a trumpet (shofar) repeatedly, louder and louder. As Moses spoke, he was answered by sound of gongs. The purpose was to hold the people in awe."[7]

Eerdmans' explanation of the various details of the theophany, recounted in the biblical narrative, will remind us of the description of the extended and secret preparations made by the elders of the Australian tribes for the initiation of adolescent boys. When we consider that the Hebrews and Kenites had advanced thousands of years beyond the cultural level of the Australian aborigines, living in the

Stone Age, the differences of those preparatory actions seem to recede and the similarities become transparent. Also with those tribes of New Guinea and Central Australia, mysterious loud noises are heard and various other terrifying phenomena are seen. "The fear of God" is put into the initiates who are waiting, full of awe, for the appearance of the animal-like monsters that they worship and whose commandments are transmitted to them by the elders of the tribe.

There is, it is true, an essential difference in the concept of the deity. To those miserable natives of Australia the gods or spirits appear as menacing beings, masked as ugly and terrifying animals. The Hebrews imagined Yahweh as the omnipotent Lord of Heaven and Earth whom no mortal was allowed to see. But that difference exists only for the believers. When Baudelaire once visited Théophile Gautier, he found there a friend of this writer, Charles Asselineau, who took the little figure of an idol from the mantelpiece to examine it. The figure was carved from a fig tree by a Congo Negro and showed a head twice as big as the body with a mouth split from one ear to the other and two deep holes in place of the eyes. Asselineau said: "What a terrible figure!" and, disgusted, threw the idol back to its place. "You had better be on guard!" said Baudelaire. "What if that were the true God! . . ."

The comparison with the natives and their crude religious concepts prepared our way to the second question that poses itself at this point: Does the fact that man-made preparations were devised and carried through efface the truth of the divine revelation? Otherwise put: Do we believe the Lord revealed Himself at Sinai in spite of those human agencies?

Let us first state that the question is an improper one if asked of an historian of civilization or a psychologist, both inquiring into the evolution of religion. The query should be directed to the theologians who are competent to give pertinent information. One of them, Rabbi Goldman, wrote recently about the theophany at Sinai: "If what is here related goes back to fact, then the Bible and with it also the religion of the Occident goes back to God. If, on the other hand it is folk-lore or fiction, then the one and the other are man-made."[8] Maurice Samuel, who edited and introduced Goldman's book, adds by way of commentary that "if one denaturizes the theophany at Sinai into naturalistic terms, the Bible as a whole disintegrates."

With regard to the operation of human agencies preparing the theophany, the alternative is certainly debatable from logical as well as from psychological points of view. It would be very possible that all preparations were devised by man and all external circumstances contrived by the Kenites or Levites, and yet that the descent of Yahweh could have been a reality. Strictly speaking—and I do not see how one could speak otherwise on such issues—it would mean only that the point where the miraculous or superhuman enters the scene were removed from one place to another. In the Eucharist the priest takes wine and bread and speaks the sacramental words: *"hoc est enim corpus meum"*—*"hic est enim calix sanguinis mei."* The priest has made all mechanical preparations for the transubstantiation. The appearance of the bread and wine remains the same as before. Yet the priest has summoned the living Christ into these substances: The bread has become His body, the wine His blood. The pious who believe in the divine presence within those elements at the Mass, sustain even more sweeping assumptions than the Children of Israel who believed in the descent of the Lord at Sinai. Essentially it is the miracle, "faith's pet child," as Goethe called it, that is unquestionably accepted here as well as there. It has, however, to be conceded that faith was more accessible to half-nomadic tribesmen of the second millennium before Christ than to us.[9] The "leap of faith" is necessary here and there, but we have to jump a wider abyss than our ancestors did thirty-three centuries ago. In order to do that we have to take a longer run.

That "leap of faith" is, of course, impossible when the abyss has become so wide that it cannot be spanned. It is again fashionable in America today to speak of a "conflict" between science and religion. There is actually no such conflict, as the two areas are so remote one from the other that no common ground upon which to argue exists. Freud once said: "The polar bear and the tiger cannot fight."

16.

The Sound and the Fury

As the curtain rises in the great
play of the primitive initiation, mysterious and frightening sounds
are heard. This off-stage music, produced by the simplest and most
crude of instruments, continues to accompany the main actions of the
ritual.

In a paper presented in Vienna in January 1919, I made the most
important of those instruments, the Australian bull-roarer, the subject of a special investigation.[1] This musical instrument, which is in
many ways puzzling, is "perhaps the most ancient, widely spread and
sacred symbol in the world."[2] It is nothing but a flat, narrow piece
of wood with a hole in it. By a long string threaded through this
hole, the bull-roarer is very quickly whirled in the air. Swung around,
it produces a kind of muffled roar. This strange instrument is spread
all over the world and is found in Asia, Australia, Africa, and even,
in a distant form, as a child's toy in Europe.

This instrument called the "bull-roarer," nothing but a thin slat
of wood with a hole for the insertion of a string, is considered holy
among primitive people. Women and children must not see it. It
plays a very important part in the religious and magical ceremonies.
The instrument was used by paleolithic man. Some prehistoric speci-
mens, made of bone, have been discovered by archaeologists. Andrew
Lang[3] concluded from them that the religion of early prehistoric man
had similarities with that of the Australian natives. We know that an
instrument of a similar nature was used in the mysteries of Dionysus.
The Australian tribes call the bull-roarer with the same name as their
ancestors or the supreme being. Its sound is often identified with
thunder and represents the voice of the spirit. Most tribes in Central
Australia, for instance those described by Strehlow,[4] use the bull-
roarer during the initiations. Swung by men, its use should keep the
women away. They are told that the roar is the voice of a being

Twanyirika, who is supposed to take the boys away into the bush until the wound from their circumcision is healed.[5] The bull-roarers are afterwards shown to the boys while the instruments are carefully concealed from the women. The elder brothers of the novices tell them: "Here is Twanyirika, of whom you have heard so much, they are Churinga (sacred things) and will help to heal you quickly." The boys of the Unmatjera tribe are told, before being circumcized, that Twanyirika will carry them away if they reveal the secrets of initiation.[6]

While the use of the bull-roarers occurs with great frequency in the initiation ceremonies of the primitive tribes, other methods of frightening the waiting boys by mysterious noises are not unknown. As Schellong reports from Kaiser Wilhelm Land, the novices who are in the stomach of the Balum-spirit hear frightful noises. They come from the elders of the tribe who are outside where they make all necessary preparations for the circumcision of the youths. These old gentlemen strike their shields, shout, blow through their fists "for the unmistakable purpose of greatly intimidating the trembling youths within." Father W. Schmidt described the initiation among the Karesau Islanders whose adolescents hear mysterious sounds of flutes supposed to be the voices of the spirit. When the sound becomes louder, it is interpreted as the expression of impatience of the spirit to eat the young people.

There are many factors in the primitive customs and beliefs concerning the bull-roarer, which will interest the student of comparative religion, the anthropologist, and the psychologist. In my essay aforementioned I sought to illustrate and interpret many facets of the problem of the bull-roarer. Only a few aspects of the problem will receive mention here: the conspicuous role those instruments play during the initiation, their interpretation as the voice of the supreme being of the totemistic tribal ancestor or of the dead, and their terrifying effect.

Let us return to our comparison: That curved horn of the ram called *shofar* plays a role in Judaism quite similar to that of the bull-roarer in the ceremonies of the Australian natives. It is a sacred instrument, which women and children were originally forbidden to hear. This very primitive wind instrument sounded terrifying on Sinai before law was given to the Children of Israel. I refer the reader to my often-quoted paper for more details and restrict myself here to the discussion of the ram's horn, perhaps the oldest ancestor of all wind instruments, at the occasion of the covenant on the Sacred Mountain.

God warns the people not to touch the mountain but "when the trumpet soundeth long, they shall come up to the mount" (Exod. 19:13). When the theophany begins, the voice begins, "the voice of the trumpet sounded long, and wailed louder and louder, Moses spake and God answered him by voice." But the people asked Moses that he should speak to them and not God "lest we die."

It does not need much sagacity to conclude that the voice the people heard out of the fire is the very sound of the ram's horn. It will not contradict, but rather confirm this conclusion when other biblical passages state: "And the Lord God shall blow the trumpet" (Zech. 9:14). The sound of the *shofar* is the sound of the God Yahweh of the Hebrews just as the sound of the bull-roarer is the voice of Daramulum or Balum of the Australian aborigines. The young black boys who squatted in the stomach of those monsters were as frightened by those sounds as the Israelites at the foot of Mount Sinai were by the crude, long-drawn-out sounds of the ram's horn.

We shall not follow here the track leading back to the comparison of the totemistic god of the Australian primitives with the prehistoric belief of the Hebrews in a horned deity, a bull or a ram. It is, however, God's voice that sounds through the *shofar,* the ram's horn. "Yahweh roars," says the prophet Amos.

The Kenites blew the trumpets on Mount Sinai as later the rabbis were to blow the *shofar* on festival days, thus unconsciously imitating Yahweh who is calling all Children of Israel. The god of the Kenites with whom the Hebrew tribes fused was Yahweh, the fire-god of Sinai. But the Kenites traced their origin back to Cain and to Cain's descendant who was Jubal, the first musician (Gen. 4:21). His name has the same root as *jobel* which signifies ram's horn or trumpet.

The significance of terror, fear, and awe in the origin of religion as well as of morality becomes transparent in the education of the young men in the Australian bush and in the Sinai Peninsula. It is not accidental that it is the voice of the tribal god which frightens the Hebrews into submission. More than three thousand years after the Sinai experience the poet William Wordsworth still addressed duty as "stern daughter of the voice of God!" Modern man is still dismayed by that strict voice. It is as hard on the ear as it was when it was first heard at the revelation.

17.

The Mask of Moses

The hypothesis that Yahweh has inherited many features of a Kenite fire-god is, it seems to me, preferable to the assumption that He resembles a volcanic god. If a naturalistic concept of the circumstances of His appearance on Mount Sinai is adopted, they can be better understood as preparations of desert smiths than as the eruption of a volcano which is not to be found near Mount Sinai, and whose outburst three days later would be difficult to predict. Let me add only one detail to the preceding ones that will support the concept of a Kenite fire-god: the episode of Korah and his company (Num. 16). Moses orders Korah and the other rebels to put fire into their censers and to stand in the door of the tabernacle: "And there came out a fire from the Lord, and consumed the two hundred and fifty men that offered incense" (Num. 16:35). Here is thus a veritable ordeal by fire. We could present other moments, such as the bush burning with fire, as representing Yahweh, and the sacrifices brought to Him in the form of burnt offerings, as well as other pieces of circumstantial evidence for the concept of a Kenite fire-god.[1] We have to leave the decision in this complex problem to the experts and return to our comparison of the phenomena of the revelation with those of primitive initiation.

For the sake of variety we turn our attention to some essential features of the puberty and initiation rituals to which scarcely any parallel can be detected in the biblical narrative of the revelation. In those primitive ceremonials the tribal gods, or the spirits who threaten the novices with death, appear before them and the youths are frightened by their sight. But Yahweh is invisible. The Lord orders Moses to warn the people not to break through to Him to gaze or else many of them will perish (Exod. 20:21). No mortal is allowed to see God and stay alive. In most native tribes of Australia and Africa the newly initiated are not only allowed, but ordered to look with great attention at the often totemistic gods or demons who will approach them. The novices in Liberia, during their long stay in the magic forest, are under the strict supervision of *soh-bah* (educators) who do not want to be recognized although everybody knows them.[2] No one dares to call them by name. The *soh-bah* disguise themselves by a long coat made of leaves and by a wooden mask covering their heads. Thus made unrecognizable, they perform various dances. They stand in high respect since the people are all convinced that they are in communion with the spirits of their ancestors or, perhaps, are these spirits themselves. They are generally feared since they can harm those whom they hate. The circumcision of the boys of other African tribes is performed by a high priest who wears a mask of leopard skin and painted spots during the operation.[3] To the adolescents in New Guinea who are gathered in the ghost house several ghosts appear—for instance, bird ghosts who wear feather masks. Among the Duk-Duk of New Britain a great part of the initiation ceremony consists of the instruction about masks and dresses by the guardian to the newly initiated. Among the Ingiet of the Bismark Archipelago, the magician possesses the power of controlling the spirits and he leads the youths to a secret place, the abode of the spirits, where their images are kept. Most of the masks of the magicians or leaders of the Melanesian and Polynesian's initiations are totemistic. They are costumes making the person resemble the totem held sacred by the clan.

There are many examples from Australia, Africa, and America proving that the elders of the tribe or the priests and magicians, to whom the most essential part of the initiation rites is assigned, use masks and costumes that make them resemble the spirits or gods of the tribe. The representative examples mentioned here are sufficient to show that nothing of a similar nature is present among the phenomena of the revelation with which we compared the primitive puberty rituals.

Nothing? From the storehouse of biblical traditions I will now choose some significant facts whose analytical interpretation proves that there were at least remnants of a similar tribal custom among the Hebrews of the time of the Exodus. It cannot be denied that my choice gives the impression of arbitrariness, but this is unavoidable. It is more important to ascertain whether the chosen feature is pertinent or not. The details of that significant fact are transmitted to us in Exod. 34:30–35. It is reported there that Moses, coming down

from Mount Sinai, did not know that the skin of his face shone
after he had talked with the Lord "face to face, as a man speaketh
unto his friend" (Exod. 33:11). It is obvious that the shining or
hardening of the face is assigned to the presence of the Lord. When
Aaron and the Children of Israel saw the leader, "behold, the
skin of the face shone and they were afraid to come nigh him"
(Exod. 34:30). When Moses called, they returned to him. When he
spoke to them later on, he put a veil on his face which he took off
only when he spoke with the Lord. "And the Children of Israel saw
the face of Moses, that the skin of Moses' face shone; and Moses
put the veil upon his face again, until he went in to speak with him"
(Exod. 34:35).

The passages presenting the tale of "Moses with the shining face"
have found various interpretations and commentaries.[4] The generally
accepted conception is that the "shining" is a reflection of the "glory"
of the Lord upon whom no mortal may gaze. ("And it shall come
to pass, while my glory passeth by, that I will put thee in a clift
of the rock, and will cover thee with my hand while I pass by . . .
my face shall not be seen" (Exod. 33:22–23).

The face of Yahweh is terrifying to the degree that the sight of
it is death-bringing. The people could not endure the radiance upon
Moses' face and they fled from him. We follow Eerdmans' interpretations which point out that the Exodus narrative can be traced back
here to two unrelated and independent sources that were closely
woven together. In one of the versions the relation of Moses with
the Kenites plays a role. Egyptian papyri explain why the ancient
natives of the Nile country did not like the smell of smiths: "The
skin of their fingers is like that of a crocodile and their smell is the
smell of rotten fish." The shine on Moses' face is to be understood
rather as the hardening of the skin that is exposed to fire for a long
time. Moses was together with the fire-god and his skin wears the
reflection of that prolonged stay with the Lord.

Eerdmans' interpretations[5] seem to me to be a great extent
plausible. His emphasis on the nature of Yahweh as of an original
fire-god of the Kenites is, however, less important than his reference
to one source of the tradition in which Moses appears as a "demigod."
Other passages of the Scripture present a similar portrayal of the
"man of God." Eerdmans could have added to the biblical passages
supporting his hypothesis a psychoanalytic interpretation that leads
the concept of "shining" or hardening of Moses' face to its logical
conclusion. The changed face is the replica of Yahweh's face. In

other words, it is a mask of the tribal god. It frightened the Children of Israel, who were in awe of the Lord and who had asked Moses that God should rather speak to him than to them directly because they were frightened by the sight of Yahweh. Already Gressmann interpreted the veil of Moses as a mask which is the countenance of God.[6] The veil is, so to speak, the second phase of the disguise, following the first form of the shining countenance. According to the concept of antiquity, in taking over Yahweh's attributes Moses becomes the dazzling, frightening God Himself.

We discover here, in the distorted tradition, a resemblance with the masked priests or elders of the primitive tribes in whose initiation the novices are intimated by the costumed representatives of spirits or of dead ancestors. Even the totemistic form of those demons or gods returns from its repression in a late version of the Moses figure that appears as horned as though he were the personification of an original bull-god of the Hebrews. Michelangelo's grandiose marble statue of the "man of God" in the church of St. Pietro in Vincoli in Rome shows this horned form, and Vasari reports that the Jews of the Roman ghetto wandered on the Sabbath to the statue "in order to worship Moses."

There is a famous exclamation of Heinrich Heine to whom Mount Sinai appears as little when Moses stands upon it: "This mountain is but the pedestal upon which stand the feet of the man whose head towers into Heaven where he speaks with God. God will forgive me that sin: at times I even went so far as to think that this Mosaic God was but the reflected effulgence of Moses himself." Do these sentences of the great poet not sound as though they were an intuitive insight into the secret nature of Moses? Even the reflected effulgence is perceived.

There is, says a contemporary writer, an element of danger in the greatness which the Children of Israel attributed to the superman who led them from Egypt. That danger is that Moses' greatness "would surpass the bounds permissible to humanity and become tinged in a special sense with divinity."[7] He points out that in the Passover Seder, the annual festival devoted to the celebration of the Exodus, the role of Moses is completely suppressed.[8] His name does not appear in the text of the Seder celebration, which emphasizes the immediacy and singularity of God's redemption: "I will pass through the land of Egypt in that night; I and no other; and I will smite all the first-born of Egypt, and I, no flaming seraph; and I will execute judgments against all gods of Egypt, and I, no messenger."

It is as though in that exclusion of a mediator any tendency to deify Moses were anticipated and eliminated.

If, as we assume, the fire-god of the desert smiths lent some distinctive features to the character of Yahweh, they disappeared soon after the conquest of Canaan. The memory of the flame continued to live in the transformation into "the glory of the Lord" (Num. 16:42). A last effulgence of His sight, originally forbidden and terrifying, now blissfully appears in the wonderful sentences of the priestly blessing, filled with divine kindness towards man: "The Lord make His face shine upon thee. The Lord lift up His countenance upon thee and give thee peace."

18.

The Ten Commandments of the Savages

Everything becomes uncertain about the Exodus-Sinai phase when critical research compares the scarcity of objective data available with the biblical story. Everything: it has been doubted that Hebrew tribes ever were in Egypt, whether there ever was an Exodus from this country or a leader called Moses. Mount Sinai is, as George Leigh-Mallory said of Mount Everest, "still there," but many modern scholars do not believe that the Hebrew tribes of the second millennium ever went there as the Scripture asserts.

There are, however, gaps within the general uncertainty, patches of relative clarity in the pervasive darkness. The Decalogue, or the "Ten Words," as the Bible says, do not form a part of that lighter area. Scholars generally agreed to disagree about the following questions: Who was the writer and who were the editors of the Decalogue? What was their original arrangement? What was its primal form and what is the relation of the code transmitted in Exodus 34 and of the code of curses in Deuteronomy 27? What is the original meaning of each of the ten words? Several scholars do not believe that there were ten commandments since in Exodus 34 there are twelve rather than ten. The comparison of the two versions of the Decalogue adds many new problems to the already unsolved ones. So does the comparison of the Decalogue and of the moral code of other ancient religions.

Added to those questions are others more subtle than these, for instance some concerning the two tablets on which the commandments are written. Some scholars were indiscreet enough to ask: How large would those tablets have had to be to contain one hundred and seventy-two words? What was their division on the two tablets? Had Moses, at the age of eighty years, the physical strength to carry them from the top of Sinai down to the camp of the Israelites? Besides and beyond those questions, there are queries concerning the economic, religious, and cultural situation of the Israelites. A fixed, recurrent day of rest such as the Sabbath is possible for an agricultural state; it is impossible for nomads or semi-nomadic people. Just as unimaginable is the presence of slaves and oxen and of houses instead of tents for the Hebrew tribes during their wanderings in the desert. The prohibition of "graven images" is not imaginable before the eighth century.

From all those considerations it has been concluded that the code we call the Ten Commandments is a late descendant of a much simpler and shorter code that must have differed considerably from the one we know.

From the affluence of discussions that threaten at this point to overflow this presentation, we pick one issue that is linked with the subject of the preceding chapter. Moses reminds the Children of Israel: "These words Yahweh spake unto all your assembly in the mount out of the midst of the fire, of the cloud, and of the thick darkness, with a great voice . . ." (Deut. 5:22). "These words" are, of course, all the commandments and Moses wants to remind the fugitives from Egypt that they all heard them.

All of them? The rabbis doubted that: God speaks of Himself in the first person only in the first commandment—perhaps also in the second. In the others He speaks of Himself in the third person. What does this change in person mean? The great philosopher Maimonides (1125–1204) argues that the Lord spoke to Moses, not to the people who heard only a mighty sound, "a great voice" and not distinct words. The Israelites perceived only the first two commandments in the same manner as Moses. But these first two proclaim the existence and unity of God, which constitute principles arrived at by means of reason. The remaining commandments are of ethical and authoritative character and do not contain truths arrived at by intellect. The last eight were revealed to Moses alone who explained them to the people.[1]

Another commentator, the Jewish theologian, Samuel David Luzzatto (1800–1865) is not satisfied with Maimonides' explanation: if people heard only sounds, they did not hear the first commandments either. A third commentator, Hasdai Abraham Crescas (1340–1410) expressed serious doubts about the fact that a people in slavery, whose spirit was broken and whose vision was dimmed by hard labor, could have comprehended the highest metaphysical concepts from mere sounds and in a fleeting moment. Also other rabbis doubted that the Lord delivered a long address to a large multitude. Thus they were wavering between having Him let everything out in one utterance and having Him speak only the first two commandments to the people. We will stop here and not follow the explanations and comments of the theologians and their scholarly successors.

Archaeology and biblical criticism have shown us how many resemblances exist between the Decalogue and the code of the Babylonian empire builder, King Hammurabi (about 1728–1686 B.C.), the famous chapter 125 of the Egyptian Book of the Dead, certain Assyrian and Hittite laws, codes proclaimed hundreds of years before Moses was born. It was mostly through the Canaanite influence that the Babylonian and other codifications entered the Mosaic law.[2] The idea that a god gives the law was old when it first appeared in the biblical story. The upper end of the black diorite on whose surface almost eight thousand words are inscribed, shows Hammurabi who receives the law from the sun god Shamesh exactly as Moses received the two stone tablets from Yahweh. Yet the Decalogue is a unique landmark in religious evolution and cannot, although it is a compilation, be compared with the moral codes of the other religions of the ancient Near East.[3]

However interesting the relations of the "ten words" to those other precepts are, our main attention remains focused on the resemblances between the Mosaic codes and the laws that are taught to the adolescent boys in primitive initiation. But are there any resemblances of this kind?

Rudyard Kipling pleads:

> *Ship me somewheres east of Suez*
> *Where the best is like the worst,*

> *Where there aren't no Ten Commandments, an'*
> *A man can raise a thirst.*

There might not be any Ten Commandments in a Mandalay to which Kipling's desire goes, but the "Four Noble Truths" of the Buddhists and the series of commandments of the Mohammedans of Burma show some conspicuous resemblances with the morality of the Hebrew Decalogue. There are, of course, not any Ten Commandments with the Australian and African tribesmen who still live in the Neolithic Age, but there are, in their place, rudimentary rules of behavior that their adolescents were taught at the initiation. It would be worthwhile to collect an anthology of the "Decalogues of the Savages." Nothing of that nature has ever been attempted. The instructions given to the novices differ, of course, in their nature and scope in various tribes. They are often combined with lessons about the tribal lore and legends, and introduce the young boys into the sacred mysteries. Before all they are especially warned not to divulge anything they see or hear, and implicit obedience toward the elders of the tribe is strongly impressed upon them. But besides that the duties of the tribesmen towards the women and the aged as well as towards the community, especially in time of war, are instilled in the boys. Avoidance of selfishness and greediness is stressed and taught.

Here are a few representative examples of those primitive codes: The chiefs of the Loritja, about whom the missionary Carl Strehlow presented an excellent report,[4] tell the young people after they are subincised: "You are always to go about with young men; you are not to go in the neighborhood of women; you are not to have any intercourse at all with the other sex. If we hear that you go after women and girls, we shall cast you into the fire." The mentor of the Yacs in Africa announces the following precepts: "You, my pupil, are now circumcised. Your father and your mother, honor them. Do not go into the house unannounced, you might find them in tender embrace. You must not fear girls; sleep together, bathe together." Then follows advice not to have sexual intercourse during menstruation. The missionary, S. Bamler, relates that the youths of the Tami Papua are told: "Do not put yourselves under other people's roof," which means "do not seduce other men's wives." The young men of the Karesau Islands in Australia were told that they must no longer quarrel with men, and when their fathers reproved them, they should not oppose them. The Binbinga-tribe novice is admonished that "he must no longer speak to, or even look at the Tjuanaki men who are his tribal fathers-in-law." He is told that "he must not quarrel with older men." Among the Loritja tribe the circumcised young men are told: "You are to be obedient, as we are obedient. You are to behave as we do. We are very prone to anger; when a circumcised youth does not behave, we will kill him. If you wish to live, behave well, lest you will be cast into the fire."

Thus the precepts of the primitive elders are accompanied by threats just as those of the Decalogue are by curses. When the Muruquin initiates try to blow the trumpet which is supposed to be the father of the tribe, the old men for the first time command all of them to "respect their fathers and mothers, never tell lies, not to run after women and the uninitiated."[5] In the Marita rites of the African Kikuku, the older men speak gravely and sternly to the initiates. Usually it is the boy's uncle who tells him that the time has come when he must understand that life is full of responsibilities. Irresponsible childhood is now ended. After the four months of seclusion, the boys are lectured to this effect: "You have been, during your boyhood, poorly behaved and irresponsible, and lacking in proper respect for your elders. You are weaklings who must be made into men worthy to take your place in the tribe and fight its battles against its hereditary enemies." Among the African Basutos the initiated are adjured to "be men, avoid father and mother, obey your chiefs."[6] The puberty rituals on the Fiji Island, Viti Levu, show many primitive features, rarely observed elsewhere. At the end of the ceremonies all the young men take a bath in the river and are presented to the high priest. He admonishes them to fulfill the obligations of the adults and to obey the tribal rules. He threatens them with the curse of the gods, should they divulge the mysteries of the Nanga, and forbids them to eat certain foods. In most Australian tribes the rules and prohibitions are communicated to the novices after their circumcision or subincision.[7]

Accumulation of further instances from savage and half-civilized people could not strengthen the impression that the rules and precepts inculcated in the novices during the initiation are the primal ancestors of the Decalogue. The differences are understandable when we take into consideration the divergent social and cultural levels. They are too obvious to be discussed. The common features of the essential content and of the social purpose, the educational aim, and the role within the group are very conspicuous. While the scholars do not tire of finding new analogies in the Babylonian, Canaanite, Egyptian and

Hittite codes, they have failed to trace the "ten words" back to that primal model in the Australian bush. The parallel of the Decalogue and of these tribal prohibitions and moral concepts is so convincing that it forms a cornerstone of our comparative concept.

There are several codes of the ancient Near East that challenge comparison with the Book of the Covenant, but none of them equals the greatness of the Decalogue in its selectiveness, precision, and simplicity. It has been called "the universal alphabet of religion for all mankind."[8]

In this connection I cannot refrain from allowing myself some remarks on the margin of my subject. The Ten Commandments present perhaps the Alpha of religion, but certainly not its Omega. The evidence of world history and especially of our time, proves that men have not yet learned even the beginnings of that alphabet. The governments of the world order their people to commit mass murders as though they had never heard of the Sixth Commandment. At this critical moment mankind is faced with a question of destiny. Will the swing upwards that started in the initiation of neolithic Australian tribesmen, and was continued in the initiation of the Hebrews in the desert, be futile or will that inner demand prevail? The question is not what the future of mankind will be, but whether or not mankind will have any future.

19.

Circumcision and Covenant

We are still dealing with a comparison of two phenomena that, as far as we know, have never been considered similar: the revelation on Mount Sinai and the puberty rites of savage tribes. Such a comparison of a unique prehistoric event and of periodically repeated tribal ceremonies seemed at first blush venturesome, even bizarre. What should the theophany of the

Lord on Mount Sinai before the Hebrews have in common with the initiation of adolescents into primitive society of Australian, African, and American savages? Are we led astray by the will-o'-the-wisp of some superficial similarities? If there were any objective and verifiable likenesses or connections, would they not have been observed, described, and evaluated by scholars of comparative religion and of high biblical criticism long ago? Nothing of this kind has become known to us.

We have, however, reached a point of no return. If we have been deceived by some accidental similarities, we shall soon find out. But if, as we thought, a new and valid insight has emerged, its percussions would cast a surprising light on the most important event and focal point of the three great monotheistic religions. There would also be a radical change in our ideas about the Sinai revelation.

One aspect of our central thesis needs to be made more explicit. We have assumed that the biblical narrative of the Exodus-Sinai events is a report of an initiation of the Hebrew tribes, founded on an old tradition and welded with the account of the historic events of their Exodus from Egypt and their infiltration of Canaan. This basic assumption presupposes that initiation rites, originally performed at puberty, appear in the biblical story expanded to a whole people. It is described there as a social and religious initiation of all Hebrew tribes. The transition to such a presentation that may and may not correspond to historic truth was, of course, facilitated by the fact that in the puberty ceremonies of most people, not individuals, but whole age groups are initiated.

If we take that extension to a collective initiation for granted, some differences that still separate the basic ceremonies of savages from the Sinai-Exodus events are to be understood through distortions, omissions and accretions of the biblical presentation. The central idea of death and resurrection appears thus in the biblical narrative, in the guise of the notion that none of the emigrants from Egypt will be alive and enter Canaan, and that a new generation will take possession of the Promised Land. In the initiation ceremonies of Australian tribes the novices returning from their long seclusion behave as though they were infants. They act as if they were "born yesterday" and have to learn to walk and talk. Among most tribes they get new names after initiation. The new Hebrew generation, born during the years of wandering in the desert, appears in the Holy Scripture as a new nation brought into existence in their exile. The people are, from then on, called Israelites or Sons of Israel. They now adopt the name given to Jacob by the angel with whom he wrestled at the crossing of the river Jabbok. Some biblical scholars, for instance U. Cassuto, assume that the name of the people is to be considered primary compared with that of the ancestor.[1]

But besides that replacement of young men of the same age group, or of individual initiation to a collective one, we find all essential features of the puberty ritual again: the long seclusion and segregation, the avoidance (or missing) of certain food and the eating of sacred food (manna), the appearance of the tribal god, the indoctrination of the novices with certain social and religious prohibitions, and the commandments under threats of curses.

If our basic assumption is correct, we would expect that these features would be followed by others which we found in the puberty rituals of Australian and African tribes; namely mutilations, circumcision or subincision. It is at this point that the biblical narrative comes, in a manifest form, closest to an account of a primitive puberty ritual—of course, displaced to a whole people. Here all biblical scholars and historians cannot disavow the similarity with the initiation of savages. As a matter of fact, none of them discussing the tribal circumcision which the Priestly Code reports (Josh. 5:2–9) fails to mention this connection of the general circumcision of the Israelites under Joshua.

All experts point out that the custom is an ancient one whose archaic character appears already in the use of stone knives. In that biblical passage emerges again the idea that "all the people that came out of Egypt that were males, even all the men of war, died in the wilderness by the way after they came out of Egypt. And their children whom he raised in their stead, them Joshua circumcised." It is as though the old concept of death and resurrection had to be mentioned again in connection with the important part of primitive initiation. It was not yet forgotten that circumcision was an important rite of the Passover festival (Exod. 12:43–48, Josh. 5:2–9).

Whatever was the significance of that ritual originally, the sacrifice of the prepuce became very soon the tangible sign of divine initiation. It was demanded in Yahweh's name. Jeremiah, who appears in this direction as predecessor of St. Paul, let the Lord say:

"Circumcise yourselves to the Lord, and take away the foreskins of your heart, ye men of Judah and inhabitants of Jerusalem" (Jer. 4:4).

Circumcision, originally a part of the puberty ritual, was usually performed only in the presence of the same sex as the novice and in a secluded place.[2] There is no doubt that, with the ancient Semitic people, circumcision was considered a necessary premise for marriage. In some Arabic tribes marriage ceremonies were preceded by circumcision.[3] George Barton assumes that circumcision was the Semitic puberty rite.[4]

The notion that circumcision was originally a tribal mark of the Hebrew people cannot be correct because almost all Semitic nations, with the notable exception of the Philistines, performed circumcision on their males when they reached the marriageable age. G. A. Barton assumes that circumcision was, in the beginning among the Semites, probably "a sacrifice to, or a mark of consecration to the goddess of fertility, and was designed to secure her favor in the production of offspring."[5]

By the time of the Priestly document, circumcision was considered in Israel as the sign of the covenant between the people and Yahweh. Yes, the expression *b'rith* (covenant) is often used in the sense of circumcision and *b'rith malah* means in Hebrew the covenant of the circumcision.

We encounter here a remarkable difference between the Hebrew ritual of the circumcision and that of the primitive tribes, a difference worthy of our attention. The Hebrews circumcised their young men perhaps at first in the house of their fathers, but "as early as the Geonic time, the ceremony had been transferred from the house of the parents to the synagogue, where it took place after the service in the presence of the whole congregation.[6] It seems to this writer that the original Semitic circumcision performance must have taken place in the society of men as among the primitive people where the operation forms a part of tribal initiation. The difference I mentioned is the following: While among the Jews circumcision is the token of the covenant between Yahweh and His people, anthropologists agree that "distinctly religious ceremonies in connection with the rite are extremely rare" among savage tribes of Africa and Australia.[7]

As mentioned before, in the collective circumcision ritual of the Hebrew tribes after crossing the Jordan, the Exodus account comes closest to a report of a puberty festival. In the concept of a covenant between the Lord and the people of the Hebrew tribes the biblical narrative seems to be the most remote from the character of the primitive puberty rituals as they are described by anthropologists and missionaries, who had ample opportunity to observe the life of Australian and African aborigines. Apparently there is no connection between the two. Yet more detailed examination of the initiation will come to the conclusion that the germ of that concept of a bond between the tribesmen is already present in the puberty rituals of savage tribes.

The institutions of age classes and men's societies were explored by Heinrich Schurtz in his book on *Alterklassen und Männerbünde*[8] almost sixty years ago. This ethnologist shows that men's societies develop from age classes that have their natural center of gravity in the puberty rites. It is tempting to compare the closer social union of the age groups in primitive societies with the ties existing between students of the same age in our colleges and universities. We know that often friendships, founded in younger years, are continued long after the end of the studies (the old "school tie"), and are renewed in clubs. Schurtz points out that the germs of the secret societies, to be found with almost all primitive people, can already be detected in certain features of the puberty rites which young men of the same age are experiencing together. The other source of the tribal unity is secured by the attempt of the older generation to bridge the gulf between them and the young men. These endeavors tie the parents-and-sons generation together almost as intimately as the "fraternities" with which we can compare the age groups of the primitive social organizations.

We can exclude from our comparison the concept of a covenant of God with the people, because, as Ernest Wright justifiably pointed out, that concept "cannot be treated independently of election, because it merely puts into concrete terms, almost metaphorically, the meaning of the relationship involved in election."[9] The idea of a covenant between a god or—in totemistic tribes, an animal guardian—and individuals is not alien to primitive tribes. In the puberty rites of the American Indians the young men who obtain such an animal guardian, or manito, often draw blood from different parts of their bodies to seal their compact with the totem. The Indians of Honduras offered their blood to their nagual, "whereupon such friendship was contracted between them that, when one of them died, the other did not survive."[10] We have here a primitive kind of blood union with the deity.

Blood plays a special role in sealing the compact with Yahweh. W. Robertson Smith points out that the relationship between Yahweh and Israel was that of a natural kinship, constituted by the formal covenant at Mount Sinai where the blood of the sacrifice was applied to the altar on the one hand and to the people on the other (Exod. 24:4 ff).[11] It is not difficult to imagine that the primitive blood covenant between the young people and their totemistic guardians developed during many centuries into the kind of bond between the god and his worshippers which we find in the Old Testament. The roots of the covenant idea are certainly to be discovered in the situation of the initiation. The evolution of the concept of a natural kinship between God and the clan to the stage when he became the God of the Hebrew confederation cannot be followed at this point. The origin of the blood brotherhood sealed by sacrifice of an animal would certainly be worthy of a special inquiry.

The emergence of Israel into nationhood, this making a people out of a rabble of slaves, is still full of problems for the historians. Yet many of the puzzling features are removed by the comparison with the primitive initiation. The revelation on Mount Sinai was considerably helped by human agencies. Nietzsche once wrote: "On the heights it is warmer than one thinks in the valleys."

20.

The Confederacy

It is astonishing that the biblical scholars and commentators have not paid more attention to the primitive initiation situation in their endeavor to explain the confederation at Mount Sinai. Only the narrow departmental point of view could have prevented them from recognizing that the social and religious beginnings of the Hebrew tribes are founded on the same principles which determine the initiation of primitive societies. C. W. Harley points out that the common initiation of the boys into the Poro society leads many Liberian tribes to form age groups which later serve as social units in peace and war. The function and influence of the Poro society "is felt even outside tribal limits and many details of the organization are intertribal . . ."[1]

The developmental gaps between the organization of the natives of Central Australia and that of the early Hebrew tribes are to be filled without too great an effort of the imagination. Only a few links have to be supplied. The roles that men play in the organization of larger forms of society are explainable when one traces them back to those associations which were formed during the initiation rites. We learn, for instance, that many tribal groups of Central Australia which live separated from each other are united on the occasion of initiation festivals. Anthropologists describe with many details how messengers to other groups are sent out on such occasions. These groups come together at a certain place; important decisions concerning much larger groups than individual tribes are made at those meetings.[2]

The biblical report about the confederacy of the Hebrew tribes suggests to many archaeologists and biblical scholars, for instance Martin Noth,[3] an analogy of the Sinai (or Quadesh) bond with the Greek Amphictyony, that union of different people centered in a temple for the common performance of certain religious duties. There are indubitable analogies and similarities between the two social organizations (besides fundamental divergencies), but would it not have been more advantageous in the interest of scientific research to trace both concepts back to their primal source? In my view the prototype of these coalitions is the association of men formed around the initiation rituals of primitive tribes. In carrying the analogy between the Israelitic covenant and the Greek Amphictyony to the uttermost limits, some historians of Hebrew evolution have forced a door that was always open. A part of the acumen used in that inquiry might have sufficed to discover the hidden gate leading to the pattern of primitive initiation as the origin of both social and religious institutions.

Turning our attention to the barbarous and crude prototype, we choose at random some instances of blood covenant between the young men as well as the bond between older or parent generation and the young men of savage tribes.

The young men who are subjected to circumcision at the same time form a very close union. The Australian Narringari call these groups by the name of *"wirake."* The young people of the Herero who are circumcised together are considered friends. The chief's son is often the leader of the Negro age group which shared the puberty rites with him. The friendship among such youth groups lasts for their whole life.

The description by Spencer and Gillen of the Kuntamara ceremony in Central Australia may be cited as a representative example of the other kind of primitive blood covenant. "On this particular occasion,

after the performance on the corrobboree ground, all the men gathered together in the bed of the creek, where the youths were camped
and performed the kuntamara. Each man took a sharp stone or glass,
and cut himself until the blood flowed freely, the newly initiated
youths following their example . . ."[4] Afterwards the circumcised
young man touches the head of his father with a little of his own
blood, and then strokes the head of his grandfather. The meaning of
this ceremony is to unite the men who had been circumcised long ago
with the youths who have just been initiated. The natives assert that
the ceremony aids the healing of the boys and strengthens the bond
among the tribesmen. In order to form a special friendship the youths
of the Mara and Anula tribes drop some blood from the circumcision wound on the man upon whom they are lying during the operation.

Father W. Schmidt reports the following ceremony of the Karesau
Islanders: All the men of the tribe, as well as the boys, have to drink
from a hole into which blood from their penes has flowed. Since the
tribesmen who were circumcised long ago pierce their penes at this
occasion and their blood is collected there and mixed with water, the
situation reminds us of the collective circumcision as well as of the
blood covenant of the Hebrew tribes.

It is not essential for our purpose that the biblical narrative projects events of a much later time back into the age of Moses and
Joshua, and that the Hebrew covenant in the form reported in the Bible
is perhaps to be dated some centuries later. What concerns us at this
point of our investigation is not how the covenant evolved from a
primal coalition of some Hebrew tribes, but what it finally became:
namely, a people. After one has attentively studied the details of a
picture, one has to step back and to look at it from a distance to get
a total impression of the work of art.

A last glance at the Australian puberty ritual will show us that
not only the Sinai covenant, but also the Balum festival, has political
significance above and beyond the promotion of young people to
the status of adult manhood. Lowie points out that the initiation
unites, at intervals of ten to eighteen years, the Bukaua, the kindred
Jabim, the Tami Islanders, and the Papuan Kai. During the course
of the ritual all feuds are suspended, foreign guests are invited, and
intertribal amity is promoted. The comparison with the primal coalition of the Hebrew tribes can hardly be escaped.

What about the religious significance of the Balum mysteries for the adult men who conduct the performance? Is there a complete absence of any religious faith? One is tempted to think so when one learns that the tribesmen want only to mystify and terrorize the women, to whom they declare that the Balum, a voracious demon, wants to eat up their sons. That monster will be pacified only if he receives a fat pig for every boy. Circumcision is explained as the wound resulting from the bite or scratch of the monster who is spewing the boys out again. The terrified women do their best to fatten the pigs for the insatiable Balum, whose raucous voice they hear in the bull-roarers the men are swinging.

Is all this only a hoax propounded to frighten the women? Only a story for the intimidation of mothers and children? Lowie and other scholars have justifiably pointed out that the irreverent and frivolous ideas of the men need not exclude their faith in some mysterious being that is an incarnation of some spirits or ancestors. The fact that novices receive instructions of a moral nature in the name of those tribal gods or totems confirms the assumption that the Balum mysteries have a crude religious significance.

To round out the analogy that we have constructed, we need only refer to the original customs of Australian and African tribes whose young men, after having recovered from the circumcision operation, go out to fight with other tribes. Anthropological literature has many examples indicating that in primitive cultures a novice might be expected to prove his bravery and virility by killing an enemy.[5] Instead of accumulating quotations of such instances from the abundant evidence about native tribes, we turn back to the phase of the biblical report on the Exodus-Sinai events to the account of the conquest of Canaan, following the crossing of the Jordan. We know that the traditional story reports that the circumcised Hebrews abode in their places in the camp till "they were whole" (Josh. 5:8). They had no manna any more, but ate of the fruit of the land of Canaan.

The historicity of the Israelites' tradition of the conquest of Canaan is not doubtful, although many modifications must be made. There were perhaps forays and infiltrations rather than wars, but in a short time the Israelites settled in some district of the hill country. There is no adequate reason why we should follow here the social and religious evolution of the new nation in the pre-monarchic age. The last phase of the analogy we have constructed between the Sinai events and the primitive Australian initiation confirms the striking parallelism between the two phenomena, so removed from each other in culture pattern, time, and place. We came to the close of that comparative inquiry in following the sequence of circumcision, recovery in camp, and combat. We have thus completed a circle that widened to such an extent that it encompassed some the most primitive and some of the most sublime phenomena of human civilization.

21.

The Next Assignment

We have now arrived at a check point. It has been a strange road that has led us there. We were catapulted from the peak of Mount Sinai or Mount Horeb into the Australian bush—from the grandiose buildings of dynastic Egypt into the primitive huts of savages of our time. With the hero of an old German tragedy, we feel like exclaiming: "Thought, where have you taken me?"

Here is the blueprint of a comparison of the Exodus-Sinai events transmitted to us by the Holy Scripture and of the initiation festivals of primitive tribes, described in detail by contemporary missionaries and anthropologists. The biblical report, often altered and distorted, still shows traces of the form and essential content of a puberty ritual. Transferred from a generation of young men to a whole people and welded to the tradition of their Exodus from Egypt, the narrative presents the contour of that original picture covered over by later paintings. What does it all mean? Does the underlying resemblance we discovered represent a direct line of evolution in the history of man? Do we have here a new approach to an old problem that appeared to be solved and was shelved long ago? When we tentatively put the picture of a primitive initiation festival in the place of the revelation report, does this not amount to replacing a rebus by a crossword puzzle? The inquirer who was mystified by the hard problem of revelation is now perplexed by the possibility that a puberty festival emerges out of the fire and smoke surrounding the

Sacred Mountain. The supernatural has withdrawn to cede its place to the incredible; a transcendental phenomenon has been replaced by a fantastic one.

Archaeology, history, and higher biblical criticism have agreed that the Exodus narrative of the theophany is a composed story condensing the religious and political development of some centuries and tracing it back to a single mythical experience of the Hebrew tribes. This view is now almost common to the experts. It is neither doubted any longer, nor is it re-examined. Firmly cemented convictions and faithfully preserved concepts of this kind are a greater obstacle to the progress of research than the uncertainties and obscurities of the material. "Most of our trouble," someone nicely said, "is caused not by the things we don't know, but by those we do know that just aren't true."

Our own endeavor has been directed toward a reconstruction of the prehistoric events whose memory continues to live in the biblical account. We have been asking: What is the secret of Sinai? What is concealed in the revelation? We have been aiming at the discovery of the primal traditions that were orally transmitted from generation to generation. We do not doubt that even these original traditions did not give a precise and true account of those events, but they certainly came closer to reality than the biblical report transformed by the alterations and distortions of its many editors and scribes. We hope that we will be better equipped to understand the character of the Sinai revelation after unravelling those later changes and penetrating to the core of the oldest Hebrew traditions.

In his recent presidential address to the American Historical Association, William L. Langer regrets that professional historians have in so great number become buried in their own minute research and specialized frames of references.[1] They lack the "speculative audacity" of the natural scientists. He expects that the historians, like their cousins in the natural sciences, will have new ideas, new points of view, and new techniques. "We must be ready from time to time to take fliers into the unknown, even though some of them may prove wide of the mark." He refers specifically to the urgently needed deepening of historical understanding through exploitation of the concepts and findings of psychoanalysis and depth-psychology. It is in this spirit of "speculative audacity" and of psychoanalysis that the following attempt at reconstruction is undertaken. As such it presents a piece of that special branch of research I prefer to call archaeological psychoanalysis.[2]

This writer, a psychoanalyst for more than forty-five years, is well aware of the pitfalls and dangers to be encountered when working in the area of a somewhat remote science. The scarcity of data and the abundance of scholarly treatises on the subject warn him to be cautious and to move forward with considerate slowness.

PART THREE

A Discovery in Archaeological Psychoanalysis

22.

Attempt at Reconstruction

In the great contest or duel between Yahweh and the Pharaoh, the Passover festival plays the decisive role. The Israelites asked the Pharaoh for permission to go into the desert and celebrate a festival to their God. The fight to obtain this permission is the content of the legend—which many scholars consider to be an "etiological" one—whose intention is to explain that the festival rites had been ordained by Moses. The biblical narrative implies, however, that the festival was long cherished by the semi-nomadic tribes, but one that could not have been celebrated in the years of bondage. It was perhaps the only one common to the Israelites who no longer had much in common, whose associations with one another were loose, and whose traditions were faint.

What was the character of this festival? We mean, of course, the original character since all experts have agreed that its original nature was transformed through its becoming connected with the Exodus from Egypt. The Bible does not tell us how the festival began, but how it came to be preserved. Passover is, in fact, "the heart of the cultus of Israel."[1] and is the nucleus about which many observances gathered.

Is it possible to reconstruct the distinctive features of the original Hebrew festival which has acquired a new character and was adapted to the new purpose of the commemoration of the Exodus? We doubt it, but the attempt at reconstruction is well worth the effort since Passover is certainly the most important feast of ancient Israel and its history reaches into a phase long before the entrance into Canaan—which means long before the Israelites became an agricultural people.

Before we attempt to reconstruct the nature of the original Passover rite, I have to remind the reader that many features of the festival described in the Bible originate in the adaptation to the later tradition of the departure from Egypt. This tradition is itself at least of double character in so far as one motive is crossed by another. It appears first as though the departure has the purpose of undertaking a journey into the wilderness to hold a feast for Yahweh followed by a return of the Israelites who were bondsmen to the Egyptians. Pharaoh bids Moses not to go away (Exod. 8:28). But the Israelites take to flight and they become runaway slaves. There is, on the one hand, the stubborn reluctance of Pharaoh to let the Israelites leave. There is, on the other, the report also by Manetho that Israel was expelled from Egypt.[2] Even according to Exodus the Israelites were driven out of Egypt—perhaps the first expulsion which was to be followed by so many others in the history of the Hebrew tribes. Pharaoh said to Moses: "Get thee from me, take heed to thyself, see my face no more for in the day that thou seest my face thou shalt die." And Moses said: "Thou hast spoken well. I will see thy face no more."

There are some features in the Passover tradition which, if psychology interpreted, might lead us to a track back into its prehistory. The most conspicuous trait of this kind is the connection of the festival with the dedication of the first-born. This motif occurs so often and so clearly that there cannot be any doubt that it belongs to the very early form of the festival. We have to separate these original festivals from the cult legend connecting them with the emigration story from Egypt which was inserted later to glorify the god of the people at the paschal feast "through an exposition of the historical events that created the people."[3] The narrative as we read it in the Bible is, of course, no report, but weaves a national halo around the Passover that commemorates the liberation from slavery.

We cannot enter here into the vivid and long discussion of the Passover rites, of the redemption of the first-born and the instances of the sacrifice of the first-born. J. G. Frazer has collected abundant evidence for his conviction that at the roots of the Passover ritual lies an ancient Semitic custom of sacrificing the first-born. This ritual was later mitigated by the custom of redemption, but occasionally re-emerged in the course of ancient Israel. There is no doubt that the Canaanites and Phoenicians sacrificed their first-born in times of national danger. Eduard König[4] and other biblical scholars believe that the Israelites took this custom from their neighbors under the false impression that it would please Yahweh. According to Exodus

(13:2,12) all the first-born, both of man and of beast, shall be given to Yahweh, either actually sacrificed or redeemed by a vicarious sacrifice. The main part of the Passover legend is centered around events connected with the first-born and we have to conclude that this element was once the predominant one in the character of the festival.[5] It has, as we shall see, preserved this role in spite of the new significance given to the ritual.

The two major events allegedly commemorated by the Passover were connected with the last plague when the first-born sons of the Egyptians were smitten, except in those houses on which the paschal blood was smeared, and the hasty departure of the Israelites from the land. The sacrifice of the lamb as the substitute for the sacrifice of the first-born child is, of course, a later form of that custom. The blood of the lamb was sprinkled on the doors of the houses of the Israelites. When Yahweh went out to smite all the first-born sons of Egypt, he would pass over (which is indicated in the word *passah*) the houses thus marked. The Passover changed thus its character from a ritual of the sacrifice of the first-born son to a feast by which the offering of a male kid or lamb in its first year redeems the human first-born.

The contrast between the treatment of the Egyptian and the Israelite first-born is, in psychoanalytic interpretation, dissolved by the assumption that here a succession in religious evolution is presented as an antithesis. There was a time, long before the age of Moses, in which the tribal god of the Hebrews was supposed to demand the sacrifice of the first-born males. One need think only of the patriarch of the Hebrew tribes to find convincing evidence for this thesis; Abraham is "called" by God to sacrifice his beloved son. The biblical narrative makes this demand appear as temptation, but this is clearly a late interpretation. But here we already have definite traits which in their succession point in a certain direction in spite of all secondary elaboration and distortion of the original tradition. We have here the introduction of circumcision, the covenant between Yahweh and Abraham, the near sacrifice of the boy at puberty age, and the redemption of this sacrificial object by a ram—just as later the sacrifice of the first-born will be replaced by the paschal lamb. Add to the aforementioned features the detail that Abraham had to make a journey of three days into the land of Moriah to offer his son as a burnt offering to God. What are we reminded of here? What occurs to us when we hear this report and when we recall the other story of the slaughter of the first-born and the Exodus from Egypt? Do we not detect here a faint echo of the tales anthropologists and missionaries tell of the puberty rites of Australian and African aborigines? *Is there not a concealed resemblance between the essential traits of the biblical Passover and those of the primitive initiation of the young people?*

We remember that the young men of Australian tribes are supposed to be swallowed or killed by Balum or a ghost who will release them only if he receives enough roast pigs. The monster gives the boys back after those pigs are offered to him. In the procedure—very realistically carried out for instance in the Kai tribe—the novice is supposed to be swallowed up and vomited out when a pig is offered for his redemption. The pigs are, of course, eaten by the men of the tribe who function as guardians or sponsors of the novices.

We have here, in the area of primitive customs of Australian aborigines, an early pattern of what we find again in modified forms in the biblical narrative of Yahweh's demand that Abraham should sacrifice his son, and of the killing of Egypt's first-born sons by Yahweh. Here as there, the redemption of the human sacrifice by an animal as vicarious victim: a ram or lamb with the Hebrew tribes, pigs with the Australian primitive tribes.

Putting the initiation ritual of those savages beside the biblical report of the Passover celebration and neglecting for a moment the difference in the cultural level of Australian aborigines and the half-nomadic Israelites in Goshen, what conclusion may we draw from the coincidence of our material?

It seems to me that at least one hypothesis seems inescapable: The Passover celebration in the wilderness was a puberty or initiation festival of the tribes which were later known in their confederacy as Israelites.

True enough, many questions remain to be answered even after we accept the preliminary assumption we have made, but for the moment we wish to emphasize that the Passover, for whose celebration the Hebrews pleaded with the Pharaoh, was a puberty feast to be performed in the desert or at Kadesh, and that it was celebrated again in Canaan. It is connected with the proclamation of tribal laws in seclusion, with the appearance of the tribal god, with a confederacy of the Hebrews, and with circumcision. Those tribes asked for permission to celebrate it and they did celebrate it. It certainly marks a very important event in Israel's history, but its connection with the Exodus story is, in my judgment, a "secondary elaboration." Passover, or a festival akin to the biblical celebration, must have been a traditional periodically repeated ritual of greatest importance to the half-nomadic tribes in Goshen and neighboring lands.

It might be objected that we have failed to establish the conclusion that the original Passover was an initiation ritual by investigation, step by step; that we jumped to that conclusion. While we still ponder the possible objection, new confirmatory material occurs to us—material from the wellsprings of our historical memories. To mention only two bits of inner evidence regarding the connection between the Passover rite and primitive initiation rites in respect to the sacrifice of the first-born son to the terrible god: Does this principal theme not return later, namely in the Passion of Christianity, accomplished at Passover? Does not even that most crude and primitive trait of cannabalistic eating of the victim re-emerge in the most sublimated form of the Last Supper at Passover? Christ distributed the bread to his disciples saying: "This is my body" and gave the cup to them saying: "This is my blood of the covenant which is shed for many." The original character of the most ancient Passover celebration re-emerges here from its prehistoric recesses. Has this theme not reoccurred time and again since the Middle Ages in the form of the blood accusation of the ritual murder against the Jews who were said to use blood of children at the Passover celebration?[6]

These and many other legends can be cited as confirmatory evidence for our thesis about the original character of Passover as the initiation celebration of the Hebrew tribes. However, it is not our main purpose to verify this or even to make it plausible. The characterization and determination of Passover as a puberty ceremony is only a station on our road; our destination is the solution of the revelation mystery.

When we accept the designation of the ancient Passover festival as initiation, the revelation or the theophany would be the heart of the whole succession of events around the Sinai. Granted that the oldest Passover had that character which we attributed to it, what is its place in the history of the Exodus? Why is it connected with the emigration or the flight from Egypt? And where are traces of that original nature of Passover in its celebration in Judaism today? Is it not conceived as commemoration of those events?

We have to remain aware of the danger we run if we draw too many conclusions from that comparison because he who wants to prove too much, proves nothing.

23.

Commemoration

The noted mathematician Norbert Wiener reminds us[1] that the true scientist is one who has the power to see simultaneous aspects of a particular problem and to convert his fleeting impressions into something permanent. Professor Wiener explains that a scientist who is able to cram all the ideas of what the problem really involves into a single comprehensible concept has more than half solved the problem.

Let us freely admit that such simultaneous conversion of images into a single concept is difficult when the phenomena under inquiry change their character and are frequently shaped into something new and seemingly unconnected. Yet, the task of integration is not impossible. Concealed threads are eventually found to run from the present form and from the more recent ideas to the concealed and repressed original thoughts. This is as valid for individuals as for groups, for the dreams and symptoms of a person as for the institutions of society. In the area of religion, the present is, according to J. G. Frazer, "the best guide to the interpretation of the past, for while the highest forms of religion pass away like clouds, the lower stand firm and indestructible like rocks."[2] Those primitive elements never entirely disappear; they go underground and continue to live in a changed and modernized form often unrecognized or misunderstood. The forgotten and disavowed is disguised, but the repressed matter is immortal and periodically sends its descendants or offspring into the light of a new day.

We have found the traces of a suppressed significance of the Passover ritual in the biblical story, traces of a forgotten time in which the first-born sons of the Hebrew tribes were slaughtered at the primitive altars of Yahweh's predecessors. Abraham's sacrifice of his son reminded us that the Passover has its model in the prehistoric past of the many clans which, later, became the Hebrews. The question that emerges here concerns the boundaries we have to draw in this particular investigation, or what we shall regard as central. What is that "single comprehensive concept" into which our ideas have crystallized? It would be tempting to follow a line investigating the succession of treatments to which the father-generation submitted their adolescent sons. Some psychoanalytic theories have emphasized[3] the following notion: In the earliest phases of culture the sires killed the rebellious sons. Later on, the boys were banished or castrated. Circumcision appears in a following phase as a mitigated form of that cruel operation. At the end of that social evolution a puberty ritual develops which enables the male offspring to remain within the community when they have renounced their aggressive and incestuous wishes. Residues of those older and more primitive phases are still recognizable in somewhat veiled forms in the biblical narrative. They coexist with newer trends in a manner similar to the way in which old symbols and shapes appear in the structure of cathedrals which were built over a period of centuries. We can pursue the motive of redemption for the sacrifice of the son from Abraham to the night in Egypt in which the blood of a lamb, smeared at the door of a house, signified a redemptive mark for the slaughtering god.

If our interpretation of the original character of Passover as initiation ritual is correct, traces of that forgotten significance should still be discernible in the feast as it is celebrated today. This means that we expect to be able to discern residual features of the original Passover festival in the ritual of 1959, about five thousand years later.

Are there such traces? The traditional Passover of the Jews was celebrated this year 1959 according to the Jewish Calendar on April 23rd and ended on April 30th. It was observed in many thousand families in the same way. Matzoth was broken, the cups of wine were lifted, prayers were said and the story of the Exodus from Egypt was recited. In this festival there are many features of the final miracle in Egypt when the Almighty destroyed every first-born son of the Egyptians, but "passed over" the homes of the Israelites marked by the blood of the paschal lamb.

In the time of the Temple, the offering of the paschal lamb on the eve of the Passover formed an important part of the observance of the festival. This part of the ceremony has become obsolete with the destruction of the Temple, but the roasted shank bone is still on the Seder plate as a symbol. Such symbols, remnants of concepts reaching into hoary antiquity, abound on the table around which the members of the family assemble participating in a common worship.

Even today, three millennia after the Exodus, disguised memories exist from the time when Yahweh was a "god of bolts, bangs, and burns."

Manifestations of the memory of those decisive events in the history of the nation—better still, of the history by which the mixed multitude became a "nation"—appear in the Passover ceremonial in a symbolic and mostly "edible" form. There are, for instance, mixtures of apples, almonds, spices, and wine to symbolize the mortar of the bricks made by the Jewish slaves for the Pharaohs. Roasted eggs will recall ancient temple sacrifices. Reduced to a detail of the table order, historical memories are revived in such symbolic forms. It is not our plan to follow the devious and circuitous ways through which the rabbis arrived at new interpretations of details of ancient ceremonials. Our exploration is headed toward another goal, and the analytic view of the Passover ritual which we are exploring marks only a crossroad on our journey. There are, however, some features which prepare us for the character of the things to come.

There is, for instance, the following detail within the order of the Passover table: bitter herbs to recall the tears of Jewish mothers when the Egyptians took their sons from them. Of what are we reminded here beyond the memory of the cruel command of the Pharaoh? What associations of thought emerge from hidden recesses at this point? The boys in Ceram are admitted to the Kakian association at puberty.[4] They are conducted into a shed where they are believed to be murdered by the devil; a sword or spear dripping with blood, is thrust through the roof of the shed—a token of the boys' heads that have to be cut off. At this sight the mothers weep and wail, crying that the devil has murdered their sons. Describing the puberty rituals of the tribes in New Guinea, R. Neuhaus reports that the mothers of the Bukaua do not sleep on the night preceding the departure of their sons. They cry continuously and caress and fondle their boys whom a terrible monster will devour in the morning. The line whose direction we faintly perceive goes from the Australian boys and their sorrowing mothers, to the Hebrew mothers in Egypt whose sons were taken away to be slaughtered; and our thoughts go beyond this point when the figure of the Holy Virgin emerges, crying over the body of her divine son. The tears shed by the Hebrew mothers when their boys were taken away from them have a prototype in the sorrow of the mothers in the Australian initiation. This line can be followed until it arrives at the image of the Mater Dolorosa.

But there are other and more significant threads running from the Passover ritual to the puberty celebration of primitive tribes. Let me mention only two of them, both from the observance of the Passover festival. During that occasion the "Song of Songs" is recited. How does this jubilant and erotic poem come into the Passover service, and what is its place there? According to the rabbis, the Passover celebration originally commemorated also the awakening of nature in the spring. Is there not the verse: "For, lo, the winter is past" (The Song of Solomon 2:11). Beyond that, the "Song of Songs" was supposed to teach the espousal of Israel the beloved and God the lover, which took place at the time of the first Passover. The rabbis followed up this interpretation by extending it to the feast of the weeks that is celebrated fifty days after Passover and commemorates the revelation on Mount Sinai and the proclamation of the Ten Commandments. They assert: "God betrothed Israel as His bride on Passover and wedded her on Shabuot."[5] What is behind the poetic language of this comparison? It cannot be accidental that the obviously sexual "Song of Songs" is transferred here to the relationship between God and His people. We have learned from the reports of anthropologists and missionaries that the puberty rituals mark a phase at the end of which the young boys, who are now considered men, indulge in sexual orgies and enjoy a time of licentiousness. In some Australian tribes, the old men—representative of the father-generation—boast of their sexual experiences and encourage the young men to follow their example. The ceremonials in which the old and young men mingle their blood have the character of a homosexual intimacy. We understand that the transference of the concept of such a close relationship led to the idea that the Feast of Weeks is often termed the marriage anniversary of Israel to God.

Let me add a little vignette to this picture of the Passover week. During the Sabbath a portion from Ezekiel (37:4 ff.) is recited. Here is the grandiose vision of the prophet who sees the open valley full of dry bones, to whom Yahweh says: "Behold, I shall cause breath to enter into you and ye shall live." At the command of the Lord, Ezekiel prophesied and the bones came together, the sinews and the flesh came upon them. Skin covered them, and the wind breathed into them. They lived and stood upon their feet. The Lord God proclaimed that these bones were the whole house of Israel and said: "O my people, I shall open your graves and cause you to come up out of your graves and bring you into the land of Israel." The analogy of this concept with the notions of many initiations, in which the bones of the novices were removed and the candidates later resurrected by the medicine man, has not yet been pointed out.[6]

The vision of the future of the Jews recited during the Passover week is often quoted by the poets, who see in it an anticipation of the reunion of all Jews and the gathering-in of the fugitives. As far as I know, it has not yet been pointed out by the many commentators that the material of Ezekiel's comparison is taken from old and forgotten, yet living, folklore. Displaced from a generation to a whole people, the old central motif of the puberty ritual reappears here in a new form. The theme of death and resurrection which pervades the initiation festivals of the primitive tribes emerges in this vision as a disguised fantasy. The young men are supposed to be killed and then to be awakened to a new life in those Australian and African tribal ceremonies. It is not accidental that the vision of Ezekiel, the messenger of God, is recited during the Passover feast.

24.

The Bush Burned with Fire and Was Not Consumed

It is notably difficult to recognize some primitive motif when it is disguised, elaborated, and transformed—when it appears in the garb appropriate to a progressed civilization and in a cultural environment thousands of years removed from its original structure. Much precious time and effort in research are wasted through failure to recognize old, familiar material in such modernized and altered shape. New discoveries in history and in neighboring sciences are thus prevented from being brought to life and remain "miscarriages" of research. We realize then that our initial mistake did not lie in the fact that we found nothing where we searched, but rather that we did not choose the right place to initiate our search.

The Passover festival has sometimes been recognized as the "nucleus of the Hebrew ritual,"[1] but the other step—which was to follow the autobiography of the Hebrew tribes—was not taken. There is even an isolated hint to be found that the sojourn in the wilderness, the Passovers of the Red Sea and the Jordan were all regarded

as significant interim—as *"periode de marge"* in van Gennep's terminology. Thus, Heidel quotes some rabbis as saying that the great
redemption of Israel would take the form of a return to the Holy
Land and that the crossing of the Jordan is a return from death.[2]
Old traditions broadly suggest "that the sojourn in the wilderness
was a sort of entombment and that on the tenth or fifteenth Ab there
was a resurrection." Yet the other conclusion that there is a remnant
of that most important feature of death and resurrection in the puberty ritual is not drawn. The great departure, the Exodus from
Egypt, the sojourn in the wilderness, and the return to the Holy
Land is nowhere compared with the initiation which is the prototype
of all feasts of savage tribes.[3]

Neglect of the concealed clues whose interpretation would have
led to tracing the Exodus-Sinai report back to its origin was especially
fatal in the misunderstanding of the birth of the Jewish nation. The
smoke enveloping the Sacred Mountain has blurred the vision of
historians and biblical scholars who did not recognize that the organization of that greater form of Hebrew society had its roots in associations centered around the initiation. Tribes of Central Australia,
living far from each other, come together on the occasion of these
ceremonies. Messengers with invitations are sent out to different
groups to come to a certain place. At these meetings, described by
Spencer and Gillen,[4] important decisions are made concerning larger
groups than those consisting of tribes. It is a time "when the old men
from all parts of the tribe come together and discuss matters. Councils
of the older men are held day by day." It seems to me that this was
also the case in the emergency situation of the Hebrew tribes depart-
ing from Egypt. It was at the occasion of the puberty festival that the
first form of a confederacy was born out of a crowd. Here are the
roots of the covenant whose rudiments reach into pre-Mosaic time
and whose dissociated branches continued to exist, dispersed over the
world.

We see in those supertribal meetings at the occasion of initiation,
also the beginning of an oral tradition that will later exist as national
history. There, as Spencer and Gillen point out, "all the old traditions of the tribe are repeated and discussed and it is by means of
meetings such as this that a knowledge of the unwritten history of
the tribe and of leading members is passed on from generation to
generation." Tribal custom is preserved through many centuries. As
we noted, some of its most significant ramifications are found in the
narrative at the Passover table.

The thesis at which we have arrived, namely that the revelation at Mount Sinai is the heart of a puberty ritual, may have first seemed far more the result of precipitate guesses than that of logical conclusions. We ventured to connect the sojourn in the wilderness and the birth of a nation with the central motif of death and resurrection in the initiation rites of the savages. We did not hesitate to put the god of the Hebrew tribes on the same level as the totemistic demons or monsters that appear before the trembling boys of the Australian clans, although we are well aware that this god could not have been a totemistic animal or plant—that a difference of several thousand years of evolution separated the tribes in Goshen from the Australian aborigines.

No doubt there was that distance, but not even the Egyptians who looked down upon the Hebrew tribes as barbarians had entirely emancipated themselves from a late form of totemism. Their religion was, in spite of the evolution into higher polytheism, full of traces of totemistic worship and totemistic animals. The reader need not be reminded of the cult of the Golden Calf—or rather bull, because the word "calf" is used mockingly as a form of derision—and of the bronze serpent worshipped in the south, to remember how much totem-cult continued to live in early Israel. We are concerned here less with the cults of the Hebrew tribes, or rather of that human flotsam that went out from Egypt into the wilderness, but with the particular problem of the totem of Moses. The "totem of Moses"? But was Moses not the innovator of Hebrew religion? Was he not the founder of the "Mosaic" faith and his god Yahweh who called to him and said: "I am the God of thy father, the God of Abraham, the God of Isaac and the God of Jacob"?

Moses, who grew up at the court of the Pharaoh and who was "learned in all the wisdom of the Egyptians" (Acts. 7:22) had perhaps been initiated into the mystery-cults, and no doubt worshipped the god of Egypt before his conversion—that means before that great experience on Mount Horeb, the mountain of God who appeared to him in the burning bush.

There are two reasons why we would like to deal here explicitly with this experience reported in the third chapter of Exodus. Of primary importance is this first encounter of Yahweh and the fugitive prince of Egypt. The theophany on Mount Horeb is the event that marks the turning point in the Exodus story. There Moses gets his commission from Yahweh, who sends him back to the oppressed Israelites. But that experience on God's mountain has a personal side that has hardly been considered in the commentaries and discussions of biblical scholars. The mysterious side of the scene in which Moses led the flock of his father-in-law to the far lands of the desert, and the angel of the Lord appeared unto him in a flame of fire out of the midst of a bush, has often enough been described. There is no scarcity of rational explanations by the commentators. Also parallels to the saga in the myths of other people have been shown by the scholars.[5] What is to be missed again in those discussions is the significance of the story in the light of anthropological analogies. We shall therefore disregard the attempts to explain the phenomenon of the Burning Bush from a rational point of view—for instance, its identification with the Dictamnus plant of Palestine which contains a volatile oil and can be easily kindled on a hot day or when in contact with electricity.

It is appropriate to bring the experience of the Burning Bush into relation with the totemistic worship of plants and trees of which so many survivals are discernible even in the late sources of the Holy Scripture. The reference to the Lord "that dwelt in the bush" (Deut. 13:16) had not originally the meaning of His abode being there, but meant actually the bush or the tree being the Lord. I shall not discuss the Semitic tree-worship here, since I have treated the matter in great detail in a recent work in which I have sought to show that the predecessor of Yahweh was the tree-totem, against which Adam commits an outrageous crime.[6] The reader is referred to this book in which the evidence for a prehistoric Israelitic tree-cult is presented. The Burning Bush of the Exodus story will be recognized as a late descendant of a primeval plant-totem. It appears there as the god now dwelling on Mount Horeb. To the young Moses who has fled to Midian, the totem-god reveals himself in his primitive and primal shape. Here, in the middle of a high and sublime concept of the deity, is a return to relinquished and obsolete ideas of a totemistic god.

What interests us more than this regression to a forgotten past is, at this moment, the fact of Yahweh's revelation itself and its place in Moses' life and lifework. The scene can best be understood as a vision of the shepherd and loses much of its extraordinary or miraculous character when we see it from the viewpoint of the initiation of a Midianite youth into the totemistic cult. J. G. Frazer[7] and other anthropologists exploring the various forms of totemism, have presented an abundance of examples which show how this individual initiation takes place. Here are a few instances: The American Algonquins revered their manitos. Besides these common tribe gods, each man has his own particular guardian spirit or personal totem; for instance, the bear or beaver. William W. Warren, the historian of the Ojibways, points out that they "believe in a multiplicity of spirits, which pervade all nature, yet all these are subordinate to the one great Spirit of God." Each man has, besides this god, a personal guardian spirit. This belief is as natural as the belief of the Catholics in their interceding saints which in some respects bears a likeness to it. The unfailing rigid fasts of first manhood when the novices first seek in dreams for a guardian spirit illustrate this belief quite clearly. Among some tribes of the Salish stock in British Columbia, whose ways have been well described by Commander R. C. Mayne, a young man has to get his medicine before he is admitted to the status of an adult male and warrior. It is expected that he will achieve this end by roaming about the woods, fasting and praying to the great spirit to help him to find a medicine." He sees an animal or any object first in a dream, then searches for it in nature. Whenever he encounters an unusual phenomenon, such as a suddenly appearing animal or a strange plant, he is convinced that he has found the guardian spirit with whom he will be from then on intimately connected. Among the North American Indians, the institution of initiation has as its central feature the lonely puberty watch—the candidate who, under the stress of fasting and mental efforts, dreams of the animal or plant which becomes his guardian later on. The dream or vision thus comes before the sight of the guardian spirit whom the candidate recognizes in some oracular manifestation of nature.

The biblical scholars who inquired into the vision of the Burning Bush failed to recognize in that plant an instance or survival of a tribal totem. There is, as far as my knowledge goes, no attempt in literature to conceive of the scene as part of Moses' puberty initiation. The fact that the young man appears in the story as a married man— as son-in-law of the Midianite priest Jethro—has served here to confuse the commentators who did not consider that, as in the last scene of Yahweh's attack on Moses, a commutation of time has taken place.

The lack of understanding of this story is the more regrettable since its character, conceived as part of individual initiation, opens another door. Very often, for instance with the Dea Dyaks of Borneo, the guardian spirit who reveals himself to the young man has a definite shape: "Usually, but not always, he is thought to be the spirit of an ancestor or another dead relative."[8] Among the Thompson Indians the guardian spirit is, in some cases, hereditary—passing from father to son: "Only a few shamans inherited their guardian spirits without passing through the usual ceremonies of puberty: to such favored persons the guardian spirits of their parents presented themselves, uncalled for in dreams or visions."[9] This is true in the case of Moses. The Lord calls the young man who "turned aside to see" (Exod. 3:4) and presents Himself as "the God of thy father, the God of Abraham, the God of Isaac and the God of Jacob." Only a few steps backwards are necessary to bring us to the concept that the "God of the fathers" was, in old and forgotten times, the father as God.

If my thesis that the story of the Burning Bush is the beginning of Moses' initiation is correct, is there any continuation? Are there any indications that an individual tale of Moses' puberty follows alongside the narrative of the Israelites? We will not expect any logical succession and sequence because the original saga must have been changed many times and its elements must have shifted more frequently. Other stories were inserted and the work of many editors and scribes changed the original tale to such an extent that it is scarcely recognizable. There is, for instance, the story of Yahweh's assault on Moses and the circumcision of his son—perhaps his own circumcision?—by Zippora, his wife. The obscure episode is certainly not transmitted to us in its original place, which is that of the puberty rituals. There is, furthermore, a doublet of the retirement of Moses—if we consider his years with the Midianites as a form of seclusion—in his staying on the Sinai mountain for such a long time that the Israelites thought he would not return (here again the number forty—forty days and nights). It seems that the motif of seclusion and return—a variation of the theme of death and resurrection of the primitive initiation—occurs twice in Moses' life: first at the time of his lonely watch on Mount Horeb where he has the vision of the Burning Bush, and then during his long stay on the Sacred Mountain where Yahweh reveals to him the rules and regulations for the Israelites. Here, thus, is the individual analogy or prototype to the collective initiation story of the Hebrew tribes.

Arnold Toynbee came close to a similar explanation in his general and abstract reflections on the development of civilizations. The famous historian introduces in his chapter, "An Analysis of Growth," a phenomenon which he calls "withdrawal and return." He describes the duality of these movements in the lives of individuals and of creative minorities and recognizes their importance for the work of Moses, St. Paul, and Jesus. He is, however, far from detecting in the responses of withdrawal and return a late transformation of the typical features of death and resurrection in the primitive puberty rituals.[10]

It would be tempting to follow and demonstrate the similar features in the life of that other great innovator of the Hebrew tribes, the son of Joseph and Mary—Jesus, who was called Christ. We have here again the seclusion in the wilderness, the temptations of the novice, the fasting for forty days and forty nights. The Christ saga, too, has as its center the motif of death and resurrection, which we have observed to constitute the axis of the primitive puberty celebration. In the Moses, as well as in the Christ tale, the recognition of the puberty motif is rendered more difficult by the fact that both figures appear as leaders of their people early in their history. Instead of being taught and instructed they teach the laws of the Lord. Here is a clear reversal of the role of the novices in the primitive tribe where the boys are initiated into the mores of their people. Jesus preaches in the synagogue, and Moses is the bearer and messenger of the Lord who brings the laws to the Children of Israel. Yet Jesus is baptized by John, and Moses undergoes his instruction in that scene of the Burning Bush.

It is not accidental that this vision of Moses' guardian spirit was, later on, developed into a symbol of the nation. The Menorah, or the seven-branched candlestick, is certainly an elaborated representation of a tree. But that bush which burned with fire and was not consumed, became itself the symbol of the destiny of the Jews, who continued to exist and give light in spite of an infinity of trials.

25.

Myth and Mystery

At the point we have now reached, the conflict between the author's temperament and the pace set for his research is vividly felt. Impatience demands that we should instantly begin the ascent of the Sacred Mountain. But research has a rhythm of its own and cannot be shortchanged or sacrificed to any other demands except to those of its object. Especially is this true of the research devoted to such sacred and secret themes as the one presented here. Simplification in such matters often results in distortion and haste, in avoidance of difficulties and obscurities. The prophet warns us: "Ye shall not go out with haste, nor go by flight: for the Lord will go before you; and the God of Israel will be your reward" (Isa. 52:12). In our case the reward for the control of our impatience and the pursuit of careful methods is, we hope, a new and unexpected insight into the nature of this God according to his words: "For that which had not been told them shall they see, and that which they had not heard shall they consider" (Isa. 52:15).

In expectation of such reward, we control our impatience and resume our attempts at orientation in that prehistoric world of early Israel. We discovered in the analysis of the Sinai-Exodus late disguised survivals of an ancient unwritten tradition which told of a puberty festival of the Hebrew tribes and of their covenant at this occasion. This tradition was much later brought into connection with the historical event of their departure—or expulsion—from Egypt. The indirect evidence drawn from the biblical sources, compared with the reports about the initiation in savage tribes, seems to us irrefutable. But there is not the slightest mention of puberty rituals in the Holy Scripture nor in the documents transmitted to us from ancient Egypt, Canaan and Babylon. A recent writer emphatically states: "The whole Hebrew Bible and the philosophical sacred Jewish writings don't say a single word about puberty-rites at puberty times, once generally practiced. After a repression of nearly two thousand years we hear of it again as Bar Mitzvah, still avidly kept when a boy is thirteen years old."[1]

If, as we are led to believe when we draw conclusions from the analogy with the customs of savage tribes, puberty rituals were once generally practiced and formed an important part of the religious and social life of the people of the ancient Orient, what happened? How can we explain to ourselves their disappearance or that total silence in the Hebrew, Egyptian, and Babylonian sources? These decisive institutions could not have evaporated without leaving any trace. Nor could there be any conspiracy to keep them hidden amongst the people of the Near East. Freud once asserted that mortals are not made to keep secrets; what they would like to conceal oozes from all their pores. It must be the same with groups and nations. There is enough darkness, and there are enough obscurities in the history of the world; there are many things we shall perhaps never know, but history contains few secrets which will not finally be unveiled.

It is perhaps necessary to emphasize that the Egyptian, Babylonian, and Greek civilizations had advanced many thousand years beyond the phase marked by the Australian and African puberty rituals. Even within those more primitive structures a remarkable development has been discerned by the anthropologists: with the decline of totemism and with the formation of clans, secret societies evolved from the associations formed around the primitive initiation ceremonies.[2] Those cults and brotherhoods have the purpose of ensuring closer contact with gods and spirits and of promoting law and order. The element of mystery which surrounds the puberty rituals is preserved also in the ritual and performance of those fraternities, in their masks, dresses, and sacred objects.

The secret societies of Africa, America, and Melanesia have thus persevered and taken the place of previously totemistic clans. The fraternities of the Pueblo Indians, for instance, spring directly from the union of totemistic clans into the tribe and have preserved their ancient rituals. The fraternities mark the transition into wider tribal organizations—especially where the government of the tribe is passing over to a more autocratic form of government by chiefs. The members of the fraternities are not necessarily kinsmen, while the totem system is hereditary and the members of the clan are kin.

The demarcation line between the performances of the secret societies and tribal mysteries is often scarcely discernible: as a matter of fact, the two formations are frequently discussed by anthropologists as though they were the same. There is no doubt that the mystery-cults of the Egyptians, Babylonians, and Greeks evolved from those earlier forms and resemble the religions and social secret societies of Africa and Australia.[3]

Mystery is defined by Jane Ellen Harrison as "a rite in which certain *sacra* are exhibited which cannot be safely seen by the worshipper till he has undergone certain purification."[4] The connection between the performances of the mystery-cults and the puberty rituals of the savages is not only a genetic one, but is also formed by resemblances in their essential content. We are mostly concerned here with the Egyptian and Babylonian mysteries since it is their relationship to the events described in the biblical Exodus-Sinai narrative which interests us in this context. The Egyptian mysteries were rites in which actions and recitations enacted the legend of Osiris. There is no doubt that the mysteries were antecedent to the arrival of the Habiru tribes in Egypt. We have, for instance, an explicit text, dated from the time of the Twelfth Dynasty (about 1875 B.C.), in which a high official, Igernefert, tells how he conducted the ceremonies "of the lord of Abydos," which means the mysteries of Osiris. We also have Sumerian hymns which celebrate the marriage of the nature-god with the mother-goddess at the spring equinox—a part of the mysterious acts which were deemed sacred. The Semites took over those hymns originally sung in Sumerian.

We consider here only the mystery-cults of these two civilizations because they were certainly those which had the strongest influence upon the Hebrew tribes in Egypt and in their previous homeland of Ur, as well as in Canaan where the Egyptian and Babylonian cultures met and sometimes melted. (It should not be forgotten that Palestine, from about 1550 to about 1225, remained almost uniterruptedly an Egyptian province.)

What is the essential content of the mystery-cults? In Babylon it was certainly centered around the death and resurrection of the young god Tammuz. The liturgies, which were sung, lamented the deceased god sought by his weeping mother and consort. Ishtar mourns for her lover whom she finally finds and brings back to earth. It is very likely that the dialogues and monologues of the couple were accompanied by a mystic pantomime, and that an image of the young god, clothed in sacred garb, was cast upon the waters of the canals. The mystery consisted thus in the death of a god and his resurrection, in the search of the mother-goddess for him and in the sacred marriage of these two deities. The cult of the dying and resurrected Tammuz was adapted to mystic purposes amongst which the doctrine of secret wisdom, revealed only to the initiated, has the most prominent role. The mysteries of Egypt enacted the Osiris myth and the "initiates" into those mysteries have to observe secrecy regarding them. In dramatic performances the life of Osiris and of his sister and spouse, Isis, the murder of Osiris by his brother Seth—the mournful guest—and the finding of his corpse, its restoration to life and immortality, are shown. It is probable that the search for and the finding of the god by his sister and wife Isis, was realistically carried out. We know how Igernefert, to whom Senusret III had committed the preparations for the performance, procured a barge in which a statue of Osiris, adorned with lapis lazuli and other precious stones, was placed. Herodotus and Plutarch tell of the existence of the Egyptian mysteries. Herodotus says with great reticence (II 170 f.)

"At Sais is the burial place of one whom I scruple to mention. . . .
All the proceedings in these mysteries are well known to me; but my
lips shall piously refrain from mentioning them." We have here an
example of the secrecy which surrounded the mysteries and which is
alluded to by other ancient writers.

Secrecy is certainly one of the essential elements of the mystery-
cults which they have in common with the initiation rituals of the
savages. But does not their content, the dramatic performance of
the death and resurrection of a young god, point to the most significant motif of the puberty ceremonials? The tribesmen who are
initiated into the secret societies have to undergo certain trials and
even contests, but in the ancient mysteries, the suffering, dying, and
resurrection of a god is shown. It is not difficult to guess how this
new form evolved from the previous one. Plutarch attributed the
institution of the Egyptian mysteries to Isis herself, acting in memory
of Osiris. The sacred performance, Plutarch writes, should afford an
image, a representation in mimic scenes of the sufferings the divine
hero endured, that they might serve as a pious teaching and a con-
solatory hope to the men and women who pass through the same
hardships."[5]

In a more matured phase of religious development to which the
totemistic cult appeared obsolete, the young son-god became the
representation of all adolescent men. He is the Lord of history. The
historian will not be intimidated by the fact that His ways are
proverbially dark. The scholar must ever be prepared to echo the
readiness of the noted French historian Augustin Thierry to "make
friends with darkness" ("*Je fais amitié avec les ténébres*").

The young god was now the hero of the tragedy and of the
triumph longed for by every man. It is, in spite of all diversities that
appear on the surface, the same principle that can be followed into
the Greek mystery-cults and even into the medieval Passion plays,
enacting the suffering, painful death, and glorious resurrection of
the Saviour. The aim of all the rites of the mysteries was the same:
communion with the saving deity with whom the initiated identified
himself, sharing his destiny—with whom he died and was trans-
figured. The movement of civilization, including great changes in the
social structure and advanced concepts of religion, did not greatly
affect the core of the initiation rituals. The transformation of a totemistic outlook into a religious phase in which the young son-god and
his mother and spouse were the principal protagonists only altered
the external aspects of the initiation. Initiation was still protected by

secrecy, still reserved to the initiated who were vowed to silence, and still had as its focal point the death and resurrection of the young men of the tribes.

This short survey of the social and religious evolution from crude puberty rituals to the mystery-cults of ancient Egypt and Babylon has not been undertaken for its own sake. The issue that concerns us is the contrast of the development of Israel's religion with that of the great civilizations in whose realms the Hebrew tribes dwelt. We compared the Exodus-Sinai events with the puberty rituals of savage tribes of our time and found unexpected resemblances. We could not arrive at any explanations for those striking similarities inasmuch as the Israelite tribes, living in the middle of highly developed cultures, had certainly left the world of Australian and African aborigines behind. We found, furthermore, that there is neither manifest trace nor tradition of a puberty festival or rituals in the biblical reports, with the exception of the commandment of circumcision which was perhaps taken over from the Egyptians. We then turned our attention to the Egyptian and Babylonian civilizations in our search for survivals of primitive initiation rituals. We were not able to discover any, but learned instead that the religious and social development of ancient Babylon and Egypt had replaced such original and primitive initiation by mystery-cults for several thousand years.

The view we now face is not clear. We are confronted with a startling contrast: that between Israel and her neighbors, between the Hebrew and the Egyptian and Babylonian religious situation. How does Israel acquire a single invisible god, into whose worship a whole people are initiated by a series of historical events? The God of the Hebrews has the position and the character of a father, is akin to them. In Egypt and Babylon, polytheism has at its center a young savior-god and his mother and wife, or a triad of gods in the mystery-cults. Everywhere statues and images of the deities are shown. In the Egyptian and Babylonian mysteries secrecy is observed about the initiation. No secrecy attends the introduction of the Hebrew tribes into the worship of Yahweh. The people are witnesses of the theophany at Mount Sinai. The event has, as a matter of historic fact, the greatest publicity and is again and again reported by the historians of Israel. It is, so to speak, history mythologized. Or is it rather mythology transformed into history?

Are there any secret societies or mystery-cults in ancient Israel comparable to those rituals that evolved in Egypt and Babylon from primitive tribal puberty initiations? As far as we know there is no similar phenomenon. Authorities in biblical criticism have repeatedly claimed that there is no tradition in the Scripture clearly pointing to the existence of distinct puberty rituals. A distinguished Jewish scholar, Solomon Schechter, says of the Bar Mitzvah festival that "it cannot claim a very high antiquity. As far as the Bible goes, there is not the slightest indication of the existence of such a ceremony."[6] This statement is, of course, undeniable as far as it concerns the manifest text of the Bible. If, however, our thesis is correct, one is obliged to discover a new meaning in the Sinai-Exodus tradition, to acknowledge the possibility that the puberty ritual appears in the biblical narrative transferred to all the sons of Israel.

The Bar Mitzvah festival, which marks the entrance of the thirteen-year-old boy into the community as its responsible member, is indeed a relatively late institution introduced by rabbinic Judaism. While the rite of circumcision of the Jewish male was originally performed at puberty time and is now performed on the ten-day-old child, the Bar Mitzvah (the expression means "son of the commandment") signifies the transition from boyhood to manhood. The boy has to study the Torah and is instructed in the history and religious duties of a Jew in analogy to the customs of the savage tribes during the seclusion of the novices. But after having finished these religious studies, he manfully reads the Torah to the congregation: a modern parallel to the test of the primitive Australian lad. The conservative power of ancient customs is so strong that by this event the boy becomes paradoxically a man at the age of thirteen.

With this side glance at the Jewish puberty ritual of our own day, we take leave of the comparative study of initiation and venture into the study of the perplexing problem of the peculiarity of Israel's religious development. We go to the heart of the problem when we confront the royal prince Moses, who was "learned in all the wisdom of the Egyptians" with the leader of the despised Hebrew tribes. Under one aspect we encounter an Egyptian aristocrat who was doubtless an initiate into the mysteries of the Nile—who, struck with awe, witnessed the quest and discovery of Osiris' sacred body, was deeply moved by the resurrection and triumph of the god who sailed back in his barge to the city of Abydos. Now compare the spectacle of this celebration, of the procession and the cheers of the people, of the pomp and circumstance of dynastic Egypt with the image of the lonely leader of a half-nomadic, miserable, hungry mob in the desert! Now compare the mysteries of the Egyptian rites, and their dramatic performances by images and figures of many deities with the great secret at Mount Sinai, with the revelation of an invisible God!

We have arrived at the crucial and critical point of our journey. We have come to the bridge we now have to cross. Or should we say, perhaps, to the abyss that cannot be spanned?

26.

The Leap Backwards

There was a report in the newspapers the other day that a Canadian bishop engaged as his secretary a woman who had previously been employed as secretary in the Defense Department of the United States government. Hunting through the files in her absence, the bishop came across a drawer labelled "sacred" and "top sacred." The part of the problem that will now occupy our research may well be classified "top sacred" because it concerns the mystery of revelation—the heart of our inquiry. The great challenge we have to accept is to explain the Israelite mutation which made the particular and peculiar evolution of biblical faith a possibility. The idea of progress that governed the outlook of the nineteenth century was incapable of explaining how Israel's unique contribution to religion occurred. The application of the general idea of development resulted in a view that saw the Old Testament as a document of "progressive revelation." The metaphor of growth borrowed from biology was used as a means to explain the biblical faith in the sense of development from seed to plant and fruit, or from embryo to maturity. Ernest Wright has eloquently demonstrated that the attempt of scholars to understand the religious world of Israel in developmental terms was both valid and misleading.[1] Their efforts have led to the accumulation of a tremendous number of facts and assertions without which the movement of biblical history cannot be understood; but these facts fail to explain the phenomena within the Bible and the Bible itself. The study of environment and development shows that a considerable part of Israel's contribution was borrowed from Egyptian, Babylonian, and Canaanite sources, and that her "uniqueness" consists in the alteration and improvement of this borrowed material. Several biblical scholars—for instance, W. Eichrodt and Ernest Wright—have pointed out that the main difficulty of the developmental outlook was the inability to take the story of the revelation and the covenant at Mount Sinai seriously. The unfolding of Israel's faith was thus deprived of a fixed starting point. It is precisely here that our attempt at interpretation begins.

The nature of the Israelite mutation can be sketched in a few sentences. The first feature that comes to mind is, of course, the monotheistic belief. We will not discuss at this moment the objection that it is not imaginable that the Hebrew tribes of the fourteenth or thirteenth century believed in Yahweh as the only god, and that the covenant with him excluded the existence of other gods. We are not dealing here with the question of whether the Israelites arrived finally quite a few hundred years later (after Exodus) at a form of henotheism rather than monotheism. It is even possible that the Aton religion of Ikhnaton heralded and stimulated the religious conviction of the Levite Moses, who was reared at the court of the Pharaoh. We are not interested in the historical aspect at this moment and will gladly admit that the pure and exclusive monotheism of the prophets is a late phase of the evolution of religious concepts. We agree with J. Meinhold's observation that more important than the question of where the biblical Yahweh-cult originated, is the question of what Moses made of it.[2] We now look at the problem from an elevated point of view comparable to that of the traveller on an airplane who sees the changing landscape as a whole, yet who knows that he will discern the individual objects as soon as the plane glides into a lower altitude.

The feature of monotheism (or henotheism in its initial phase) was, in my view, less decisive for the final character of Israel's religion than the absence of a female deity and the concept of an invisible god, which implies a perpetual prohibition of representations and, therefore, the reinforcement of the absence of duality of male and female in the realm of the Godhead. There is strong ground for suspecting that the absence of female deities results more from an elimination than from an original lack. The same seems to be true also of images of Yahweh. It is notable that while archaeology has found many small plaques or figurines of Canaanite mother-goddesses, no image of a male deity has been dug out in the vast debris of Israelite towns. Wright sees here clear evidence that "the prohibition against images of Yahweh was so deeply fixed in early Israel that even the enlightened and the tolerant understood that Yahweh was simply not to be honored in this way. While other practices might be borrowed this was not one of them. God was not to be seen or touched by human hands."[3]

The religion of Israel appears in history suddenly and marks a radical break with the approach to reality characteristic of other people of the ancient Orient. "With Israel," a recent historian comments, "there appears a new agent of history that is neither a civilization nor a people within a civilization like others."[4] The same scholar rightly points out that we can speak of an Egyptian or Mesopotamian, but not of an Israelite civilization.

The sudden appearance of a religion, so different from that of the neighbors, of a people so unlike those in the midst of whom they lived, is hard to understand in developmental terms. How are we to explain it in any other manner than to assume it is a new creation? This question has been posed by a well-known scholar. He does not doubt that the fundamental elements of this faith were established early in Israel's history, which means we are led to Sinai and to the work of Moses. These distinctive elements are "that something in early Israel which predisposed and predestined the course of biblical history."[5]

We are led again here to the Exodus-Sinai story as the focal point of the miracle and mystery of Israel's religion and history. Here, we are told, all the puzzling and age-old problems of the existence and faith of that strange people will find their solution. We are led to the antechamber and to the door that leads to the secret, but there is no key to open it and the massive door cannot be forced. Not only the biblical scholars, but also the historians were baffled by the special features of ancient Israel. Her history appeared to them as "deviation" (to Spengler and Toynbee, for instance), but all attempts to explain the causes of that divergence have failed or have, at most, resulted in recognizing some contributory factors.

The following attempt to explain and reinterpret the development of ancient Israel will certainly not pretend to present a solution of the many problems which the unique experience of the Jews poses, but it asks for attention as a new and original venture which promises more successful results through exploration resumed from different viewpoints.

In order to make this new approach clear, let me return for a moment to a comparison used previously. We likened the biblical record to a play with the revelation as its climax. The reader follows this drama with suspense and awe. The biblical scholars inquire into the sources from which the authors took their material, show their literary predecessors and their resemblances and differences with the drama of other nations. Experts and laymen alike are fascinated by the events whose audience they become. They are, so to speak, stage-struck. Very rarely is a biblical authority curious about what goes on behind the wings, about the work of the electricians and stage-hands. Occasionally a student of biblical history ventures a hypothesis about the work behind the scenes. I remind the reader of the explanation of B. D. Eerdmans who pointed out the activity of the Kenites, those desert smiths who "stage-managed" the theophany on the Sacred Mountain. They provided the sound and fury of Yahweh's appearance by striking the iron while it was hot.[6]

In a similar manner we dare to look behind the wings of the Exodus-Sinai drama, but our aim is different. We would like to understand the cause and character of that unique experience which the biblical narrative records. To understand, and if possible to explain, how it came about, what its psychological foundations were and to which factors it owes its deviation from the history and the religions of other people of the ancient Near East. It seems that there is a confusion between two terms as though the extraordinary and unique character of that experience excluded the possibility of a rational elucidation and historical search. Yet there are unique phenomena in the world that can be explained, and there are still unexplained phenomena that are not unique.

The uniqueness of Judaism and of its key ideas has often been questioned and sometimes denied. Yet in spite of certain similarities between ancient Israel and surrounding cultures, the facts speak loudly enough. The famous archaeologist, William F. Albright, has stated that, though the Old Testament "contains a synthesis of the best that had been contributed by the ancient East, it was transmuted by the Hebrew religious insight into a work which rises mountain-high above even the highest hills of Egypt and Mesopotamia,"[7] but no satisfactory hypothesis has yet been developed to explain that extraordinary experience and to determine how it became possible.

The preceding investigation is meant to serve as a preparation to the shaping and formulation of such a hypothesis that throws light into the darkness surrounding the beginning of ancient Israel. The comparative material collected will be used in combination with the data secured by archaeology, history, and biblical criticism, as guidelines in this inquiry which I hope will lead to the discovery of a new and decisive character—and to insights changing our views on the nature of Hebrew origins. Our aim is the understanding of the particular development of a people, of their history and their coreideas; but the method we apply is, in contrast with that of the historians, psychological—the exploration of the minds and customs of that group.

It would be tempting to assume that the Lord favored Israel because it was a late-comer within the family of brothers in the Near East. "When Israel was a child" (Hos. 11:1) the brothers had already come of age. According to the tradition Abraham left Mesopotamia on his way to Palestine in the late twentieth century, the age of the Middle Bronze and a time of great migrations throughout the Fertile Crescent. The Egyptian and Mesopotamian empires had already reached their highest point then or rather had passed it. Semitic invaders from Syria governed the Nile countries and Babylonia was conquered by barbarian mountain tribes. Semitic people of various origin had flooded Palestine. When Israel was a child, we see it already wandering from country to country, roaming through the lands in search of a home. The Wandering Jew became the symbolic figure for a dream-led people. In the strictest ethical sense they were not a racially homogeneous people then nor are they now. The blood of many tribes of Arabia, Mesopotamia, and Canaan flowed through their veins. Are those migrants identical with the "Habiru," nomadic raiders mentioned in the cuneiform sources? Were they a group of those bands of laborers, slaves, and mercenary soldiers? No one knows. The patriarchal ancestors of Israel were certainly not any longer of the caliber of hired soldiers or slaves, but were already families united by kinship and eager to find land for themselves and their cattle. We would be mistaken were we to imagine that the clans leaving northern Mesopotamia were barbarous nomads. They had been under the influence of Akkadian, Hurian, and Nuzian civilization in their original home. They themselves believed that they were not of Aramean, but of Arab origin.

The Hebrews entering Canaan met a highly advanced civilization whose essence was built upon Babylonian and Egyptian elements added to the Canaanite tradition. That part of the Hebrew tribes that went—most likely with the Hyksos—into Egypt, must have lived there a long time and some of them must have been highly

Egyptianized, as the Joseph story and the Egyptian names of Moses and of some Aaronites show. When the Hyksos, many of whose chiefs bore Semitic names, were expelled, the New Empire changed the Egyptian attitude. The "king who knew not Joseph" and oppressed the Israelites was a Pharaoh of that New Empire who had hated the Asiatic intruders. The Israelites who had lived in the northeastern delta since the invasion of the Hyksos of Egypt, were now pressed into forced labor.

There are quite a few features in the "prehistory" of the biblical narrative which puzzle us. First of all: When we meet Abraham and the patriarchs they already resembled their descendants inasmuch as they were wanderers who drove their cattle from one place to another. More than that, they were already expelled from some country or were fugitives. It is, of course, easy to guess what drove and propelled them to wander—famine, or just Mother Earth who turned her favor away from those clans ("and there was famine in the land; and Abraham went down into Egypt to sojourn there; for the famine was grievous in the land").

Yet Abraham did not leave Egypt on account of famine. He was expelled by the Pharaoh whom the Lord had plagued "with great plagues" (Gen. 12:17) because of Sarah, Abraham's wife. However we interpret that strange story, we will not hesitate to conjecture that the Hebrew clans or Abraham and his people had what we would call today "personality-difficulties" with the Egyptians—so to speak, a prelude of things to come. Here we have Hebrew clans already in Egypt, first favored and then expelled. We have the conflict between the Egyptians and the representative of those clans, and we have the plague the Lord sends to Pharaoh and his house. Do we have here a cycle that repeats itself?

Where did it begin? We don't know. As far back as we can go into the period of Hebrew origins—and we cannot penetrate farther than the patriarchal age[8]—we find a situation which is already extraordinary in several ways. The threshold of history is crossed by those semi-nomadic groups entering not a primitive environment, but countries whose civilization could look back at more than two millennia. Those tribes drifting into ripened civilizations "burgeoned . . . much more rapidly than would have been the case had they relied solely on their inner growth. The first phase of Israel's history presents therefore the picture of a more or less primitive group assuming the variegated hues of the neighboring civilizations." Salo W. Baron, who thus characterizes the period of origins, emphasizes that Israel in a peculiar way "skipped many phases of normal development."[9] We have observed individual analogies of such often offensive "skipping many phases of normal development" in various Jewish types who came from the ghetto into the middle of a highly industrialized Western civilization.

We are here especially interested in the destiny of that part of Israel that entered Egypt—perhaps with the Hyksos—while the other tribes had remained in Palestine. There is no doubt that the great religious renovation, that mass conversion in the desert or in Shechem, originated with the clans which left Egypt and were joined by the Palestinian Hebrews. What were the vicissitudes of those clans? What was their religion before Yahwism? We are here in a situation similar to that of a biographer who has to present the story of a person's life without knowing anything about his first five years. He finds documentary evidence that a great change took place when the child was at this age. But what preceded it? Life does not begin at five.

Those great events took place in an age which J. H. Breasted justifiably called the "First Internationalism" because in that bridge between the Mediterranean Sea and the Arabian desert Babylonian, Egyptian, and Canaanite civilizations had formed a milieu of itself. The great innovation takes place on the background of the much older civilizations of the ancient Near East that had brought forth ethical concepts whose finest parts were taken over and reshaped by the Hebrews. They were far from being the exclusive contribution of the Hebrews, yet the Hebrews who gave them a new imprint in their literature made them the dominant ideas of the Western world.[10] More than once have Orientalists expressed their astonishment about the extraordinary fact that the great moral legacy should have descended to Western civilization from a politically insignificant people living at the southeast corner of the Mediterranean— from a tiny nation unable to form a state for more than a couple of centuries.

The religious and political transformation of the Hebrew clans was initiated by that group of Israel that had been very much Egyptianized. Whether it was Moses or Joshua, the leaders of the clans which formed the covenant between Yahweh and the people and built the bond among the tribes, they were men who had absorbed the essential part of Egyptian civilization and had assimilated the cultural, rich life of the cities on the Nile. The preceding chapters, comparing the Exodus-Sinai story to the primitive initiation of savage

tribes, have prepared us for the direction into which the new movement of the Israelite tribes is pointed. Its character must have been
that of a turning away from the religion and the ideas of the Egyptian
people who had become their oppressors—a turning away and a
return to older, forgotten, and relinquished ways of their forefathers.
The revolutionary change that marks perhaps the greatest shift in the
adventure of man in the last six thousand years was a return, a
powerful regression to a denied and deserted tradition. The quintessence of Moses' innovation is a break with the recent acquisitions and
a reversion to the old. Thus, is it a step backwards? No, not a step
but a leap back in time.

27.

The Advance in Regression

Every attempt to define the factors
underlying the unprecedented progress of Israel is limited by the
fact that the biblical tradition is the only source at our disposal. This
being the case, how can we hope to be exact in establishing the
directions of developments and in describing the currents and counter-
currents of change? The recorded tradition is a few centuries remote
from the events and is colored by the views of late editors and priests
and stands in the service of certain tendencies of national and religious glorification. We can only hope that the conclusions we are
going to draw will be justified by internal evidence.

Almost more difficult than the description of those currents is the
presentation of their speed, of the rate of their movement. How can
we depict in general terms the speed of a stream, of a river such
as the Danube, the Mississippi, or the Nile? It is obvious that the
speed is different in various places, swift in one spot and slow in
another, rapid and then hesitant, steady and then bubbling. The
development we are trying to grasp eludes description if we do not
want to follow it in detail and in slow historical succession.

It is excluded that the ethical and religious code as it was reached at the phase of the prophets belonged to the age of Moses. Yet for the purpose of this presentation we have to neglect the precise historical characterization of the development. This means our presentation will necessarily be an abridgment. It will condense the development of some centuries in an accelerated manner. Let me return to a comparison mentioned before: A biographer has only scanty material about the life of a person before his fifth year, but at this age a series of events take place that change the course of this person's destiny—for instance, moving to a new country, death of the father, or similar happenings of paramount importance. There are now an abundance of memories, although altered by later tendencies, regarding those early events preserved and often revived. Can the biographer evaluate the effects of those outstanding occurrences without insight into the conditions and circumstances of the child before his fifth year?

We pick up the thread where we left it: we expressed the opinion that the great "conversion" of the Hebrews—to use a modern term —must have started in the midst of the highly civilized and much Egyptianized portion of the Israelite clans in the Nile valley. It is scarcely imaginable that a religious and tribal transformation of tremendous consequence could have originated among those uneducated and miserable slaves, oppressed and forced into hard labor in the northeastern delta. The great reformation of the Israelites is also, in biblical tradition, indissolubly tied to the memory of a powerful leader-personality of extraordinary force and ability. It needed such a person of almost superhuman energy to weld the Hebrew tribes into unity and to compel them to leave Egypt and her fleshpots. There were certainly trends of rebellion against the Egyptian oppressor in the clans living in the plain around the old capital of the Hyksos in Egypt (Tanis or Zoan, Psalms 78:12, 43); but the mighty impulse for collective action had to come from a man who had emancipated himself from the ways of the Israelites.

There were also movements demanding the return of the Jews to the land of their forefathers in the ghetto of Eastern Jewry, but it was an emancipated Jew, born and bred in Western civilization, whose untiring efforts lent momentum to Zionism and prodded it into action. It is not my intention to compare Theodor Herzl with Moses, but rather to compare the cultural atmosphere in which the founder of modern Zionism grew up and the milieu in which the greatest son of the Israelites became a man. The analogy concerns only the position of the emancipated Jew who, as a leader, returns to his people—not the culture patterns, because I feel that in many ways the Egyptian civilization of the New Empire was superior to that of the time of Dreyfus and of the Vienna under Franz Josef.

Yet the comparison is not accidental because it is founded on a certain resemblance of the situations and of the external conditions that propel mass movements among the Jews. It is no matter that the Zionist cause cannot compare in its significance with the Exodus from Egypt and the "first return" to Palestine. I have already pointed out how noteworthy it is that we find already in Israel's earliest history a situation similar in all its essential features to those that we see again and again in her subsequent development. There is already Abraham's migration from one land to another; there is already the expulsion and the tradition of an early conversion to a faith different from that of the ancestors who "served other gods" (Josh. 24:2). I am quite convinced that the conditions similar to those of the past century in Europe were already present among the Hebrews of the New Empire in Egypt. In the old Austro-Hungarian monarchy in which Theodor Herzl lived and died, a minority of the Jews shared the life and interests of the German, Hungarian, and Czechoslovakian peoples. They were emancipated and assimilated into the Western civilization, to which they made remarkable contributions. The majority of the Jews lived in the ghettos of the East, in Galicia and Poland, and clung to the religious customs of their forefathers. To continue our analogy: It is probable that even the majority of the Hebrews who dwelt in Goshen had adopted certain of the civilized customs and attitudes of the Egyptians in whose midst they lived. Yet the difference between the separated Hebrew and his assimilated co-religionist must have been almost as great as that between a Jewish peddler in the ghetto of Cracow and a Jewish journalist or lawyer in Vienna. This was certainly the case already in the age when the Hyksos were tolerant towards the Hebrew clans in the Nile delta and when some Hebrews functioned as officials and administrators at the court of the Pharaohs. One has only to recall the high position enjoyed by Joseph in the days of Potiphar—but such cases were certainly exceptional.

When the hated Asiatic usurpers were defeated and expelled and Pharaohs of Egyptian aristocracy governed the country, everything changed again almost overnight. The New Empire radically removed all traces of the old regime and restored order to Egypt. The victorious revolution and reformation after the expulsion of the Hyksos (about 1550) was also felt by the Hebrew clans which had been tolerated and perhaps even favored by the Hyksos. The radical change must have been similar to that of the rise of the Nazi regime in Germany and was perhaps also characterized by a new attitude towards "foreigners," who were treated more and more as inferior barbarians. The change was certainly not performed in a few days—nothing in the ancient Orient was done with modern speed—but proceeded in waves with increasing intensity. The Pharaoh's oppressive order—to slay all male children of the Hebrews—constitutes the ancient prototype of Hitler's persecution. We may imagine that the cruelties of the new Pharaoh occurred to the Israelites in wave after wave—or rather blow after blow—until there had set in the forced labor that made their lives bitter with hard "bondage in mortar, and in brick, and in all manner of service . . ." (Exod. 1:14). It is likely that the Hebrew clans read the handwriting on the walls of the cities they had to build in forced labor and knew that worse yet was to come. Though not as sophisticated in their brutalities as were the Nazis, the ancient Egyptians also knew how to torture their Hebrew slaves.

Without entering into a discussion of the legends around Moses, we have asserted that the rebellion and the liberation of the oppressed had been directed by a leader who had assimilated the Egyptian civilization, and not by a sheik or chief of the tribes working under the cruel demands of their taskmasters in Goshen.

Several biblical scholars have expressed their astonishment that there are so few signs that the Hebrews were influenced by the Egyptian culture. Thus T. J. Meek remarks that it is "one of the enigmas of history that the Hebrews were so little affected by the religion of Egypt, when both history and archaeology show such intimate contact between the two."[1] A. Lods states that the cult of Egypt had apparently not any deep influence on the half-nomadic Hebrews at the time when their national religion took shape: "the divergence between the two people was too great."[2] A. L. Elmslie assumes that "the shepherds occasionally saw as spectators rather than participants the worship of the native Egyptians."[3] One has to consider that the Hebrews of Goshen lived geographically and culturally at the margin of Egyptian civilization. Only a small minority of the Hebrews shared its benefits with the urban population.

We meet thus in pre-Mosaic Israel in Egypt a characteristic division, social and cultural, among the Hebrews, almost the same division and difference that was discernible many centuries later in the

Jews of the great cities of the West. We have here emancipated layers of society, to a great extent assimilated to Egyptian civilization, and perhaps taking an active part in it; and lower classes living a segregated and closely knit life, relatively unaffected by the cultural life of Egypt. This majority living in Goshen was, of course, a scant minority in the midst of the host nation. Professor Salo Baron assumes that the Israelites would have been socially segregated even if they had not been oppressed on account of the ritualistic rigidity of the Egyptians and points to the fact that in the period of greatest friendship and conviviality under Joseph's regime the Egyptians "might not eat bread with the Hebrews for that is an abomination unto the Egyptians."[4] This scholar wonders whether this pre-Mosaic ghetto in Egypt did not already cast its shadow over all the future history of the people. There cannot be any doubt that the later separation and segregation of the Israelites was in large part the result of their own wishes, born of their desire to avoid the hostility and cruelty of their hosts. But all processes of this kind perpetuate the result of a segregation originating externally and enforced by superior powers.

What happened when the new regime began to oppress the Israelites? What were the effects of that change, especially upon those emancipated and assimiliated Hebrews, when their brethren around Tanis were placed in bondage and treated with extreme cruelty? The comparison with the situation at the outbreak of Nazism in Germany whose contemporaries (and sufferers) we were, suggests itself. The despair and confusion, the misery and sorrow among the tribes in southern Egypt must have been similar to the emotions experienced by the Jews in Germany. The Hebrews were a mixed people of composite origin and of different cultural and social layers. Yet, in spite of these divergencies, there was a kind of solidarity among them and an awareness of a common past. In Egypt and during their migrations, the Israelite tribes retained a vivid memory of their previous dwelling in Palestine and of their blood relation with the Palestinian Hebrews whom they were soon to join. Here again is an analogy with the psychological situation of the Jews in Germany and their relations with the Jews in other countries.

Precisely those Israelites who had been accepted and favored by the Egyptians must have felt their humiliation deeper than the others and reacted to the cruelty and hardships with greater bitterness. Their offended pride and their bruised feeling of worthiness caused them to experience the change more than the herdsmen and laborers in

Goshen who took the brutality of the Egyptians and the turn of their fate more fatalistically. It was the cultured Hebrews, these who had most loved Egyptian culture and appreciated its superiority, who were most affected by the feeling of loss and degradation, the certainty of being wronged and unjustly despised—and who experienced most vigorously scorn and hate against the oppressors. Nonetheless, these emancipated and assimilated Israelites—the élite of the group —clung to the cherished Egyptian civilization. Even the slaves and laborers in Goshen recalled the miserly security and material benefits accorded to them by their oppressors. Even in the desert, those ancient "praisers of bygone times" expressed homesickness for Egypt when they were suffering under the privations of the desert.

The final result of that intense ambivalence was no longer doubtful. It grew as the tyranny of the Egyptian taskmasters became more insupportable. A passionate hatred welled up in them to suppress a lifelong love. It was turned against all Egyptian ways and customs—against Egyptian religion and social organization. The movement, increasing in intensity, had thus the character of a determined turning away from Egypt and her traditions, of a total rejection of all assimilation and incorporation of the faiths and ideas of Egypt. The obliteration and annihilation of the Egyptian acquisitions went so far that it erased and effaced all traces of the influence experienced by many generations of the Hebrews. The removal and hateful destruction of all Egyptian concepts was all the more radical since it flowed and was nourished from the hidden source of disappointed love and frustrated hope. Biblical scholars and historians have found traces of those disavowed and denied influences in many manifestations of Israel's morals and literature, because even the most energetic expurgation and expulsion cannot remove everything. But those traces do not contradict the dynamic force of the negative and rejecting powers operating in Israel. They are only the memorials of that passionate ambivalence. They resemble fragments of an old love letter inadvertently inserted into a document of the most determined farewell and irrevocable repudiation.

This is the character of the forces of refusal and rejection that rebuff all the Egyptian influences we have described. But where are the powers that pulled the Hebrew tribes in a particular direction while they violently cast off Egyptian religion and social organization? Where is the attraction corresponding to the repulsion and aversion? Where is the action related to that vehement reaction? We could infer the nature of these forces from the path in which the Hebrew exiles, or refugees, moved—even if we did not have the biblical tradition. The story of Moses, who became the leader of the Exodus, shows the direction and the aim toward which the movement was heading. After he had murdered an Egyptian brute, Moses fled to Midian. He found Yahweh worshipped by those Midianites with whom the Levite family of Moses seems to have had some connections. The Kenite desert smiths had perhaps preserved the monolatry of old nomadic times as well as its simple life. Their tribal god was conceived as father of the clan. Moses and his successors developed and elevated these concepts of the Kenites who dwelled far from the centers of Egyptian civilization: "Is not he (the Lord) thy father that hath brought thee" (Deut. 32:6)? That Egyptian prince, Moses, had found the way home to his people when he turned away from the culture pattern within which he had been educated. He had been sobered and deeply disappointed by the brutality of the Egyptians toward the Hebrews. The sight of those cruelties must have affected him in the same shattering and shocking manner as the barbarities of the Nazis, four thousand years later, affected the German Jews, who proudly considered themselves members of the "Nation of Poets and Thinkers" ("*Volk der Dichter und Denker*"). Imperceptibly, but with increasing intensity, the attraction of the life of the Kenites, with whom he felt akin, was experienced.

Proceeding from this individual, but highly representative, example, the inner upheaval of the Israelites who had been assimilated to Egyptian civilization, will be better understood. Their deep disappointment and bitterness led them to that extreme reaction and rejection of Egypt. In their frantic flight from their oppressors they felt again the half-forgotten emotional ties with their own clans. They followed the call of their leaders, Moses and Aaron, who gathered them together and organized the Exodus.

The combination and the confluence of those two forces, the rejection of the Egyptian civilization and the attraction of old Hebrew tradition, resulted in the initial form of what is called the mutation of Israel's religion and culture—so difficult to understand when conceived in the simple evolutionistic terms of the school of Wellhausen.

For the sake of clarity, it might be good to present a sort of "balance-sheet" of the state of the Egyptian religion and that of the burgeoning faith of the Hebrew tribes after the Exodus. We are well aware of the simplification and condensation necessitated by a synoptic diagram. We do not pretend that the following illustration covers every detail of this extraordinary story.

EGYPT	HEBREW
1). Polytheism.	1). Monotheism or Henotheism. Perhaps, as Freud assumed, influenced by renewal of Ikhnaton's solar monotheism.
2). Osiris and his sister and wife Isis and their son Horus.	2). Removal of a son-god and mother-goddess as well as of their sexual relations. The only god is the deified father.
3). Abundance of magic, sorcery, amulets.	3). Repression of all magic and sorcery.
4). Plenty of sculptures and images of gods and divine things.	4). Forbidding of images. The invisible God.
5). Osiris mysteries with initiation.	5). All Hebrews initiated into Yahweh's cult.
6). Belief in immortality and care of the dead.	6). No belief in the life hereafter.
7). Class society.	7). Democracy.

Only the main features of the opposed faiths are contrasted here. Nothing is indicated concerning the remnants of Egyptian concepts in early Israel and the seeds of common Semitic ideas to be found also in dynastic Egypt. Moreover, we do not go beyond the result of the co-operation of the two forces in the initial phase of Israel, neglecting all the later developments.

The Hebrew tribes in Goshen had reached a dead end in their efforts to assimilate themselves to the Egyptian pattern when they became slaves and serfs of the Pharaoh. Moses and other leaders opened a door to redemption for them, pointing to a new road that led back to a phase they had left behind, and then leading them beyond this phase. Those leaders had absorbed the best of what Egyptian civilization had to offer, and used it unconsciously when they turned determinedly and grimly away from Egyptian culture, eager to found a people from the debris of desperate Hebrew clans. The astonishing progress they made was the effect of two dynamic forces; one pushing them away from the pattern of their torturers, and the other attracting them, through the pull of old traditions they had almost relinquished and to which they now returned.

Let us summarize: The great innovation is the creative outcome of a regression. The new religious advance at first took the form of all religious revolutions—namely, that of a regressive and reactionary drive against the way of the fathers. The Hebrews tried to purge themselves of the theological notions and practices of the Egyptians which they had acquired during the last two centuries. They got rid of them all except circumcision and Ikhnaton's tendency toward monotheism. In their return to the faith and ways of the forefathers they improved and modernized them—thus reaching an advanced phase, far beyond the stage of the original cultural environment that sent them forth.

By what figure of speech can we express the typical character and significance of the way this progress was achieved? Two instances from remote fields present themselves for purposes of comparison. The foxglove is a plant with tall stalks having many bell-shaped flowers. From its leaves and seeds a very valuable medicine is obtained, used for stimulating the heart. For a long time physicians rejected the idea that this plant had curative powers. They spoke of this as an old wives' tale until Withering, in Birmingham, introduced it into medicine in 1775. The second instance lies close at hand. Modern psychiatry had, for some centuries, brushed aside the folklore or superstition that dreams were prophecies foretelling future events, and explained dream production as the result of physiological stimuli. Freud showed, at the beginning of this century, how much psychological understanding can be obtained in the interpretation of dreams; he conceived of them as meaningful psychical productions. In returning to these seemingly superstitious and relinquished concepts of dreams Freud evolved his distinctive view which set forth from the evidence that dreams were disguised wish-fulfillments. In this, as in numerous other instances, a revolutionary innovation was essentially a return to an old abandoned phase that is revived, changed, and brought to a higher and more advanced form.

The great metamorphosis whose tradition is preserved in the Sinai story, interlaced with the Exodus narrative, was initiated and propelled by the Israelite group which had been assimilated to the Egyptian civilization. Moses and his Levites convinced the Hebrew tribes that they had no other way of redemption than flight and, later on, that they had reached a point of no return to Egypt.

The last thirty years have seen numerous attempts at an explanation of the beginnings of Israel. A recent survey of the pertinent literature expresses the widespread feeling that up to date no entirely satisfactory treatment of the subject exists. The reviewer comes to the conclusion that the recent contributions—for instance the books of Martin Noth[5]—leave many questions unanswered: "Most serious of those is, in my opinion, that the origin of Israel and its faith is left quite without adequate explanation."[6]

I will not presume to attempt a precise description of the manner in which the rabble of fugitives, united with the Hebrews in Canaan, became organized into a twelve-clan league. There is no doubt that Moses and Joshua used all means at their disposal to bring about a cohesive group, and the union of the various clans into a covenant. The refugees from Egypt who had never lost their feeling of solidarity with their brethren in Palestine influenced them in a powerful effort to return to the faith of their common forefathers. The process of turning away from the civilization to which they had been assimilated for so long and from the worship of Baal and Ashtaroth, was a Canaanite doublet of the Egyptian movement. The biblical narrative shows how much more difficult and slow the return to the old Hebrew tradition was in Palestine. Finally the mother-goddess and her divine son and lover were removed, and Yahweh, the father-god and the god of the fathers, became the only sovereign also in Canaan.

My own impression resulting from an admittedly cursory study of recent literature is that the failure to understand the genesis and early history of Israel originates in the neglect of the two dynamic factors characterized in this book. Any attempt at exploration that does not consider the co-operative and cumulative effect of the rejection of Egyptian civilization and of the return to the faith of the fathers, misses the point—or rather, misses the two points—of the Israelite mutation, of the unique development of Hebrew history. This most challenging problem can only be solved by a reappraisal and reassessment of these two intensive powers. The development starting at the Exodus-Sinai phase took then an upward turn. Israel had to step backward in order to jump higher. The leap backwards was the prologue to a movement that skipped several phases of evolution and arrived at a higher and more advanced phase of civilization.

28.

A Holy Nation

The time has now come to deal at least casually with the much-discussed problem of Israel's election. It seems to me that this problem, also, can be brought closer to a solution if approached in the light of our analogy between the Exodus-revelation events and the initiatory patterns. Can Israel's attitude to her election as it appears in the Bible be compared with the pride of other nations? There are significant differences which cannot be overlooked. If the Egyptians were proud of their nation, they had good reasons for their attitude. Theirs was an empire covering the greatest part of the then known world, theirs a civilization of such age and amplitude that they looked down on other people as barbarians.

The emphasis of the Hebrew belief in their election is not on the people, but on Yahweh. The Israelites will be honored not for their own sake, but because they are His people. All honor belongs to Him. But—we come back to the old question: Why did He choose them? "How odd of God . . ." Only one reason is given by biblical testimony: It was just "because Yahweh loved you" (Deut. 7:8). Hosea confirms it:

> When Israel was a child I came to love him,
> And out of Egypt I called my son.

Well, if this explanation be accepted, no other reason seems necessary. Was that love reciprocated? Certainly not in the beginning. The biblical narrative indicates that Israel did not want to be chosen. The Haggadah tradition says that the nations rejected the Torah, while Israel accepted it only under enforcement.[1] There are traditions that Israel was willing to fulfill the obligations connected with the

140

covenant. Yet there are other traditions stating emphatically that Israel had to be threatened with extinction in order to make her yield to the demands of God.[2] The chosen people were not always proud of being chosen. Yahweh complains:

> Because they have transgressed my covenant
> And against my law have rebelled.

The Lord speaks (Isa. 1:2):

> Hear, O heavens, and give ear, O earth:
> For Yahweh hath spoken
> I have nourished and brought up children,
> And they have rebelled against me.

Hosea compares Israel with an unfaithful wife. If Yahweh is self-admittedly jealous, He has good reason to be. In her long career of "whoring after strange gods" Israel was many times unfaithful to Yahweh: with the pantheon of the Egyptians; with the gods of the Babylonians, Canaanites, Persians, Greeks, and Romans. There are, indeed, few deities who cannot boast of having enjoyed her favors.

It is also not correct, as some biblical scholars assert, that Israel reacted with humbleness when the prophets accused her of unfaithfulness. The feeling of unworthiness and guilt came much later. At first, when caught in the act, she treated Yahweh with the contempt which, in the words of Anatole France, a woman feels for the man whom she has deceived.

We turn from synthetic attempts to explain the election concept, to Freud's interpretations.[3] Freud points out that the claim of the Hebrews to be especially near to God is what made them exceptionally proud and confident. Their self-confidence became, through Moses, anchored in religion. The worshippers of this god, who grew slowly to universal grandeur, took part in his greatness, felt uplifted themselves. To make his meaning clear Freud uses a simile: the confidence a Briton would feel in a foreign land made unsafe by revolt. The Englishman feels very self-confident because he knows his government will protect him with all its might. As a British subject, he is proud of the greatness of his empire. Consciousness of the greater security and protection similar to that of the British subject is enjoyed by the Hebrews: "pride in the greatness of God goes together with that of being chosen."

Freud's psychological characterization of Jewish pride is undoubtedly correct as far as it goes; but it could perhaps go further. The tracing of the Jewish faith in their preference to the greatness of their god is certainly the most important factor in the idea of election. Yet it is certainly not the only factor and we do not understand where it comes from, what were its preliminaries. We cannot trace the steps by which that faith came into existence. Originally the power of Yahweh was very restricted and the ancient Israelites did not deny the existence of the gods of other people. The Israelites are the people of Yahweh as the Moabites are the people of Chemosh. Israel is called *am Yahweh* (Judg. 5:11; II Sam. 1:12; II Sam. 2:24) or *am Elohim* (II Sam. 14:13; Judg. 20:2) as Moab is called the people of the other God *am Chemosh* (Num. 21:29). Even after Yahweh grew to his august position and grandeur, it was not denied that other gods were powerful too. When we think of the many biblical passages in which the superiority of Yahweh is contrasted with the gods of other nations, the attitude of ancient Israel is, in the best case, comparable to that of a little boy who boasts to another concerning his father's superior prowess.

Freud's explanation presents only one aspect of the idea of election and leaves unexplained how this idea arose in the middle of a tiny and powerless people. The situation in which we find ourselves is the following: If we assume that the conviction of election was an early one and dates from the time of the Sinai revelation, it becomes difficult to imagine how it came into being, since the god of the Israelite tribes was a poor and crude deity of limited power. Let us now consider the idea of election a very late one—in accordance with the view of many biblical authorities and with Freud. Yahweh was then conceived as the Lord of Heaven and Earth and his majesty acknowledged, but what about the people He had chosen? Their God had proved to be impotent.

However we elaborate the idea, it is not easy to understand where the concept of the chosen people originated. The miserable clans in Goshen, Egyptian serfs—could these people conceive a god as Lord of the universe whose favored sons they were? Neither the Babylonians nor the Egyptians developed a faith comparable to the idea of being chosen. How could the Hebrews imagine that they were under the special protection of a god and reconcile their miserable situation with that idea? Theological speculation will not help us to solve the problem. We have no recourse but to view it as a psychological question: their god is made after the image of this people.

No solution of the problem can be acceptable which does not explain to us how that strange idea came into being in the midst of half-nomadic and despised tribes. When we speak of the "chosen people," we naturally think first of choice in the sense of preference or election. To choose something—let us say a book from the library—means to pick it out from many others. It now seems to us that *not selection, but separation is the prime meaning of the term.* Is it not possible that we have overlooked that character of separateness in the concept of the "chosen people"? The thought is at least worthy of our consideration.

In the key sentence concerning election (Exod. 19:6) the Lord promises that the people, if they will obey His voice and keep the covenant with Him, will be a "peculiar treasure unto me above all people," and says: "And ye shall be unto me a kingdom of priests, and an holy nation." The characterization of the Israelites of the future as a "kingdom of priests" and as a "holy nation" is certainly unique in the history of antiquity. It signifies not only the election, but, even more, the elevation of half-civilized clans, intermingled with a "mixed multitude" of fugitives from Egypt. We take this key sentence together with another passage to be found in Leviticus (18:3): "After the doings of the land of Egypt, wherein ye dwelt, shall ye not do: and after the doings of the land of Canaan, whither I shall bring you, shall ye not do: neither shall ye walk in their ordinances." The Lord repeats: "Ye shall be holy: for I the Lord your God am holy" (Lev. 19:2).

In contrast with other commentators, we emphasize here not the holiness of the Lord, but the separation from the Egyptians and Canaanites and their ordinances. The reference of the Lord to the "doings of the land of Egypt" leads us back to Moses and his followers who forced the B'ne Israel under the yoke of Yahweh. Moses was an Egyptian of high position, according to a text of the Rameses period—even high enough to depose a Vizier. In some stories he was considered to be the heir to the throne. Other legends tell of his functioning as a High Priest.[4] He was, as the New Testament says, "instructed in all the wisdom of the Egyptians." That can only mean that he knew the secrets of the Egyptian religion and was introduced into the mysteries of the Osiris cult.[5] He was, at any rate, familiar with all details of the temple schools of Thebes. He knew the services and the whole hierarchy directed by the High Priest of Ra at Karnak—those services of washing, anointing, perfuming, and libating—of sacrifices, oracles and divinations. He was certainly aware of the privileges of that army of Egyptian priests who belonged to the richest class and who often abused their position for their prestige and enrichment. Living at the court, he must have once shared the belief that the Pharaoh was the personification of the god Osiris.

It is likely, as Freud suggested, that Moses was a follower or admirer of Iknhaton, of that "god-intoxicated man" (to recall Breasted's description) who is often called the first monotheist. This Pharaoh despised and condemned the priests of the Egyptian parthenon, took their goods, and closed their richly endowed temples. He put an end to their magical and divinatory ordinances. Ikhnaton's revolutionary reform perished shortly after his death, which was the signal for the priests to eliminate the memory of the heretic king and to restore the old order of things. In the mind of that passionate man, Moses, there lived perhaps the memory of the Aton religion— of that purified belief which the fanatical Pharaoh Ikhnaton had raised to the official religion of Egypt. But Moses saw also the furious reaction of the priests which set in after Amenhotep's death. He was an eyewitness not only of the oppressor's wrong, but also of the insolence of office, of the haughtiness of the privileged priestly class who exploited the superstitious people.

After surveying the personal and cultural milieu from which Moses emerged as the leader of the Hebrews, the pronouncement of the Lord appears in a different light. The admonition "not to do" after the "doing" of the land of Egypt "wherein ye dwelled" provides resonance to the statement: "Ye shall be unto me a kingdom of priests and an holy nation." The sentence does away with a special and privileged class of priests and with the god-king or Pharaoh.[6] It transfers and extends their prerogatives to the people, to all members of the confederation and covenant. If I may be allowed to employ a striking comparison to illuminate the meaning of that key sentence: it is as though the Lord would abolish the Catholic clergy and the Pope and then declare that the Irish are a "kingdom of priests" and a "holy nation." The hierarchy of the Egyptian priests, along with their supreme dignitary, is dismissed and its form and function conveyed to the Hebrews.

The sentence has thus a polemical character, implying rejection of the sacredness and separateness of Egyptian priesthood and of the divine king. In breaking down the wall separating the clergy from the people, Yahweh's pronouncement gives priestly character to the Israelites, and with the attribute of the holiness, the power and the glory of the election. The Hebrews inherited from the Egyptian priests the separateness of a privileged class in which they were promoted to the rank of the "chosen people."

I do not doubt that many scholars will attribute the character of an intellectual *tour de force* to my interpretation of the biblical passage pronouncing that the Israelites are a holy nation. But this interpretation of the much-commented sentence is no more arbitrary than many others and has, if I am not deceived, the advantage of psychological plausibility.

The changed attitude of those educated Israelites who had been assimilated to Egyptian culture manifests itself in the implied denial that there was a divine king and a special caste of priests as well as in the defiant declaration that the Hebrews are a kingdom of priests and a holy nation. The Leviticus passage warning the people about imitating the Egyptian ordinances serves only as added inner evidence for this assumption. Even if we regard that sentence as a late interpolation, its confirmatory significance cannot be lightly dismissed.[7]

Thus far in the present chapter, we have attempted to trace the origin of the election concept back to intensive reactions of the Hebrews and of their leader Moses to the idea of a divine king and of the privileged Egyptian priest-caste. The abolition of those concepts was accompanied by the elevation of the whole nation of the Hebrews to the rank of priests. But have we not previously asserted that the Hebrew tribes returned in that Exodus-Sinai experience to more primitive religious and social institutions? How does our theory of the source and significance of the idea of election tally with the data on initiation rites and secret societies?

An answer to this question requires the review of the transition materials on initiation with special emphasis on the significance of separation and election. The secret fraternities which evolved within primitive societies, it is evident, ensured a closer connection with the gods or spirits of the tribes and promoted simultaneously both law and order.[8] Their activities, rituals, and dances are surrounded by mystery. Admission to them is gained only after long and severe tests of initiation, similar to those in the puberty rituals. The elaborate initiation to the tribal mysteries forms the main aspect of the secret fraternities. The members of the fraternities are supposed to possess supernatural or magical powers by virtue of their intimate connection with the tribal spirits.[9]

The privileges of the neophytes who pass into the spirit world by way of death and resurrection are of various kinds, but they are different from those obtained by membership in special societies, for instance, those of warriors. In his excellent survey of American secret societies, H. B. Alexander emphasizes that they are in charge of religious mysteries: "To be sure, in a life where nearly every activity is accompanied by religious observation, this is not a clear criterion . . . in fact the secret societies tend to assume a social importance, i.e. to become priesthoods."[10] The various fraternities of the Zuni which execute the rain dances "may similarly be regarded as priesthoods endowed with special appeals to the gods of rain and vegetation." We hear about African religious confraternities that the right to prepare a charm, to use a spell, to call upon a deity, or to officiate as a priest, is jealously guarded. The attitude of the members "is that of possessors of a trade secret to be divulged only to those who themselves become members of the guild." In the Ibo area of Africa the blacksmiths and the doctors form their own societies. It is interesting to find that the title *"ozo"* (blacksmith) is the highest in the hierarchy and does not imply any expert knowledge of the blacksmith's craft. (We think here of the Kenites who were desert smiths near Mount Sinai).

The original reason for the secrecy surrounding the society is, as N. W. Thomas suggests, that all rights of initiation and membership "imply a certain amount of separation from the outside world, and a certain affiliation to the new world; this aspect is especially prominent where it is a question of admitting a youth to full tribal right . . ."[11] This process is not restricted to the puberty rituals. The paramount chiefs of Sierra Leonea, for instance, undergo a period of separation before they assume the reins of power. Sacralization implies everywhere separation from the profane world. The secret societies seem to represent a new social order bringing together members of the same tribe who are of different clans. They pass also from tribe to tribe, and even from linguistic stock to linguistic stock.

As we have observed above, the fraternities evolved from the age groups of puberty initiation that formed an important part of the tribal and intertribal communities. They also had the purpose of teaching the novices the secret ceremonies of the tribe. They held the intermediate place between the mysteries and official religion. A certain clan often possessed functions of priests, but as the example of the African Tenda shows, there was a tendency in many secret societies to initiate the whole tribe, even its slaves. Do we not have here a feature we rediscover in the extension of "holiness" to the whole nation of the Israelites?

I shall attempt to reconstruct the development of the idea of election in its earliest phases, using the clues found in the biblical tradition and in the comparative material from anthropology. Moses who fled to the Kenites who were kin to the Hebrews, was introduced to the secret society of the Midianites. Reports about the Ibo society in West Africa present here comparative material: There is the custom of taking "titles" which correspond roughly to generation grades or age grades. Originally a man takes his first title after the death of his father. The highest grade in the Ibo society is that of blacksmith which points to the character of the titles as names of trade guilds. A large proportion of that population is composed of blacksmiths. Thomas reminds us[12] that blacksmiths occupy, in many areas, a peculiar position: "they are occasionally a pariah class, but more often, as among the Ibo, have succeeded in making their society the head of the hierarchy formed by the 'titles.' In more than one case the blacksmith is the operator in initiation rites . . ."

Also the Kenites, who traced their descent back to the murderer Cain, were perhaps once considered a pariah tribe. They were desert smiths and at the time they received Moses they worshipped Yahweh, the god of Mount Horeb. Jethro was their priest and Moses married his daughter Zipporah. It is perhaps not accidental that it was in Midian that Moses was attacked by Yahweh, because he had neglected the holy usage of circumcision and that his Midianite wife saved him from the rage of God. It is likely that the Kenites circumcised their young men before marriage. The Kenites were perhaps operators in the initiation at puberty as were the blacksmiths of the Ibo society.

It seems to me that the expression "chosen people" originally had a character similar to the "title" of the West African secret societies and was later transferred from a tribe or grade to the federation of Hebrews tied together by the covenant. "Chosen" thus originally meant, "separated" from the mass of the "profane," and the term is applied to a person who is initiated into the totem-mysteries or into a secret society. The Essenes and the early Christians considered themselves in this sense "chosen."[13]

The title "kingdom of priests and a holy nation" is an extension also in the sense that it was transferred from a few clans or tribes to the whole people who had entered into the covenant. We know that long after that revolutionary reform there was again a privileged caste of priests, with a high priest at their head[14] in ancient Israel. The old order as it had been in Egypt was at least partly restored. The Levites became the priests of the federate tribes and the only true shrine of Yahweh was at Jerusalem. The priesthood there completely controlled the cult. The progress made by declaring the people a "kingdom of priests" was again lost. But the conflict between the priests and the prophets—particularly Jeremiah—revived the old contrast without hope that the solution of the problem could be found.[15]

The discussion of this later phase reminds us that we have to add a third element to the two features which we made responsible for the formation of the idea of the "chosen people," namely the rejection of the Egyptian order and the regression to an earlier religious phase. There were certainly remnants of just those religious ideas that were so bitterly opposed by Moses and his followers. It was unavoidable that the disavowed and denied Egyptian concepts should invade, slowly but perceptibly, the area of the new organization of the Hebrew confederation. The very formulation of that sentence in Exodus proves that the repudiated Egyptian heritage crept into the reform. A "kingdom of priests"? There were no kings or priests in Israel at the time of Moses. The notion of holiness was attributed to the Egyptian priests and magicians.

The extension of the "kingly" and of the "holy" from individuals and from a small caste to a people has world-historic significance. Seen from a certain angle, it is *the first formulation of a democratic religious concept*. The élite of ancient civilizations, the Babylonians and Egyptians, had a caste of privileged persons whose sacred obligation was the religious cult, not only for themselves, but for all people. There were no such priestly privileges, nor any specially sacred persons, who had to take care of things divine in the early phases of Mosaic religion. The despised Hebrew tribes arrived at the idea that every tribesman was a priest and was holy.

The other side of the coin shows a picture that is in every regard the opposite of that democratic concept. It raises the whole nation to the rank of a distinguished and separate group and attributes to it the dignity and superiority of a "chosen people." The extension of the concept of holiness from the priest caste to the Israelite tribe amounts to the elevation of a pariah-people to a lonely and lofty height. That promotion had later the same effect upon the Israelites as, to use a comparison, the sudden promotion of the Negroes to the rank of American aristocracy would have upon that minority group today. The result of such sudden exaltation explains the extraordinary pride and self-confidence of the Jews later on in spite of agonies and tortures.

We are here only concerned with the origin of the idea of election and its historic roots in the soil of tribal initiation and cannot enter the discussion of the psychological problems connected with the idea of the chosen people. The Bible does not assert that they obtained the elevated rank by any excellence of the Israelites. There is always reference made to Yahweh: they are holy because He is holy. Yet, says Baruch Spinoza, one of the most distinguished, if not one of the most appreciated, sons of Israel, whenever the Jews think something, they declare that God told them so.

29.

The Name Ineffable

There are a few critical scholars who claim that monotheism existed in a phase previous to Moses, but there are also some who assert, as does W. F. Albright, that the belief in a single God was a creation of Moses. Several others state that the exclusive worship of Yahweh at the time of the Exodus is an impossibility and that until the time of Elijah in the ninth century, other gods besides Yahweh were acknowledged, if not worshipped. Some historians affirm that the only real monotheist in the ancient Near East was Ikhnaton of Egypt, and some deny even that. Those who assume that there was a tiny flicker of monotheism at the period of Ikhnaton in Egypt, maintain it was soon extinguished in the bitter reaction against the heretic Pharaoh immediately after his death.

The problem of the beginnings of monotheistic belief belongs entirely to the area of history. There are, however, other aspects of the question which concern the theologian and the philosopher. The quest for the first cause, in which many philosophers are engaged, is sometimes opposed to the point of view of the religious man. This is illustrated in the popular story of the discussion between a philosopher and a theologian. The priest compared the philosopher to a blind man in a dark room looking for a black cat which was not there. "That may be," said the philosopher, "but the theologian asserts he has found it."

Putting aside for a moment the arguments on both sides, what is it that makes the monotheist believe that his faith is superior to that of polytheism? Or, to continue in that comparison, is there a higher position to the claim of the theologian who sees a single cat in the black room, than to the belief that there are many animals there? One could say in favor of this argument that if there is a necessity to believe in supernatural beings, it would be advantageous to assume a single divine figure. This would, so to speak, present an advantage in economy since the requirements to be met are present in a single entity. But even this gain is ambiguous. A skeptic once remarked that the only argument he knew in favor of the monotheistic principle was a purely arithmetical one: monotheism is nearer to the truth because one is nearer to zero than three or five.[1]

The majority of historians and biblical scholars considers monotheism the great forward step of Judaism. Freud also seems to think that strict monotheistic principle was the unique achievement of Moses. Geza Roheim, A. B. Feldman and other psychoanalytic critics of Freud's views have argued that monotheism—even in its ethical aspects—is not the crown of religion. Feldman has stressed the fact that the polytheistic Confucian Chinese and the Aeschylean Greeks are, in their ethical attitudes, in no way inferior to the believers in one God.[2] On the other hand, as Roheim points out, many primitive people have a monotheistic faith and—insofar as the sky-god is the patron of the puberty rite and its taboos,[3]—they may be considered to adhere to some forms of ethical monotheism.

In his critical review of Freud's thesis on monotheism, Ernest Jones assumes that the Jews who first succeeded in concentrating the divine qualities into a single figure were not "a little proud of this advance. It has revealed the father nucleus which had always lain hidden behind every figure." In Jones' view, the advance is contained in the return to the historic beginnings of the idea of God. Now that God was a single person, man's relations to him could recover the intimacy and intensity of the child's relation to his father.[4] It is doubtful whether this attitude was an original one and if it was not transferred from the primary intimacy to the mother—which immediately brings up the question of the place of the mother-goddess in the evolution of religion. But with this question we are led back to the statement that the character of the Mosaic renovation was to a

great extent determined by violent reaction against Egyptian and
Canaanite concepts in which the mother-goddesses Isis and Ishtar
played a dominant role.

In order to evaluate a suggested move forward, one has first to
determine the point from which a progressive movement started.
What was the religion of the Hebrew tribes before Moses? It is
likely that the use of the singular in this question is itself a mistake.
Before the Hebrews amalgamated to make the confederacies of Israel
and Judah, each tribe had perhaps its own gods. These gods or
demons were probably of half-human and half-animal shape, originally totemistic in character like the banners carried by the twelve
tribes. The fact that they were superhuman did not exclude that they
were—in our sense—subhuman. These gods had in the time of
Moses certainly lost many of their original properties and had obtained some qualities of a higher kind; but they were still tribal
deities and had not "arrived."

The fact that a new religion was born in the great conversion at
Sinai, or Shechem, does not devaluate the evolutionary principle
and does not abolish the laws that determine the growth of religious
development. Some theologians who assert that the Hebrew mutation
puts Israel outside the evolutionary design have a misconception of
the historical process. The development from a few simple forms
of life to more complex ones does not follow a straight and direct
line. There are often detours on the journey, turns and returns, shifts
and regressions.

The ascent of the god to a lofty position does not rule out the
possibility that the Lord was once a crude and barbaric deity even
when his promotion appears to be a sudden and surprising one. Also
within the religious development of ancient Israel one god followed
the other. The Hebrews were by their own admission a mixed people
whose original Aramaean stock was fused with various Hittite groups
and with the Amorite population. In the older tales their god is a
mighty and dangerous demon who attacks Jacob and kills Egyptian
as well as Israelite first-born sons when he walks from house to house
and is only kept away by the sight and smell of blood at the threshold. This deity is originally a tribal god of very restricted realm, and
his dwelling place is a high tree or a mountain. His humble and poor
position contrasts conspicuously with that of the Lord two thousand
years later when his residence is in the luxurious temple of Jerusalem.

In our continuing search for earlier shapes of the deity we again
recall that saying of the Lord (Exod. 6:2–3): "I am Yahweh and

I appeared unto Abraham, unto Isaac and unto Jacob as El Shaddai, but by my name Yahweh was I not known to them." The divine words are contradicted by other passages in which the name Yahweh is used in much earlier times. God says to Abraham: "I am Yahweh that brought you out of Ur of the Chaldees" and to Jacob: "I am Yahweh the God of Abraham thy father, and the God of Isaac" (Gen. 28:13). Thus the Lord identified Himself already to the patriarchs by that name. But it is also stated in the fourth chapter of Genesis that man began to call upon the name of Yahweh. We rejected the irreverent possibility of forgetfulness on the part of an all-knowing deity and traced the contradiction to the mistake or lapse of two different groups of editors. In this assumption we find ourselves in agreement with most biblical scholars.

In contrast with them, however, the problem does not appear solved with this explanation because we are not concerned here with the solution of a logical contradiction, but with the finding of a historic truth which is hidden. In other words, we want to know if that divergence does not conceal and at the same time reveal a forgotten tradition. The occasion on which the Lord introduces Himself to Moses is certainly an extraordinary one. It is not a social encounter but a private revelation, as are the other occasions upon which Yahweh speaks to the patriarchs. The enunciation of the name of the tribal god was an essential part of the revelation.

In the sense of our interpretation, the divulging of his name belongs to the climax of the puberty rituals in which the novice was introduced into the worship of the tribal gods and their mysteries (not known to the uninitiated). It would be imaginable that Yahweh is the hushed-up name recognized only to the man who has passed the puberty ceremonials, while El Shaddai was the name otherwise used for God. The other members knew the deity as Elohim or Adonai and the name Yahweh was perhaps divulged only to the initiated ones.

There is another possibility, as A. Alt has shown,[5] that the Hebrew tribes had each their own god before the confederacies. The early Israelites thought, like their neighbors, of their gods as of members of their tribe. The Yahweh-cult was perhaps first known in Arabia; it was even later connected with the Negeb and with the southern sanctuaries like Sinai and Kadesh. It is likely that this god became prevalent at the time of Moses. Alt explains that the figures of the patriarchs were reversed as the founders of the cults associated with their names—of the "God of Abraham," the "Fear of Isaac" (Gen.

31:42), of the "Kinsman of Isaac," and "The Mighty of Jacob."
Alt's findings have been reinforced by significant northern sources.
W. A. Albright states that the material presented by Alt and Lewy
makes it all but impossible hereafter to regard the tradition about the
"Gods of the Fathers" as late or secondary. Yahweh introduced himself as god of the fathers. It was not a new religion but a renewed
one. It re-established and restored an old and forgotten faith.

We are struck not only from what comes recently from outside.
There is another kind of newness that emerges from inside and is
perceived as surprising. It is the disavowed and repressed which
returns from hidden recesses. Not only that which was never known
is unfamiliar and strange, but also that which was once known,
but has become forgotten or alienated. Many experiences in individual
psychoanalytic practice show us that experiences which are felt as
surprising are often things that were once consciously perceived and
were then banned from knowledge. Yahweh was in this sense a new-
old god. The Mosaic concept of a god is, as an acute historian
recently remarked, not a radical break with the previous tribal religion
of the Hebrews. Some of its essential elements grew directly out of
the people, still organized on the basis of clans and families. Although there is no evidence of ancestor-worship among the early
Hebrews, religion was nevertheless a clan affair. God himself was
under certain aspects related to his clan or clans as a kind of god-
parent.[6] The missing link of the name of Yahweh is buried deep in
the past of the Hebrews. A spark from old fires leaped a gap when
Moses brought his message to the serfs in the land of Goshen.

The question "What's in a name?" would sound nonsensical to
every person of the ancient Orient. What is in a *name?* Everything.
To know the name of a god or an animal means not only knowledge
but power. Adam "named" the animals (Gen. 2:19–20) and knowing their name made him their master. The name is part of a person
—as essential a part as his body. Without a name the person has no
social form or reality; he has given up his identity. The affinity between the pronunciation of the name and the personality is, according to an anthropologist,[7] as certain as a chemical reaction, with the
same fatally necessary effects. The attraction takes place of itself,
with all its inevitable consequences.

The intrinsic power of the names has certain consequences such
as the reliance upon secrecy in self-protection against magical and
dangerous use of the awesome words. Among many primitive peoples, individuals have an ordinary name and a real name known

only to themselves which they will never reveal. The same purpose of protection keeps the names of demons and gods secret. The natural consequences of those protections leads to a "name-taboo." The name of the divine beings must not be pronounced and, amongst semi-civilized people, not written. In Zululand, Tahiti, and other places, the name-taboo has marred even the everyday language by changing or distorting by alliteration or homonymy most words in which the tabooed name might be evoked.

In this context, the prohibition of the name of Yahweh inevitably comes to mind. That name is etymologically obscure and has been differently interpreted. Whatever might have been its original significance, there is no doubt that this name was too terrible to be pronounced. The third commandment says: "Thou shalt not take the name of Yahweh thy god in vain for Yahweh will not hold him guiltless that taketh his name in vain." The commandment was generally interpreted as a prohibition of blasphemy, but it originally intended the forbidding of Yahweh's name for magical purposes. The commandment is thus a prohibition belonging to the area of the name-taboo. The word "Yahweh," considered too sacred to be spoken aloud, was substituted by "Adonai," meaning "the Lord." The laity avoided the pronunciation of the sacred name and only the high priest dared to pronounce it upon most solemn occasions, and in so low a tone as to render it inaudible even to his colleagues.

The prohibition against pronouncing Yahweh's name is clearly a reintroduction of the primitive name-taboo that protected the divinity against magic but also prevented men from using magical practices. Egypt was in Moses' time the country of magic *par excellence* and its numerous gods are called by many names, some of them by a combination of names—for instance, Amon-Re. In the Babylonian civilization written texts preserve the names of several thousand gods besides those of countless spirits, demons, and goblins.

The Mosaic religion shows also in the avoidance of the name of God that its character is determined by an intensive reaction against the Egyptian religion, and by a return to a more primitive, earlier form of worship. Archaeology has not been able to shed any significant new light upon the pre-Mosaic religious belief of the Hebrew clans nor upon the traditions of the Kenites, under whose influence Moses found himself. But the new name-taboo is certainly characteristic of a people who were adverse to the magic and the incantations of the Egyptians.

It is significant in this context that we do not know what the original name of Moses was. If the tradition that Moses was brought up in an Egyptian palace is exact, his Egyptian foster-mother naturally gave him an Egyptian name with a theophoric character. Moses means in Egyptian "child" and the word is often used in names such as Amon-mose, meaning "Amon (has given) a child," or Ptah-mose, meaning "Ptah (has given) a child."[8] Baron suggests that Moses later dropped the name of the god, the theophoric part of his name "as a sign of his repudiation of Egyptian paganism."[9] The case would be comparable to one in which, let us say, an American who is called Isidore Goldstein would, from a certain moment on, assume the official name of Dore Goldstein, dropping the divinity of Isis from his name.

In our quest for the pre-Mosaic phase of Israel's religion, we came upon the prohibition of the name of God as a significant symptom of turning away from the advanced Egyptian civilization and of a return to an earlier phase of the religious evolution. But this regression does not mean a return to nature in the sense of Jean-Jacques Rousseau. The Hebrew tribes who settled on the Nile delta were contemporary to the Eighteenth Egyptian Dynasty. They were half-nomads domesticating animals. They made extended use of the instruments and tools of the middle and late Bronze Age. The return to an earlier form of religious and social development does not mean a regression to the phase of savagery such as that of Australian natives, nor even to the half-civilized level of African Negroes. Yet it is this same core that runs through the roots and the branches; and the roots of the tree extend farther than its height.

In our interpretation of the revelation at Sinai we compared the events whose memory the biblical narratives have preserved in spite of all distortions and changes of different kinds with the puberty rituals of Australian and African tribes. In following this comparison which, in my view, touches the core of the Sinai tradition, I have quite often and unhesitantly shifted from treating the puberty festivals to the initiations into the secret societies of primitive and half-civilized people. This change from one position to another was made without excuse or justification as though the two were the same. They are not the same, and here is the place to state that the Hebrews in the revelation tradition are closer to the phase of the initiation into secret societies than to that of the puberty festival.

I shall at least attempt to justify the preference in comparing the Sinai events with the puberty initiation. First it has to be pointed out that the two celebrations or initiations are, in their forms and functions, so similar and akin that they sometimes seem to overlap. According to Webster, the point of connection between the puberty rituals and the secret societies is "the elaborate ritual of initiation to tribal or totemistic mysteries which occurs also as one of the main aspects of these fraternities."[10] There is furthermore no doubt that the puberty festivals are the primary form of initiation from which the brotherhoods developed.

I have taken this original form as prototype for the comparison with the events of the Sinai revelation, because the description of those primitive festivals provides a picture of their significant features in their representative and clear shapes. This facilitates the comparison because the complication by late and secondary traits is avoided and the common elements between the initiation and the Sinai revelation come to a clear expression. There is another reason for the preferential treatment of the puberty initiation: the importance of circumcision in the savage ceremonials as well as in the Sinai tradition—although circumcision or similar operations occur also as part of the initiation into the fraternities. For the special case of the Hebrew tribes a fact pointed out by N. W. Thomas in his survey of the African customs[11] interests us here. We have to reckon with the inexactness of terminology in regard to secret societies, but also with the circumstance that a society which is secret in one area may be public in another.

We will come back immediately to this remarkable fact after having discussed an aspect of the Sinai tradition that has scarcely been mentioned until now. It was skirted when the subject of election with which it is intimately connected was considered. By this I refer to the idea of the covenant, a concept which is, in the view of some biblical scholars, the foundation of Israel's theology.[12] The covenant at Mount Sinai is so important for W. Eichrodt[13] that he reconstructs the whole theology of the Old Testament around it. Other scholars such as K. Galling,[14] H. Wheeler Robinson,[15] and Ernest Wright[16] regard it primarily as a formal expression and confirmation of the election idea. We disregard here the many discussions about the age of the original confederacy and about the tribes participating in it. Martin Noth[17] is of the opinion that Joshua (24) is an authentic tradition relating to the conquest of Canaan, and presents the extension of the Sinai covenant to the complete Amphictyony of twelve tribes.

The comparison of the sacral confederation of the twelve tribes with the attitude of the ancient Hellenic tribes and of their cult of the confederate deity Apollo is very popular nowadays with several biblical scholars. It is informative as far as it enables us to understand similarities in some functions, but it is utterly misleading if it is supposed to shed any light on the original nature of the Hebrew covenant-concept. The same is true for the reference to Hittite and Babylonian treaties as legal documents, often compared with the covenant at Shechem. The legal aspect is certainly a secondary one and belongs to a later time. All these archaeological parallels are of minor importance when the question of the original character of the covenant is raised. None of these analogies reaches the heart of the problem. They are to be compared to the small fish which the fisherman throws back into the lake because they cannot be used. There is no doubt that the fry was in the lake and was caught, but the small fish are discarded by the fisherman who wants to bring big and choice fish home.

In the research regarding such problems it is desirable to blot out all preconceived ideas about similarities with contemporary legal institutions. George E. Mendenhall argues[18] that the statement that Israel's religion is based on covenant implies that a form of action which originated in a legal custom has been transferred to the field of religion. He concludes that a study of the forms of the covenant as we know them in ancient legal documents may possibly serve to bring into the chaos of opinion some objective criteria for reconstructing the course of Israelite history and religion.[21] The legitimacy of such an approach is not doubtful but its usefulness is highly questionable, even when the argument is disregarded that the pre-Mosaic tribes were a much too primitive group either to know or to understand the highly developed forms of legal treaties brought in as analogous.

The very primitive ceremonies and symbolisms in the covenant described in the biblical account, the rites of the sacrificial meal and of the sprinkling of blood on the altar and the people—thus uniting God and his worshippers—point in another direction. The origin of the blood covenant is to be found in the initiation into the secret societies of brotherhoods between members of different tribes. This means that the covenant presents a form developed from the primitive groups united by certain laws and customs and introduced into the cult of gods. We learned that the secret societies are intertribal and comprise members of different clans and people and that a god is regarded as the third participant to the covenant.

The old fraternities and secret societies of primitive tribes would

thus have two offsprings in later development of religious organizations: the mysteries as we encounter them in Abydos and in Eleusis
in which the death and resurrection of a young god were dramatically
displayed, and the covenants, solemn initiations into the cult of a god
together with an intertribal confederacy of many clans formed into a
new community, bound by stipulations as in the case of the Hebrews
by the laws of the Decalogue. Both sacred institutions, different in
their forms and functions, are late developments of the initiation
rites of puberty, of age classes, and have grown from the same roots.
This interpretation of the covenant (*b'rith*) of various Hebrew
tribes—some of which were not even Israelites—and of some others
who joined the confederacy in the time of Joshua, traces the Sinai
events back to a festival of initiation into fraternities or bonds of men
out of which the covenant between its members and Yahweh grew.
A legendary and grotesque trace of that original form of intertribal
solidarity can be recognized in the anti-Semitic propaganda describing a conspiracy on the part of the "Elders of Zion." It was mentioned
before that the frontiers between the association of age groups which
have gone through the common experience of puberty initiation and
certain forms of brotherhoods as well as secret societies are fluent. It is
perhaps correct to say that the phase to which the Hebrew tribes
regressed was one which hovers between those two forms.

The concept of *b'rith* or covenant would then be a late result of
the development of a union of various kindred tribes which Moses
led forth from Egypt and which he welded into a confederacy whose
god was Yahweh, and which was united by various laws, customs,
and traditions. The final act of unification came later at Shechem
where Joshua bluntly asked the Israelites (Josh. 24:15) "And if it
seem evil unto you to serve the Lord, choose you this day whom ye
will serve; whether the gods which your fathers served that were on
the other side of the flood, or the gods of the Amorites, in whose
land ye dwell: but as for me and my house, we will serve the Lord."
It is very difficult to reconstruct the history and religion of the
Hebrews from the traditions preserved in the biblical narratives. A.
Lods[19] once likened the effort to reconstruct the patriarchal age from
the Genesis tradition to an attempt to reconstruct the age of Jesus
from traditions not older than St. Louis IX (thirteenth century) or
Francis I (sixteenth century). The gap between the situations that
gave rise to the traditions and the finished form of those traditions
remains great and unbridged. The same is, of course, valid for the
traditions concerning the concept of covenant as it appears in the

Bible. This interpretation of the covenant idea whose origins I have found in the primitive fraternities is a bolt in the dark, but the mysterious night is sometimes illuminated as by lightnings around the peak of the sacred mountain.

Tracing the confederacy of the Hebrew tribes back to the secret societies solves some problems, but raises others. The union of the confederate tribes that had made a covenant in the name of Yahweh is conceived here as a late offspring of the fraternities of primitive or half-civilized people. A secret society without secrecy? But we have learned that there are analogous cases of such paradoxical kind in Africa where at some places a society is secret while in others it has lost this character. In the Sinai tradition the initiation into the new cult is open and public, common to all people, including women and children. The revelation of Yahweh takes place in view of the people, gathered around the sacred mountain. The secrecy is not kept any more; cult and rites are made known to all, but is there really no secrecy any more? There is, but it is displaced. It is transferred to the deity, to his name and countenance.

30.

God's Incorporeality

The hypothesis presented here grew from an intuition or hunch which was followed until it became an opinion and finally a theory which was put to the test on the ascertainable facts provided by archaeology and biblical criticism. In developing the theory the logic of probability was employed. I pursued, thus, a course of investigation not inadmissible when the data are sparse and cloudy. The purpose of the research worker is to discover and communicate a likely pattern of events. Karl Popper once remarked that genuine science does not primarily seek to prove, but challenges refutation.

The theory developed here tries to reconstruct the events that are at the core of the biblical tradition about the Sinai revelation. Its aim is not that of history and archaeology which try to arrive at a factual description and chronological account of events, but to present the general historical truth upon which the biblical account is based. This writer does not pretend to be a scholar, but dares to be an explorer in excessively neglected areas and even at that he has to confess that his research does not follow the systematic course of scientific investigation. The present study is best viewed as an adventure of discovery: it searches for the solution of certain problems, neglecting others, and is eager to find new land in the spirit of the *conquistadore,* as Freud once called himself. Following the shadow of my great teacher, I arrived at the theory that at the foundation of the biblical narrative of the Sinai revelation is an historical truth—namely the initiation of the Hebrew tribes into a new religion in the manner of the primitive puberty festivals, or the admission into the fraternities of half-civilized people. The outline of the description of such an intertribal initiation is, in my view, recognizable in the biblical description of the Sinai revelation that presents the events as a supernatural phenomenon. The description preserves the tradition of the periodically occurring initiation festivals which appear in the Bible intermingled with the report of the Exodus of Hebrew tribes from Egypt. All this goes hand in hand with an embroidered and glorified narrative of the flight of oppressed serfs.

The alterations and distortions of that tradition are not only determined by different tendencies of later editors of the reports handed down to them, but also by hesitant attitude toward divulging the secrets of initiation. The very elaborate ceremonies of this kind are shrouded in secrecy. Women and uninitiated are carefully kept away from the rites that make claim to occurrences contrary to nature. That esoteric quality of the initiation rites can be observed in most primitive societies. The young men of the Kwoma of New Guinea are, for instance, shown a carved head representing a powerful spirit. They are told that this "is a hoax . . . but the secret must be carefully guarded from the women and children."[1] A remnant of that secretiveness can still be felt in the mystery surrounding the Sinai narrative, and is perhaps responsible for some of its darkness and contradictions.

But did we not assert that the old tradition presenting an initiation as theophany changed the secret character and transformed the report into an impressive narrative of Yahweh's appearance on the Mount Sinai before the eyes of all the Hebrews? Could not the whole people face the theophany? No, this god cannot be faced. He should be heard but not seen. It was already said that not all secretiveness of the primitive initiation was relinquished. The secret no longer concerned the rites; it was now concentrated upon the nature of the deity. The great mystery was the person of Yahweh, while the ceremonies were a public affair and the events on the sacred mountain took place before the whole people who were awed by the manifestations of the theophany. The obviousness of that majestic descent of Yahweh provided an excellent chance for certain circumstances to escape attention.

We have already noticed some remnants of that secrecy: for instance, the prohibition regarding Yahweh's ineffable name. We take it for granted that God is not visible and has no name, but to the ancient Egyptians and Babylonians, as well as to the pre-Mosaic Hebrews, such a concept bordered on the absurd. God may appear in a terrible and terrifying shape, but he could be seen and, if one dared, touched. The prohibition of "any likeness of anything that is in the heavens above, or in the earth beneath, or in the waters under the earth" is more important than the interdiction regarding the utterance of Yahweh's name. No one knew what God looked like, because He was invisible.

It was not important that his feet could occasionally be seen, since neither his face nor his figure was known. They were protected against indelicate and irreverent scrutiny. Sir Richard Burton tells us of a Moslem dignitary who was not in the least perturbed when his wife fell from her camel, inadvertently revealing her underparts to a large company of Englishmen. Had she not kept her face veiled through the mishap? God revealed himself, but he did not show himself. The Israelites heard his voice but they did not see his countenance: "For ye saw no manner of similitude on the day that the Lord spake unto you in Horeb out of the midst of the fire" (Deut. 4:15).

The prohibition involving images of God and of divine things shows clearly enough the character of a passionate reaction to the Egyptian religious ideas. Moses, who introduced the imageless cult, grew up in a milieu with a profusion of images, sculptures, and statuettes of gods and demons. Grandiose temples of Osiris and Amon-Re and colossal statues of the Pharaohs who were gods met his eyes, together with the symbols and representations of gods in amulets and statuettes of worshipped animals and other objects that are "in the heavens above or in the earth beneath, or in the waters below the earth."

Monumental and miniature figures presented a vivid picture of the Egyptian pantheon. Dramatic performances of the events in celestial realms exerted an irresistible appeal on the imagination, and left indelible impressions in memory. The festival at Abydos, called Sed, presented the passion of the life, death, and resurrection of Osiris in lively and lifelike scenes. The people were so impressed by this spectacle, duplicated on a smaller scale in other cities, that they prayed that after death they might be privileged to participate in the dramatic celebration. Moses certainly witnessed the incantations and libations before the figures of the gods and the amazing performance of magical practices of their priests. Not born, but bred in this atmosphere of image-cult and magic, Moses must have abruptly turned away from its emotional power and thrown himself into its very opposite, presented by the surroundings of his Midianite relatives. The environment of Moses in Midian was diametrically different from that of Pharaoh's court where Moses had been reared. Here were the huts and tents of desert smiths and shepherds on the fringes of the desert. In that great experience on Mount Horeb, Moses' first impulse was to approach and to explore the strange sight of the Burning Bush. But then he hid his face "for he was afraid to look upon God" (Exod. 3:6). Here is the prologue to the later prohibition of seeing God in images of animated and unanimated objects.

The repression of the image-cult by Moses was performed with characteristic impatience and passionate zeal. His enforcement of that revolutionary prohibition was unconditional and severe. It was too much and it came too soon. The people shouted demanding a visible, tangible god, the image they were accustomed to worship. A revolution was brewing among the Hebrews and was bloodily suppressed. We can readily assume that the protest against an imageless cult was raised again and again. David tolerated Teraphim (perhaps to be identified as household gods) in his house and King Hezekiah broke a bronze serpent in the temple, which Moses himself was said to have made, into pieces many centuries after the leader's death. Remnants of the old idolatry continued to live a long time, but the idea of the invisible god became gradually supreme in Israel.

The prohibition against worshipping God in a visible form was, in Freud's view, the step which raised the concept of the deity to a higher and loftier level of spirituality and opened the door to further changes in the idea of Yahweh. By the dematerialization of God,

Moses gave the Jews an increased self-confidence. That progress in spirituality remained with them and it has helped to build a dike against brutality and the inclination to violence which are usually found where athletic development becomes the ideal of the people.[2] In another passage[3] Freud remarked that the religion which began with the prohibition against making a picture of its God has developed in the course of centuries more and more into a religion of instinctual renunciation.

Freud brings to our notice that the progressive spiritualization of the Jews initiated by the worship of a nameless and invisible god had a drawback. The harmonious development of spiritual and bodily activity, as achieved in Greek civilization, was denied the Jews. But he adds that in this conflict their decision was at least made in favor of what is culturally the more important. I have always wondered why Freud did not mention two other effects and implications of that biblical prohibition. This is the more conspicuous since these two characteristic features are not to be found in any of the ancient civilizations. The first consequence of that Mosaic prohibition is the logical and psychological result of its displacement and generalization. The second commandment forbids the making of any pictures of images of "anything that is in heaven above, or in the earth beneath, or in the waters under the earth." The law covers a lot of animate and inanimate objects which could be conceived as gods or as divine. Here was a bold break with the customs and the tradition of the people and it certainly needed a permanent religious pressure to enforce that law.

The effects of the prohibition, especially in its enlargement and generalization, must have been a suppression of all creative endeavors of an artistic nature and finally a weakening and diminishing of the skills and talents used in nature-drawing, painting, and sculpture. That pressure, originally coming from outside, became internalized in the course of centuries and led to a lack of activity and ambition in the field of artistic creation, especially in the fields of visual arts.

As a matter of historic fact, the achievements of ancient Israel in the area of architecture, painting, sculpture are, as compared with those of other people, negligible.[4] So powerful were the after-effects and repercussions of the biblical prohibition, that the Jews even in modern times have produced fewer masterpieces of art than other nations. Only in the last three centuries have Jewish artists achieved remarkable progress in artistic creation, owing to the lessening and lifting of religious inhibitions. It is certainly remarkable and highly characteristic of the tenacity and forcefulness of the religious tradition that it could result in an impoverishment and almost an atrophy of those creative impulses for three thousand years.

It seems to me that another consequence may have resulted from the violent reaction of Moses and his circle to Egyptian culture, a consequence which blocked the road to artistic development of visual arts. Scholars have collated the late and rather poor beginnings of the theatre and of stage presentations with the injunction (Deut. 22:5) against masquerading. In my view this prohibition is itself the outcome of the rejection of the Egyptian mysteries and their dramatic presentations of the vicissitudes of the gods. Only late in the day and hesitantly did the Jews develop an inclination for theatrical performances.

There is yet another consequence of the prohibition regarding the creation of images of God that is perhaps even more important. Since the deity was not to be reached through the creative powers of imagination, mental activity and thought had to be turned away from direct speculations concerning His nature. His incorporeal and invisible character had to be affirmed in all speculation which became re-directed to His words and to the law He had given to the sons of Israel. The result of this commutation was not only the spiritualization of the idea of God but a progressive intellectualization of religion.

We have an excellent analogy of this process in the psychology of obsessional neurosis. The patients, who anxiously avoid thinking certain sexual and aggressive thoughts, are compelled to brood over remote issues that are unconsciously connected with the forbidden and repressed objects and actions. Since meditation on God's nature was taboo, His sacred words and will became the subject of extended and minute obsessive thoughts, so that every word and every letter of His Torah were discussed and became not only debatable, but also disputable. The eternal deliberations and arguments of Talmudic Judaism were marked by preoccupation with all trifling details of the law. Such permanent circling around the minutiae of the sacred Torah was not only the expression of high and zealous reverence, but also the manifestation of bitter aggression and of persistent doubts that had returned from the repressed to which they had been banned. The law of Yahweh was his shadow but his substance was not in it. As in the symptomatology of obsessive thoughts, the objects of theological thinking were more and more critically examined. They were, as a German psychoanalyst once put it, annihilated, demolished, and pulverized (*zerdacht*) by means of intellectual exploration. The fatefulness of an original, intensive attitude of ambivalence showed itself in such effects of a powerful religious inhibition.

The spiritualization of the concept of God was not the only effect of raising the deity to a supernatural and lofty region inaccessible to mortals. The elevation to a sublime region and rank also had an adverse side. A god without name, without body and countenance, who could not be known, was in danger of evaporating and disappearing. With his incorporeality he lost much of his reality. With his invisibility and untouchableness, he lost his substantiality. He could not be known—in the end his existence became unimaginable.

He began modestly as a tribal god restricted in his power to a narrow region, but this domain became so extended that it finally comprised heaven and earth and the universe. For Spinoza God is identical with nature (*"deus sive natura"*). That which is all-embracing is infinite and indefinite, but it is also inaccessible to human thought. Talleyrand once asserted that all that is exaggerated and over-blown cannot exist (*"tout ce qui est exageré est inexistant"*).

It would be misleading to assume that the rejection of the image-cult was only due to emotional motives. It is also a manifestation of the growth of the human mind and of its critical faculties. What can be seen and touched can be observed, can be scanned and sized up. The prophets spoke with biting sarcasm of the gods of wood and metal. The unseen cannot be examined. One might say paradoxically that the less visible God became, the more vividly was His presence felt.

31.

The Birth of a Collective Super-Ego

There are recurring misconceptions of the character of Israel's early religion originating in a misunderstood evolutionary system. Ernest Renan's once-famous explanation of Mosaic monotheism as a "minimum of religion," natural to desert nomads, belongs to the area of such doubtful theories. Julius Well-hausen, Hugo Gressmann, and other scholars found the roots of the biblical prohibitions concerning images in the artistic impotence of the Israelites and in their lack of a plastic urge. How mistaken—to put it charitably—this theory is, can be recognized by instances from primitive people to whom the crudest wood or stone presentation of a face, a trunk and limbs, appears as image of the deity. The simplest roughly formed doll of most elemental shape will be loved by a child. Besides and beyond this argument the lion-seal of the eighth century and the ebony tablets of Schomron of the ninth century show a strong plastic sense in a very realistic work of art. Elias Auerbach, who points this out, justly remarks[1] that not lack of artistic capability but the will of Moses who regarded the image-cult as an abomination prevented the people from making likenesses of Yahweh. Yet that other obsolete explanation of the roots of the biblical prohibition is still to be found in the books of historians. Science, as Anatole France once said, is infallible but scientists err all the time.

The principle of evolution is not refuted when we follow the development from the crude masks and animal hides behind which the old tribesmen hid intimidating the novices at the puberty festivals to the presentation of gods in statues and pictures of dynastic Egypt. The prohibition of the image-cult appeared to us as a break with the Egyptian tradition, as a violent and passionate reaction of Moses to the customs and religious thought of the milieu in which he grew up.[2]

In his book on Moses, Freud propounds the theory that the great progress in Moses' work originates in the monotheistic belief borrowed from Egypt. He emphasizes the influence of this monotheism on the Jewish people, "how it formed their character for good through the disdaining of magic and mysticism and encouraging them to progress in spirituality and sublimation."[3] I have already pointed out that the monotheistic faith as such does not deserve such high and exclusive merit. Freud appears to overrate its value in the evolution of religion, as do many eminent theologians. His characterization of the spiritual evolution of Judaism is correct but appears to me to be too general. The advance seems in his view limited to the avoidance of magic and mysticism. The upward thrust attained by the concept of an invisible and nameless god is not followed in its psychological implications by Freud. Yet only a few steps blazed along the track made by his genius may enable us to arrive at other profound insights into the character of that amazing progress heralded by the Sinai revelation.

The child is prevented from following all of his impulses by fear of punishment from the parents, especially by the fear of losing their love. This inhibition presents an external obstacle to the satisfaction of his drives and can lead to what Freud calls an "instinctual renunciation." That fear of punishment, kept alive by memories, is replaced in the later individual development to a great extent by a new standard which is established within the ego, by an agency which observes, criticizes, and prohibits one's own inner impulses. We call this factor determining the moral standard the "super-ego." This new agency which perpetuates the external inhibiting factors is the successor and representative of the parents, who have now become internalized. The father who warned and forbade is not there any longer in the outer world, but he and his censures and commandments have become an inner possession. The super-ego now sets the standard of morality and limits instinctual satisfactions. The super-ego developed from an identification with the father whom the child sees as a model and it now functions as a father-substitute. The influence of the parents is later continued and replaced by racial, national, and family traditions handed on through them, as well as by the demands of the immediate social milieu which they represent. The super-ego takes over later contributions from successors and substitutes of the parents, such as teachers, admired figures in public life, or high social ideals. In the case of the Hebrews, tribal ideas and the model of the leader Moses have taken the place of such parent substitutes.

Since we are dealing here with a certain function of the super-ego in collective life, a comparison from a neighboring area will be illuminating. A little boy is warned to be careful when he crosses the street and to walk across only after all cars have passed. Later on his father or his mother is not there any more, but when the child has to cross the street, he now follows their commandment. He will look right and left before he crosses the street in later years and never think any more that his father once warned him of its dangers and told him to take the necessary precautions. Also here the persons of the parents have become internalized, transmuted to voices and memories of voices and finally merged with the self.

Matthew Arnold once spoke of "something not ourselves which makes for righteousness" and which many philosophers call God. God indeed corresponds in collective life to a deified super-ego projected back onto the outer world. Also, historically God is the successor and representative of the father since his figure was formed in the image of the father of the primal society. In individual development God has inherited the idealized features of the father of the child's early years.

All this is well known and we have only reviewed it here because the new train of thought leads us to the core of the problem that interests us in connection with the introduction of the Hebrew concept of an invisible God. New research, especially that of Otto Isakower,[4] has made us understand that the auditory sphere may claim an exceptional position in the development of the super-ego of the individual. In the building up of that new agency of the super-ego, certain experiences and impressions are necessary. Purely optical impressions without words by themselves would be insufficient for the establishment of ethical judgments. For the preliminary stages of super-ego formation, language, audibly perceived, is indispensable. The nucleus of the super-ego is to be found in the human auditory sphere.

The impact of the idea of the invisible deity on the formation of the super-ego of the people is obvious. The "ten words" heard by them at the sacred mountain correspond to the commandments—originally to the forbiddings ("you shall not")—of the father and thus will become the core of the inner authority that will be the successor to his external presence. That unseen voice speaks words men will live by in the future. The Ten Commandments will be then heard as resounding voices inside the people. God need not be seen. It is only necessary to harken to his inward words. The Lord speaks: "I will put my fear in their hearts, that they shall not depart from me" (Jer. 32:40). It is no longer fear of external punishment from a god whose figure could be seen by the people that prevents them from satisfying all their impulses, but inner demands. Through this same voice will people make moral decisions and follow what these decisions imply. It will warn them ("How long will they forget me?" asks the Lord). Memory will remain intimately connected with responsibility and with the sayings of parents, never consciously remembered, but never forgotten. Timeless ethical demands conveyed in the Decalogue will be heard also in the "brave new world" to come.

A good deal would have to be added to the theory presented here, but I have to restrict myself to a few remarks. It is clear that the ego borrows strength and will power from the model of the father, both for conquering forbidden impulses and for meeting the inner moral demands. It is his figure that will be decisive in the conflict with the forbidden drives and his standard which will be maintained. (The Jews are to be a holy nation because their Heavenly Father is holy.) The capacity for development of a super-ego, peculiar to men, depends upon the introduction and incorporation of admired objects whose actual presence has become superfluous. Freud reminds us that the establishment of the super-ego shows itself in that "it is a phenomenon of reaction to a fantasied overcoming of, and doing away with, the father." In establishing his power forever the super-ego replaces the father to some extent "making the effects of his presence superfluous to a certain degree by taking over his sphere of influence." A person who has erected those prohibitions in himself is not any longer so much in need of the external veto which still remains in existence in the background.

The process of replacement of the father by the super-ego and the resulting dispensability of the father-ego foreshadows the future evanescence of God. The disappearance of the idea of a god who functioned as the externalized conscience of mankind does not mean a decrease of the moral principles he represented. The super-ego that according to Freud "testifies to the internal gain on the part of the parental authority shows the decline of his external power." The new agency within the ego has reactive character. It enthrones the father's power after victory over him and after having made him superfluous.

It cannot be accidental that the inward word became triumphant when God was no longer visible nor tangible. Here are the origins of faith. There is a German proverb: "The eyes believe themselves, the ears others."[5] What the eyes lost in the perception of God's image, the ears gained. The Hebrew tribes recalled the great experience at Mount Sinai that had left indelible traces in their memory because it had reached them through their ears, which made it more durable than impressions received through the eyes. They hearkened to the unseen voice and were pulled by invisible strings.

The progress in spirituality which made the Sinai experience the decisive turn in the human adventure is the establishment of a collective super-ego, of an inner standard within the people created by the introduction of Yahweh into the formation of the ego. This new agency is the greatest achievement of Moses—not monotheism. *The greatest contribution of the Jews to human culture is the creation of an invisible deity and of its successor and heir in the form of the collective super-ego.* I have always believed that the emphasis placed on the Shema Israel, the Jewish creed ("Hear, O Israel, the Lord is our God, the Lord is one") has to be shifted to the first two words. Superficially seen, the statement proclaims faith in monotheism, but it really testifies to the moral law now heard inside. It does not say: "Look, Israel!" but "Hear, Israel!"

32.

The Return of the Repressed

We cannot take leave of the discussion of the ethical aspects of the Sinai revelation without at least emphasizing one law which points to the future of moral evolution, to a social concept that has to be considered the forerunner of democracy. The laws of the Torah assume the existence of slavery to be normal, yet they prescribe a very humane treatment of the slaves. How did such an order of social justice come into the ethics of the Hebrews whose codes were in so many ways similar to those of other people of the ancient Near East? Someone has justly remarked that there is no substitute for experience. The moral demand to treat slaves kindly is a result of the sufferings the Hebrews themselves had undergone. They are reminded of it "because you were slaves in Egypt."

In contrast with the views of shallow freethinkers, to whom the biblical revelation narrative is nothing but an empty and senseless legend, we conceived of it as a tradition which is built on historic truth. We think that the core of that tradition is the memory of old puberty rituals of Hebrew tribes and of a reintroduction of an initiation festival made impossible by the Egyptian oppression. We acknowledge thus, in contrast with the false rationalists and also with a great group of biblical scholars, that the revelation story has a core of historic truth which has to be detected by splitting the religious shell and by removing the supernatural aspects that conceal it.

A last piece of inner evidence may be cited in favor of our thesis. The development of Christianity within Judaism will be found to complete the circle. The essential features of the "new-old" religion of Moses, of Yahwism, were determined by the rejection of the Egyptian pantheon and its religious customs and by a regression to an older and almost forgotten tribal worship. It is perhaps advantageous for the purpose of the following presentation of circumstantial evidence to put the negative or reactive aspects of the Mosaic innovation in the foreground. They are the elimination of the cult of a son-god and of his mother as his consort and the prohibition of image-cult and of the name of God. The Jewish credo ("Hear, Israel, the Lord is our God and only the Lord") is not directed against pagan polytheism in general, but wishes radically to exclude the son-god and his divine consort.

If the thesis presented here is valid, the suppressed impulses which manifested themselves in the Egyptian and pagan religions ought to be expected to reappear in a later "breakthrough" and the forbidden institutions and aspects struggle to return. This reemergence is not to be considered only as a sign of the probability of this special interpretation. It is an instance of a law of emotional development which at some points follows a course as certain as that of the processes described in physics and chemistry. The expectation of that reappearance of the forbidden gods and cults is analogous to a psychological phenomenon we know as "return of the repressed." To take a case at random: Let us consider the neurotic patient who suffers from compulsion neurosis of the kind the French call *"délire de toucher,"* and who avoids touching many things, such as money, with his bare hands because they are unclean and he could infect himself. At first he may even use gloves when he has to touch these tabooed coins. Since the used gloves have to be cleaned again chemically before subsequent use, he prefers, for economical reasons, to use paper napkins and finally even toilet paper. In order to isolate those pieces of paper, he puts them neatly in a certain place after their use as a measure of protection. Later on, this patient begins to throw them carelessly into a corner of his room. Since he does not allow them to be removed, a mass of "dirty" toilet paper accumulates there. Behind the increasingly severe procedures of neurotic defense by which he protects himself against uncleanliness, we recognize his struggle against the temptation to soil himself. His measures of protection appeared at first sight as exaggerated results of extreme tidiness, originated in the demands of toilet-training of the child. While the neurotic symptoms at first have the character of violent warding-off of forbidden impulses, they change as the illness is prolonged. They become compromise-formations between the repressed and the repressing forces, in our case of cleaning up and becoming soiled. Finally, the forbidden impulses break through into action in undisguised form and he becomes the rebellious child who reacts against too severe toilet-training by defiantly throwing pieces of soiled toilet paper around.

In the context of our own presentation, the image-cult and the magical performances and, before all, the idea of the son-god and of his divine mother and mistress, correspond to the part of the repressed concepts. The revolution initiated by Moses had eliminated those essential elements of the Egyptian religion.

The most important figure of that pantheon which was removed by Moses was that of the divine son who finally took the place of god-father after he had died and was resurrected—in this case the figure of Osiris who was replaced by that of Christ after many centuries. Yahwism was a pure father-religion. There was no place within it for a competing son nor for an adored mother-figure. We should, of course, not expect that the myth of Isis and Osiris would return from the repressed in its original form. Christianity grew from the soil of Judaism and, although Egyptian elements are still perceivable in its formation, Canaanite, Babylonian, Hellenistic, and Persian influences have been more pattern-forming in its early development, which was, above all, determined by old Hebrew concepts.

There is a special resistance and embittered reluctance on the side of the Jews against even the potentiality of assuming a son-god beside Yahweh. One would like to know more about the hidden cause of that particular dislike of an idea of that kind. If one could trust one's intuition, one would conjecture that the avoidance of such a thought-possibility might have its roots in an intense tendency to protect the life and power of the father-god which are endangered by the rivalry of a divine son who tries to usurp his father's throne. It would even be imaginable to bring the mysterious circumstances of Moses' birth and the absence of his real father in connection with the attitude characterized here. This is speculation, although not idle, and we want to regain the firm ground of history.

We assume that there was once a figure of a son-god like Osiris, Attis, Adonis, and Heracles in the religious concepts of pre-Mosaic

Hebrews. The biblical story of Isaac's sacrifice by Abraham and his redemption by a ram testifies to the role of such a son-figure as do various other half-mythological tales of the Scripture. We can only assume that the revolution instituted by Moses erased the concept of this son-god together with the figure of Osiris, who corresponds to it in Egyptian religion. But the new situation persisted for only about a thousand years. Imperceptibly, and in disguised forms, the idea of a divine son crept back into the consolidated formation of Judaism. It appears already in the figure of the suffering servant of Deutero-Isaiah, that great unknown Babylonian writer of the sixth century.

Here, if not in earlier texts, there emerges at last part of the destiny of that figure, namely, of the suffering god and his redemption. In the Egyptian, Babylonian, and Greek mythologies, the son-god suffers agonies and a cruel death and is resurrected to join (originally to replace) the god-father. But not only Osiris, Tammuz, Adonis, and Heracles are predecessors of the Christ-figure.[1] The suffering servant of the Lord, as Deutero-Isaiah characterized him, heralds the appearance of the Saviour. "He is despised and rejected of men; a man of sorrows, and acquainted with grief; and we hid, as it were, our faces from him; he was despised and we esteemed him not. Surely he hath borne our griefs and carried our sorrows." That prophet sees the servant who is the personification of captive Israel stricken and afflicted, but he sees also his redemptive mission: "He was wounded for our transgressions; he was bruised for our iniquities."

It is very likely that Christ had this picture in mind and lived vicariously the life of that predecessor depicted by the prophet. All the eschatological concepts of pre-Christian Judaism announce the re-emergence of a figure similar to the son-god, especially that of the Messiah who will come "at the end of days," redeem his people and triumph over all enemies. At the end of this phase of religious development, the figure of Christ emerges as the youngest representative of the divine son of the ancient Near East, who, like Osiris, Attis, Adonis, suffers, dies, is resurrected and "sitteth on the right hand of God the Father Almighty."

With the passion, resurrection, and triumph of the Saviour, the repressed and banned concept of the rebellious and finally victorious son-god found its re-entrance into Judaism which rejected him again and again. "No Jew," wrote Heinrich Heine once, "can become a true Christian, for no Jew can ever believe in the divinity of another

Jew." In proper psychological interpretation, this would mean that no Jew can think through to the end the idea of killing and replacing Yahweh. The emotional resistances against this thought, the reluctances, hidden in the prehistoric past of the Jewish people, are too strong ever to be conquered.

Together with the figure of the son-god, that of his divine mother and consort was revivified. Ishtar of the Babylonians, Cybele of the Phrygians, Isis of the Egyptians, Aphrodite of the Greeks—those are her predecessors who lived a phase of perfect happiness with their son and lover, cried and mourned over his body, saw him resurrected, and were reunited with him. The great mother-figure of the ancient civilizations who was the goddess of sexual gratification and of fertility returned from the repressed as the Holy Virgin, as a figure purified and sanctified or deprived of her sexual appeal role in the life her divine son. Even her re-emergence within Judaism could not reach the more primitive and sensual character of the earlier figure. The restraining influence of Jewish morality still was too powerful and did not allow the reborn myth to go all the way back to the ancient figure who was mother and mistress, as Isis once had been in the days when Moses looked at the scenes of the play in Abydos where she was united in embrace with her resurrected son Osiris. The first generations of Christians, who were all Jews, still shied away from the idea of the mother-son incest of the gods.

Every scholar acknowledges that the forbidden image-cult and the magical use of God's name returned from banishment with Christianity. The smoke of incense, the amulets, the incantations that were inhaled, seen, and heard in the temples of Osiris and Amon-Re, were there again. Images and sculptures of the trinity were worshipped. Thomas Aquinas said that the same deference has to be rendered to Christ's image as to Himself, and Bonaventura demanded the same for the image of the Virgin. The magical power of names was revived: "In my name shall they cast out devils." The formula, "In the name of Jesus" or "In the name of the Father and of the Son and of the Holy Ghost" became sacred. The belief in the magical power of the "name" that had been general in Egypt was restored. Even the mysteries of Abydos had a kind of continuation in later phases of Christianity. As in the dramatic presentation of the death and resurrection of Osiris, the *Passio Domini,* his crucifixion and resurrection, the mourning of his mother and the triumph of the pious at his return were dramatized in the Passion plays. The development in terms of the return of the repressed has come into its full rights.

We discover that characteristic features of that most impressive initiation festival can still be discerned in the elements of the story of Christ as we uncover a familar face beneath a veil. It gives me great satisfaction to learn that noted American psychoanalysts[2] now acknowledge that the biography of the young Christ follows the typical lines of a puberty initiation, a theory which I presented in a paper published in 1915.[3] Christ's life and crucifixion, with the typical motifs of death and resurrection, presents in narrative form a picture of the puberty rites of primitive societies. In spite of all alterations, many features are easily recognized as belonging to those rites; the withdrawal from the community, his preaching in the temple at the age of twelve (reversal of the instruction of the novices), his trials and sufferings and death, as well as his resurrection, corresponding to the rebirth of the youth in the initiation ritual. It is significant that Christ goes away from mother and sisters, just as the novices at puberty in savage tribes are removed from the women and taken into the society of adults, to "be about his father's business." Even the formula, "I and the Father are one" points to the communion with the generation of fathers in primitive societies. The other side of the ambivalent attitude of the father-generation to the son is represented by the report of the suffering the fathers inflict on the son ("The Son of man must suffer many things, and be rejected of the elders, and of the chief priests, and scribes, and be killed, and after three days rise again" (Mark 8:31). The baptism by John is called being "reborn," corresponding to the concept of the initiation rites, and is part of the ideas connected with the admission into the society of adult men. ("Except a man be born again, he cannot see the Kingdom of Heaven.")

If, then, we recognize in the crisis in Christ's life a portrayal of puberty rites and regard his figure as that of the representative of the boys who go through many sufferings before they are granted the privilege of being considered grown-up men,[4] if this divine figure is that of "the Universal Novice" (to use H. A. Bunker's poignant characterization),[5] how do we explain the fact that in the Christ story not many young men, but a single person appears as passing through the initiation? The contrast between the concept of the revelation in Exodus and the new covenant, between the scene on Mount Sinai interpreted by us as the initiation of Israelite tribes and the scene on Calvary, becomes here especially conspicuous. In order to understand that difference, one has to follow the development which led from the primitive puberty rituals via the secret societies to the mysteries of the religions of antiquity.

In the initiation rites of savage tribes of Australia and Africa there sometimes appears the figure of a man (or several men) who is covered with blood and seems to be dead. He is shown to the terrified novices until he suddenly jumps up and runs away. Later on, the rites developed into mysteries in which the dying and the rebirth of a young god as a representative figure of the puberty boys are dramatically presented. In identifying with the passion and the resurrection of this god, the novices are supposed to be saved and to be admitted into the circle of the men (or priests) of the tribes.

Christianity, which originated in Judaism, joins, especially in its Pauline form, the world of those ancient mysteries among which the Orphic initiation and the passion of Heracles played a major role. Christ, who was later often compared with Orpheus or the son of Jove, is the last representative of the suffering and resurrected young son-figures with whom the age groups of puberty identified; with whom they were supposed to die, to be reborn, and to gain eternal salvation. This is the development from the phase of primitive puberty initiation to the stage of the ancient mysteries with which Christianity is so intimately connected in essential ideology.

Judaism had followed a very different course in its religious history. Moses' revolutionary movement meant a leap back into a more primitive form of initiation, but one breaking the limitations of age groups. Israel became as a whole people initiated into the secret society of Yahweh-worshippers. In Christianity, in its Hellenistic form, a young god, representing the young men in their rebellion against the father and atoning for that crime—in Israel, a whole nation identified with the lonely figure of the father-god. The advance of Christianity in joining the more recent forms of the oriental mystery-religions resulted finally in a relapse into polytheism and paganism. The regression to simpler forms of initiation, hidden behind the revelation tradition, led later to a rigid monotheism, but also to a progress in spiritualization of the idea of God.

Christianity marks the great crisis in Israel's history. It was originally a movement to bring the God of Israel to the gentiles and its divine role was that of "Israel's apostle." Yet its evolution brought about a relapse into idolatry which was banned by Moses and the prophets. A Christian theologian, A. Roy Eckhardt, raised the question: "Can the Christian Church supersede the synagogue in the struggle against paganism?" and answers: "No, because the church itself is subjected to pagan distortions."[6] Another eminent Protestant theologian, Paul Tillich, states that the existence of Judaism is important because it is "the corrective against the paganism that lives along with Christianity."[7]

In brief: The image-cult and magical use of names were reintroduced into Christianity according to the dynamic pattern of the "return of the repressed." The re-emergence of those banned concepts marks the end of this chapter of Israel's long journey. It does not, however, mean the end of the story.

33.

The Living Past: Retrospect and Prospect

This book does not deny that it is an attempt at a reconstruction of the hidden traditions underlying the biblical narratives of the Exodus-Sinai events. It belongs to the area of what was once called "conjectural history" and freely professes this character as well as the fact that its main hypothesis is based on circumstantial evidence and likely inferences. The great astronomer, Laplace, once suggested that the amount of evidence which needed to be marshalled in favor of a particular hypothesis was directly proportionate to its antecedent improbability. If this improbabilty is infinite, no amount of finite evidence could carry conviction.

In our case, the situation has not been so parlous. Nothing in our material barred the way to the prospect of high plausibility and probability. Considering the nature of the sources to be investigated we have no right to expect more. The revelation is attested to by no other report than that of the Bible. We have only God's word for it.

My major thesis has been that the biblical narrative presents a distorted old tradition of an initiation festival of some Hebrew tribes, later on amalgamated into the League of the Twelve Tribes. This report was combined with a much-altered account of the Exodus or expulsion of those tribes from Egypt. The internal evidence I have been able to proffer for the original character of the Sinai narrative is not incontestably conclusive. It is based on far-reaching similarities between the phenomena and the social and religious functions of revelation and primitive initiation. A specialist in such matters might wish to dispute this claim; to his mind, the differences might seem to be so essential as to make comparison inadmissible: for example, in primitive puberty rites only a generation of boys is initiated, while the revelation takes place before the eyes and ears of a whole people. We have been able, we believe, to eliminate that difficulty with the help of anthropological authorities who point to similar cases of extended initiation. There are other arguments not so easily countered, involving divergences which apparently make a lot of difference. At least the miracles before and during the Exodus cannot be lightheartedly dismissed as being on the fringes of the biblical tale. Some of those miracles are of a magical nature—for instance, those reported in Exodus (7 and 8)—and are alleged to have been copied by pagan magicians. As such they could well be fitted into the frame of primitive initiation rites. But some are conceived as direct divine interpositions. Not all miracles reported from the age of Moses and Joshua are as beneficial as the majority of the miracles in the New Testament. The Lord shows Himself ruthless, reckless, and remorseless in His attitude toward the Egyptians, while He led His people out of Egypt "with a mighty hand, and with an outstretched arm . . . with signs, and with wonders" (Deut. 26:8). He shows Himself as very partial: except when He punished His stiff-necked people, He treats them well and redeems them; while He is a force of evil, a "destroyer" to Pharaoh and the Egyptians. There is a conspicuous and poignant contrast: He slaughters the first-born of the Egyptians and spares those of the Hebrews. He performs a miracle at the Red Sea (or rather the Lake of Reeds) where the waters are divided and the B'ne Israel pass over on "dry ground." The chariot wheels of the Egyptian army are mired in the mud and all men are drowned in the returning water.

It is easy enough to dismiss this and other miracles ascribed to Yahweh during the Exodus as sagas, as legends. Our task is to put them into the framework of the hypothesis we have advanced. How can this be done?

Let me first state that we dare not claim to possess more than an outline with many suggestive points in it. Only the central element, the initiation character of the Sinai events, is in full light. The background is all darkness. Yet we can at least guess some of the contours of the designs in this Rembrandtesque picture, and we can try to draw their shapes as they appear to us.

We may begin with the miracle of the Red Sea. Before discussing it the reader will be reminded of the meaning of the different treatment Yahweh applies to the Egyptians and the Israelites. Apart from other considerations, according to psychoanalytic principles that contrast means that an original identity later appears as a pattern of two opposites. The slaughter of the first-born (his sacrificing to God) was at first practiced by the Hebrews. In the Biblical report, only the Egyptian first-born are smitten, while the Israelites were spared. Only the Egyptian soldiers were immersed by the waves of the sea, the Hebrew refugees remained unharmed.

In pursuing this road we arrive, after removing all subsequent distortions and alterations, at a tentative hypothesis about the original meaning of the Red Sea saga. Again relying on the hypothesis that the Biblical narrative displaces events from the generation of young men to the whole people, we venture to assert that the core of the Red Sea story relates to an integral moment of a puberty ritual.

In most primitive tribes as well as in the secret societies, the immersion into or the sprinkling with water is an essential part of the admission. We shall not enter the discussion of the details of the rite, but only remark that in our view this water-ceremonial is perhaps a remnant of the post-circumcision procedure of the candidates. The interpretation of such immersion as rebirth-symbol is certainly valid, although it concerns already a higher level of development. The novice of some American tribes is "dragged forward and backwards several times completely immersed in water," as B. Spencer, recounts. The initiates of Southeast African tribes are, according to A. W. Howitt, led to the edge of a pool and liberally sprinkled with water. Similar rites of purification are reported at the admission into adulthood among the Basutos[1] and the expression "to throw oneself into the river" is an equivalent of being circumcised with some of the tribes in Africa.[2] In several religious societies and mysteries—as for instance, in the Egyptian Isis initiation, in the Brahmanic rites, and in those of the Parsis as well as in the Greek Eleusinia—the candidate, at or before the age of fifteen, has to undergo this baptism before admission.[3] Mircea Eliade, who presents a picture of the development of initiatory elements in Christian baptism, points out that already the Essenes and other pre-Christian Jewish movements knew baptism.[4] (The scholarly author neglects the connection between circumcision and baptism, a theme which richly deserves a separate investigation.)

W. Brandt points out[5] that male converts to Judaism have to be first circumcised, and when the wound is healed, have to take a bath during which the rabbi recites to them the commandments. After complete immersion the proselyte is a fully privileged Israelite. The Talmudic scholars conclude the necessity of that baptism from the fact that according to Exodus (19:10, 22) the Israelites were commanded to "sanctify themselves" before they received the Law at Sinai. Ablution was, of course, part of this sanctification. Here are clear traces of early initiation rites underlying the revelation narrative.

It would not be difficult to array many anthropological facts to prove that immersion into water is an essential part of the initiation, which, in my interpretation, follows the circumcision of the novices who bathed in the river. Later on, the age of baptism was moved forward to childhood, as was circumcision in Judaism, where it was originally performed in puberty.

In Christianity in which circumcision was relinquished, baptism remained as a residue of the primal puberty ritual. The ceremony of baptism contains in it death and resurrection, the most distinctive features of that primitive initiation. St. Paul wrote to the Colossians (2:12): "Buried with him in baptism, where in also ye are risen with him through the faith of the operation of God, who hath raised him from the dead." In the Epistle to the Romans (6:4) the statement is repeated: "Therefore we are buried with him by baptism into death: that like as Christ was raised up from the death by the glory of the Father, even so we also should walk in newness of Life."

It needs to be noted that our interpretation of the Red Sea saga makes a not inconsiderable claim. In our view, the saga is to be understood as an exaggerated rendering of a displaced fraction of a report of initiation festival of the Hebrew tribes. It appears in the biblical notice provided with a negative sign which we well understand as manifestation of the rejection of the Egyptian cult still to be recognized in the displacement to the Egyptian soldiers who were immersed or, rather, submerged. This accentuated contrast with the different faith appears still in the detail that Christians are by orthodox Jews called "baptized." In the mentioned displacement of submergence from the Hebrew tribe to the Egyptian appears disavowed and grotesquely overdone, a trace of the fact that the circumcision practice as well as the water immersion was perhaps taken over from the Egyptian customs.

We have spoken here of miracles as testimony of God and of His power to effect His purpose. All other miracles pale in significance when put beside the divine guidance and divine presence in history. None of the miraculous events reported in the Old Testament, from the Ten Plagues to the miracles connected with Elijah and Elisha, can be compared to the redemption of the Hebrews from Egypt. The Jew who violates a commandment acts "as if he denies the going out from Egypt"[6]—a horrible blasphemy. The deliverance from Egypt is God's claim upon Israel. It is testimony of God's love for Israel, because, as Jehuda Halevi observed, love originally came from God, not from us, in whom it calls forth responsive love.[7]

Exodus-Sinai is for Judaism "the interpretive center of redemptive history as Calvary is for the Christian."[8] Redemptive history, *Heilsgeschichte,* as the German theologians call it, is here meant in the sense that the Jew does not expect to achieve salvation by mystical experiences uniting him with God, but by making Israel's history his own, by seeing the covenant as a tie connecting him with past and future generations. "He who does not himself remember that God led him out of Egypt," says Martin Buber, "he who does not himself await the Messiah, is no longer a true Jew."[9]

Here is the place to emphasize an apparent difference between Yahwism and the other religions of the ancient Near East. In the mysteries of antiquity, for instance in those of Osiris, the candidate is identified with the resurrected god as the Christians with the Saviour. Salvation is reached by this identification with Adonis, Attis, Dionysus, and other young son-gods who have risen from death and whose resurrection promises salvation and finally immortality for their worshippers. *To Judaism the concept of salvation is alien in a theological sense:* that means it has no equivalent for this theological term and redemption is no mysterious or supernatural process. After Osiris' death he is lamented by the women, his resurrection is celebrated with loud outcries of joy by the people. In Antioch, the capital of Syria, the death and resurrection of Adonis was re-presented in dramatic form. The resurrected god was ecstatically greeted in the streets where the people shouted:

> *Courage, believers! As God is saved*
> *So shall we receive salvation from our griefs.*[10]

An echo of this jubilant certainty of salvation is still audible in the Christian Easter celebration. In the Greek church the Easter week with its mourning ends on Saturday midnight. At the stroke of twelve, at midnight, the bishop originally appeared and announced the "glad tidings" (*Evangelium!*) that Christ is risen. The crowd answered: "Yes, He is indeed risen" and the whole town resounded with wild jubilation and the noises of yelling and fireworks.[11]

It will not astonish us that nothing of this kind is reported in the biblical Exodus-Sinai narrative. Yet we asserted that this tale presents a distorted and veiled report of a great initiation festival of the Hebrew tribes! Is it possible that so essential a feature as triumph about delivery, as joy about salvation, is missing from the narration? If our reconstruction is correct, vestiges of those feelings should still be perceptible in the biblical record. *They are there:* Moses and the Children of Israel sing a triumphant song after they see the Egyptians dead "upon the sea shore." They sing: "The Lord is my strength and song and he is become my salvation . . ." and Miriam takes a timbrel in her hand and all the women go out after her with timbrels and dance. And Miriam answers them: "Sing ye to the Lord, for he hath triumphed gloriously; the horse and his rider he hath thrown into the sea" (Exod. 15:21). But aside from the rejoicing of Moses and the Israelites and from Miriam's victory song, the whole record of Exodus as well as all references to the revelation story celebrate the salvation of the Hebrews from serfdom, their escape. The redemption is here described as an event without precedence, a miracle without analogy in the history of the ancient world. This wonderful redemption is recited and the Lord's power as Saviour of His people is praised to this day in the Passover ceremonials.

A comparative presentation cannot be content with finding such an analogy. It has to find the causes for the differences in the theological assumptions of the Israelites and of their neighbors and has, if possible, to explore how it came about that salvation appears in a different form to the worshippers of Osiris, Attis, Adonis, and of Christ and to the believers in that new God, Yahweh. In the mysteries of the ancient world the resurrection of the young son-god was the guarantee of immortality, for the novices who identified themselves with him, died with him and gained eternal life with him who arose from the dead. The miraculous experience of resurrection reflects the rebirth of the novice. There is nothing of a similar kind in the belief of the Hebrews who rejected the concept of the young god who died and was resurrected.

The denial and rejection of the Egyptian Osiris-myth was so intensive, the turning away from the Egyptian theology so passionate, that it not only excluded such beliefs, but with it all cult of the dead and the assumption of a life in the beyond as well as the great interest in the hereafter that preoccupied the people of ancient Egypt. While the hope of an individual salvation and resurrection was reduced to such an extent that it is negligible, the expectation of the arrival of a Messiah who would deliver the people of Israel was the eternal consolation and redemptive certainty for the Israelites. The Saviour was not here yet. He was expected in days to come. In the rejection of Christ the Israelites, so to speak, renewed the repulse of Osiris who was believed to have died and arisen again as had his divine successor. But also the Israelites had a redemptive history or, if you wish, mythology, like the Christians and their pagan predecessors: the Exodus-Sinai story. Yahweh had redeemed His people in carrying them "on eagles' wings" into freedom.

Looking back, we wonder about those essential differences and especially about the form which the redemptive report of the Bible took. The Exodus narrative is essentially the story of fugitive serfs who rebelled and found their way to freedom. At the same time it is a tale of their religious redemption in which they discovered that Yahweh is their god. While there is scarcely any doubt that the story of the flight of the Israelites from Egypt has a historic background, the elevation of the story to that of redemption and election of a whole people as well as of their sanctification is clearly a folk myth. A scarcely noticed and insignificant flight of some tribes from forced labor is later represented as a redemptive event of world-shaking significance. At the subsoil of the biblical story we detected the jubilant, triumphant mood of the novices after they have passed all trials and labors of the puberty ceremonials. In the biblical story those trials and tribulations are projected to a whole people and the release of young men from their torments is presented as redemption of a nation, or at least of a nation in the making.

It is the fusion of a great puberty initiation narrative with a magnified and glorified story of an insignificant historic event of ancient Hebrew tribes which puzzles us and whose differentiation causes so many difficulties to research. The flight of a number of half-nomadic shepherds from Goshen, not mentioned in any other ancient source but in the Bible, swelled in the lore of the Israelites to the gigantic dimension of a world-historic occurrence. What interests us here is the merging and melting of the report of this deliverance and of the tale of a divine revelation into which the tradition of the Sinai festival developed. Many centuries after the descendants of those runaway serfs had became united into one people, the tradition arrived at a consistent shape in which their beginnings were presented and finally brought into a written history.

We may "imagine" how in the earlier phases of this tradition certain features of the half-historic departure reports were altered and became amalgamated with issues belonging to the tale of a great puberty festival: the initiation was now displaced from a generation to all members of the tribes. The alleged death of the novices in the initiation was changed in the report to a certainty that almost all Hebrews of the generation present at Mount Sinai died before reaching Canaan. The immersion in water, an essential part of the initiation, was transferred to the adventure at the Red Sea and reported of the Egyptian soldiers. The jubilant joy of the admitted novices after all trials was presented as triumph over the Egyptians and thanksgiving to Yahweh. Thus several inherent features of the puberty rituals were transferred to the area of the historical report of the Exodus in such a way that they appear as organic pieces of the departure story. This work of compression and condensation of two separate tales was certainly not finished in the time of a generation and did not exclude the possibility of later accretion and expansion of certain portions, removed from one part to another.

We do not fail to recognize that two tendencies were operating in the alterations and displacements to which the tradition was subjected. The one was a tendency to magnify and glorify the past history of the tribes and to celebrate the role Yahweh had from the beginning attributed to them. The other inclination can be described as a residue of the tribal tradition to keep the puberty initiation secret, to make it appear as a mystery in which supernatural powers directed the course of events. The continuity of the secretiveness about the initiation ceremonies, originally concealed only from women and children, explains many otherwise unintelligible features of the tradition.

We arrive here at the threshold of the last problem that arouses our interest in connection with the Exodus-Sinai narrative: namely, that of the oral tradition. There is an extended literature about the genesis of the Old Testament, and everybody is now familiar with the three main sources—the Yahwist, the Elohist, and the Priestly writers. Yet there is, of course, little known about the most important source, namely the oral tradition of the sacred stories. Their collection and written fixation does not reach back very far. Their history is rather young: scarcely three thousand years old, but tradition wears, as John Greenleaf Whittier once said, "a snowy beard."

Also history has its history, has even its prehistory, reaching back into earliest times of the tribes. It is a long way from the early traditions of the Hebrews, from the stories told when they were not yet differentiated from the Semitic stock in their Arabian home, to the writing of Israel's history by a gifted man of Judah who was living in the day of King David and who used the name of Yahweh for the Lord. It seems to be probable that those original traditions reach further back than the Early Bronze Age. Many Australian and Polynesian tribes still in the Stone Age, for instance, the Maoris in New Zealand, handed down from father to son genealogies covering several centuries. V. Gordon Childe, recently deceased pioneer in the field of prehistory, asserted that certain portions of those lists of ancestors "are extremely consistent one with another and are probably reliable" though "they start with manifestly imaginary divine beings."[12] The "autobiographical impulse," to use an expression of Thomas Mann, was there long before the sacred art of writing became known. Those early traditions have a hard core of fact although they are mixed with many legendary features. Rudolf Kittel rightly pointed out that "a dilemma like the following: the patriarchal narrative is either history or saga, or as it might be put: the patriarchal narrating is not history, but saga, is entirely wrong. That narrative can be saga as well as history."[13]

But why pose the problem here, in the discussion of the revelation story? There is no more appropriate place. The analytic exploration of this narrative opens a singular avenue to its solution and its result sheds a surprising light on the origin of oral tradition. The Bible opens with cosmogonic traditions which have long been recognized to be rooted in similar Babylonian stories and continues with the patriarchal narratives. While there is some historical value to them, they often take the form of saga. This is valid also for the Exodus-Sinai account whatever the historical kernel of this tradition might be. The decisive fact is for us at this point that there is some historical substance in the tradition of Moses and of the Exodus. I have sought to prove that the tradition preserved in the biblical tale presents a fusion of that historical report with the detailed, but veiled, account of a great initiation festival of some Hebrew tribes.

Closely considered, this hypothesis, if re-examined and verified, leads to two conclusions. The first is that we have here in the Exodus tale the only account of the secret puberty rituals of the people of the ancient Near East. There is almost no mention of such initiation ceremonies from Egypt, Babylonia, Canaan, or Phoenicia, and scarcely more than notices from ancient Arabia. We understand well why it could not be otherwise: the puberty rituals were highly secret and every exposure of their mysteries was considered an unpardonable crime, followed by death-penalty. The biblical narrative does not present a picture of that initiation as such, but its disguise in the form of a theophany and revelation before the Israelites. The initiation rituals appear here, so to speak, masked in the appearance and concealment of a single unparalleled historic event in the early life of the Hebrews. Between the lines of the biblical report we recognized the outline of an old tradition of the periodically repeated puberty festivals of the Israelites.

This new interpretation takes us to the threshold of the second conclusion to be drawn from this investigation. The biblical narrative provides a splendid documentary confirmation for this thesis because it definitely describes the instruction of the boys as the main means of the transmission of oral tradition. The Bible commands the telling of the story of the Exodus (13:8 and 4). Orders to transmit the events of national history by word of mouth are to be found in many biblical passages, for instance: ". . . but teach them thy sons and thy son's sons . . . that they may learn to fear me all the days that they shall live upon the earth and that they may teach their children" (Deut. 4:9–10) and others.

Compare now these biblical passages with the anthropological reports we possess about the puberty rituals of primitive and preliterate tribes. The novices of the Australian Kurnai are shown two bullroarers which represent primal ancestors and an old man tells them the myth of the origin of the initiation. After return to the camp the teaching continues: the events of mythical times are displayed to them in dramatic performances. The essence of the instruction, continued for several months, is "the communication of the name and myth of the Supreme Being, and the revelation of his relation to the bull-roarers and to the initiation mystery."[14] Among most Australian tribes the ordeals of the novices are accompanied by instruction through dances and pantomimes presenting mythical traditions. Before and after circumcision the novices take long journeys following the route of their mythical ancestors. The initiation is "equivalent to introducing the novice to the mythical history of the tribe, in other words, the initiate learns the deeds of the Supernatural Beings . . ."[15] But the traditional lore includes also the adventures of the ancestors which in Australia amount to little more than long wanderings and a certain number of acts. To be initiated is compared in Mircea

Eliade's words to "learning what happened in the primordial time . . . The sacred and secret lore now depends on the mythical Ancestors, no longer on the Gods." Men during the initiation period learn a sacred story. Everything that happens to the novice, for instance, circumcision, is understood by him in the light of the knowledge of events that took place in the history of the tribe which its old men teach him.

An accumulation of reports about the puberty rituals in Africa, Australia, and America would convince the student that instruction in the history and mythology is an integral part of the primitive tribal initiation. This elementary but detailed study of history, often presented in the form of dances and dramatic performances, is continued for a long time and seriously pursued. "The avidity," writes Norman B. Tindale about the natives of South Australia, "with which the newly initiated youth enters into ceremonial life and the acquiring of the hidden significance of the mythological traditions and practices of the tribe is remarkable."[16]

On the detour over the biblical revelation story we arrived at the origin and home of oral tradition. It was transmitted from the generation of fathers to that of sons during the initiation seclusion. Later changes transformed this situation, but the instruction of history remained a time-honored transmission from man to man. Women and children were not taught history. They were told stories.

History does not simply repeat itself. It returns to certain collective experiences which reappear in various forms as the motifs of a symphony reoccur in later elaboration. We resist at this point the temptation to be absorbed in the problem of how much of the mystery of Jewish survival can be understood through the analysis of the early history of the group and how much of its fate can be attributed to the vicissitudes of an early phase "when Israel was a child." I dare say that the understanding of the Sinai revelation, seen in retrospect and prospect, might illuminate the present and future of religion in the Western world. As Arnold Toynbee wrote in a recent issue of the Times Literary Supplement, "the only light we have on the present and the future comes from our knowledge of the past."

This book presents a piece of archaeologic-psychoanalytic research and applies the methods of this incompletely developed branch of depth-psychology. It tries to decode the elusive messages from the past using small signs and traits that have not yet been observed and psychologically evaluated, and following leads rising from deep recesses of the groups. It makes no claim to answer many great questions of religious evolution, but I hope it will open an avenue at the end of which answers can be found. This writer, who has spent so much of his life hearing the life stories of many patients, hopes that he has caught a leading motif of the world symphony to which he has listened "with the third ear."

NOTES

Introduction. *Vision and Revision*

1. Michael Corday, *Sous La Rose. Pages inédites d'Anatole France* (Paris, 1924), p. 69.

2. This paper was read before the Vienna Psychoanalytic Society in January 1915 and first published in *Imago* (Vol. IV, 1915–1916) and is now part of my book *Ritual* (Leipzig, 1919; 2d edition 1928), which originally appeared in English under the title, *The Psychological Problems of Religion, I: Ritual—Psychoanalytic Studies* (London, 1931; New York, 1946), henceforth cited as *Ritual*.

3. *Ritual*, p. 157.

4. *The Shofar* and *Kol Nidre*, 1915 and 1916, both contained in *Ritual*.

5. "Some Aspects of Semitic Monotheism," *Psychoanalysis and the Social Sciences*, IV (New York, 1955), p. 194.

6. Martin Buber, *Moses* (Oxford, 1946), now available in inexpensive paperback reprint in the Harper *Torchbook* series.

7. *Amid These Storms* (New York, 1932), p. 293.

1. *The Dramatic Action: The Revelation*

1. Compare K. D. Herrmann, *Der Begriff der Offenbarung* (Giessen, 1887), reprinted in his *Offenbarung und Wunder* (1908), p. 8.

2. John Baillie, *The Idea of Revelation in Recent Thought* (New York, 1956), p. 28.

3. Richard Chenevix Trench, *On the Study of Words* (New York, 1852), p. 87.

4. Emil Brunner, *Revelation and Reason* (Philadelphia, 1946), pp. 8 ff.

5. Quoted by John Baillie, *op. cit.*, p. 66.

6. Arnold Toynbee, *An Historian's Approach to Religion* (New York, 1950), p. 155.

3. *Moses as Protagonist*

1. "Dieu est le poete, les hommes ne sont que les acteurs. Les grandes pièces qui se jouent sur la terre, ont été composées dans le ciel."

2. New York, 1939.

3. *The Archaeology of Palestine and the Bible* (New York, 1935), pp. 165 ff.

4. Philo Judaeus, *On the Life of Moses,* translated by C. H. Colson in the Loeb Classics edition of *Works, VI* (Cambridge, 1956), pp. 285–293.

5. Translated by H. St. J. Thackeray (London and New York, 1930), IV, p. 265.

6. *Preparation for the Gospel,* translated by E. H. Gifford, (Oxford, 1903) IX, p. 27. It occurs to me in this connection that it might be helpful to approach the delicate question of the identity of Moses from an extreme point of view, with analogy from the borderlands between history and fiction. Moses was a Hebrew, a Levite, one of the half-nomadic tribes living in Goshen. He was, if you wish, in a position similar to that of a bedouin sheik. The question now arises: How should such a man find admission to the Pharaoh? How could he get a hearing with the emperor who was considered a god? The Pharaoh, it will be remembered, was really worshipped as the personified Osiris. What had the chieftain of an uneducated, despised, and barbaric tribe in common with the king of a people who thought of themselves as the élite of mankind, as the most enlightened men on earth? There was no common ground between the Pharaoh Rameses the second and a Hebrew fanatic. Each conversation—if such a thing were imaginable—would amount to a complete failure.

It is likely that the conversation would take a course similar to the one Napoleon's general Desaix had, more than three thousand years later, with a dervish quite near the place where the biblical narrative had the Pharaoh speak with Moses. As Anatole France tells the story in *Sur La Pierre Blanche,* Louis Charles Antoine Desaix de Veygoux, who subjugated Upper Egypt, pursued the enemy after the battle near the Pyramids with twelve hundred cavalrymen. When he arrived at his destination, he learned that an old dervish who was celebrated as a very scholarly and saintly man by the Arabs, lived near the town. Desaix had philosophical tendencies and was very affable. Curious to make the acquaintance of the man who was so highly thought of by his people, he sent for the dervish and received him respectfully in his headquarters. He started his conversation with the dervish with the help of an interpreter: "Reverend old man, the French came to bring justice and liberty to Egypt."

"I knew that they would come," the dervish replied.

"How did you know that?"

"Through the eclipse of the sun."

"How could a solar eclipse inform you about the movements of our armies?"

"The eclipses of the sun are caused by the Angel Gabriel who places himself before the sun to announce a threatening calamity to the believers."

"Venerable old man, you do not know the true cause of solar eclipses;

I will explain it to you." He takes a pencil and a piece of paper and draws figures: "A is the sun, B is the moon, C the earth . . ." When he finishes his demonstration, he says: "This is the theory of solar eclipses."

The dervish murmured some words.

"What does he say?" the general asks the interpreter.

"General, he says that it is the Angel Gabriel who causes eclipses in stepping before the sun."

"But he is a fanatic!" Desaix cries, and he turns him out, kicking him in the backside.

A conversation between Rameses II and the Hebrew chief Moses would, we think, have ended in a manner similar to that of the discussion between General Desaix and the dervish.

4. The Birth of a Hero

1. *The Dawn of Conscience* (New York and London, 1944), p. 412.

2. *From the Stone Age to Christianity,* 2d ed. (Garden City, 1957), p. 112.

3. "Was Moses an Egyptian?", *Psychoanalysis and the Social Sciences,* III, 1951, p. 189.

4. "Moses and Monotheism," *Jewish Social Studies* (October, 1939).

5. "Abraham and Monotheism," in *The American Imago,* XI, no. 3 (1954), p. 299.

6. *The Hebrew Moses: An Answer to Sigmund Freud* (New York, 1939), p. 62.

7. Paul Brunton, *A Search in Ancient Egypt* (New York, 1936), p. 178.

8. Compare Otto Rank, *The Myth of the Birth of the Hero* (Vienna, 1909; English translation, New York, 1914) and Freud, *Moses and Monotheism,* pp. 7 f.

9. "Was Moses an Egyptian?", *Psychoanalysis and the Social Sciences,* III, (New York, 1951), pp. 189 f.

10. This true story was told in *McCall's Magazine* in November, 1957.

5. The Forming of the Tradition

1. *From the Stone Age to Christianity,* 2d ed. (Baltimore, 1946), pp. 14 ff.

2. *Introduction to the Old Testament* (New York, 1941), p. 272.

6. *The Birth of a Nation*

1. A. C. Steindorf and K. C. Seels, *When Egypt Ruled The East* (Chicago, 1947), p. 256.

2. Garden City, 1957.

3. *Die Israeliten und ihre Nachbarstämme* (Leipzig, 1906), p. 222.

4. For instance: Jacob Hoschander, "The Exodus, Its Historic Date," in *The Jewish Forum*, VI (1925). The still highly controversial date of the Exodus is fully discussed, yet the decision is left in abeyance in Salo Wittmayer Baron's *A Social and Religious History of the Jews,* I (New York, 1952), p. 308.

5. Quoted by W. F. Albright, *From The Stone Age to Christianity,* p. 209.

7. *Exodus as Genesis*

1. *Record and Revelation* (Oxford, 1938), p. 67.

2. H. Richard Niebuhr, *The Meaning of Revelation* (New York, 1946), p. 110.

3. Martin Buber, *Hasidim in Religion* (New York, 1948), p. 199.

4. "Preface to Hermeneutics," in *Journal of Religion,* XXX, no. 7 (April, 1950).

5. H. H. Rowley, *From Joshua to Jesus* (London, 1950), p. 1

6. *Judaism and Modern Man* (New York, 1951), p. 288.

7. Pesik K. 102 A.

8. *Some Aspects of Rabbinic Theology* (New York, 1909), p. 24. Abraham Joshua Heschel's "A Preface to an Understanding of Revelation," in *Essays presented to Leo Baeck on the Occasion of his Eightieth Birthday* (London, 1954), p. 313, points out that remembering the revelation on Mount Sinai "we do not conjure up the shadow of an archaic phenomenon, but attempt to debate the question whether to believe that there is a man at all times or at some times in the name of God."

8. *The Setting of the Stage—The Wanderings and the Mountain*

1. Introduction to *The Ten Commandments* by Solomon Goldman (Chicago, 1956), p. ix.

2. *The Religion of the Semites* (New York, 1956), p. 117.

3. Alexandre Dumas, *Mémoires* (Paris, 1852–54).

4. Compare the article on "Mountains and Mountain Gods," *ERE,*

Vol. VIII, p. 811, and Mircea Eliade, *Birth and Rebirth* (New York, 1958), p. 65.

5. Werner Keller, *The Bible as History* (New York, 1956).

6. Theophile J. Meek, *Hebrew Origins* (New York, 1936).

7. Quoted by C. C. Robertson, *On the Track of the Exodus* (New York, 1936), p. 17.

8. New York, 1958.

9. Marcel Le Goff, *Conversations avec Anatole France, 1914–24* (Paris, 1925).

9. *Passover and the Redemption of Israel*

1. T. Erich Peet, *Egypt and the Old Testament* (Liverpool and London, 1922), p. 64.

2. Compare W. Robertson Smith, *The Religion of the Semites* (New York, 1956), p. 406, who points to the primitive character of the offerings in the details of the ritual and to the coincidence of its season with that of the Arabian sacrifices.

3. Julius A. Wellhausen, *Prolegomena zur Geschichte Israels* (Berlin, 1905), pp. 82–94.

4. *Kritischer Versuch über den Ursprung und die geschichtliche Entwicklung des Pessach und Mazzothfestes* (Bonn, 1883), p. 69.

5. *Lectures on the Religion of the Semites,* 2d ed., pp. 381 ff.

6. A. van Gennep, *Les Rites de Passage* (Paris, 1909), soon to be issued in English translation by The University of Chicago Press.

7. *The Dying God,* in *The Golden Bough,* Vol. III (London, 1911).

8. Theodor Herzl Gaster, *Passover: Its History and Tradition* (New York, 1949), p. 24.

9. S. H. Hooke, *The Origins of Early Semitic Ritual* (New York, 1938), p. 57.

10. *The Day of Yahweh* (London, 1929), p. 98.

10. *Toward a New Beginning: Beyond Higher Criticism and the New Archaeology*

1. *From the Stone Age to Christianity,* 2d ed., Anchor Books (New York, 1957).

2. Sixth edition (Leipzig, 1878).

3. Especially *Studies in Divine Kingship in the Ancient Near East* (Uppsala, 1943).

4. *The Rediscovery of the Old Testament* (London, 1946), p. 88.

5. In H. H. Rowley (ed.), *The Old Testament and Modern Study* (Oxford, 1951), p. 290.

6. *Psalmenstudien, II,* (Kristiania, 1921), pp. 213–314.

7. *Myth and Ritual* (London, 1933), *The Labyrinth* (1935), and *The Origins of Early Semitic Ritual* (1938).

8. In H. H. Rowley (ed.), *The Old Testament and Modern Study* (Oxford, 1951), p. 283.

9. *The Old Testament Against Its Environment* (London, 1950), p. 7.

10. *Ibid.,* pp. 9–15.

11. *Ibid.,* p. 29.

11. *The Meanings of Initiation*

1. Maurice Samuel in his foreword to Solomon Goldman's *The Ten Commandments* (Chicago, 1956), p. xiv.

2. 1912–1936. Compare his *The Origin and Growth of Religion* (New York, 1931) and *High Gods in North America* (Oxford, 1933).

3. *Primitive Revelation* (Oxford, 1939). See also Pettazzoni's essay in *Revue de l'Histoire des Religions* (Paris, 1923), pp. 193–229, *Archiv für Religionsgeschichte,* XXIV (1931), pp. 108–29, 209–43 and N. Söderblom, *Das Werden des Gottesglaubens* (Leipzig, 1916) and Herbert Jennings Rose, *Gods and Heroes of the Greeks* (London, 1957).

4. For an introduction to and persuasive illustrations of this method, see Jane Ellen Harrison, *Themis* (London, 1912), E. R. Dodds, *The Greek and the Irrational* (Berkeley, 1957), and Mircea Eliade, *Patterns in Comparative Religion* (New York, 1958).

5. The description concerns the Australian aborigines at the time when they were the object of careful study by anthropologists, more than eighty years ago, and is especially valid for the tribes in the interior of the continent.

12. *Primitive Initiation into Manhood*

1. H. Schultz, *Altersklassen und Männerbünde* (Berlin, 1902), p. 96 and Mircea Eliade, *Birth and Rebirth* (New York, 1958).

2. van Gennep, *Les Rites de Passage* (Paris, 1909).

3. About new names after initiation, compare Mircea Eliade, *Birth and Rebirth* (New York, 1958), pp. 28, 31, 68, 74, 75, and E. O. James, *Primitive Ritual and Belief* (London, 1917) pp. 16 ff.

4. H. A. Junod, *The Life of a South African Tribe,* Vol. I (London, 1912), p. 74.

5. G. McCall Theal, *History of South Africa,* Vol. V (London, 1893), p. 205.

6. W. S. and K. Routledge, *With a Prehistoric People* (London, 1900), p. 151.

7. Goblet d'Alviella's article "Initiation" in *Encyclopaedia of Religion and Ethics,* VII, pp. 316 ff.

8. *Ibid.*

9. A. Menes, *The History of the Jews in Ancient Times,* in the symposium, *The Jewish People,* Vol. I (New York, 1946), p. 88.

13. *Death and Resurrection*

1. Many examples of the death and resurrection concept during the initiation ceremonies are collected by Frazer in the second volume of his *Golden Bough.* Compare "The Puberty Rites of the Savages" in my book *Ritual* and Moritz Zeller, *Die Knabenweihen* (Bern, 1923).

2. B. Spencer and F. J. Gillen, *The Arunta* (London, 1921), p. 175.

3. Isaac Landman (ed.) *Universal Jewish Encyclopedia* (New York, 1948), III, p. 193.

4. *Rabbah III,* 258.5.

5. *What Mean These Stones?* (New Haven, 1941), p. 69.

6. William Howells, *The Heathens* (Garden City, 1948), p. 248.

7. Mary A. Owen, *Folklore of the Musquakie Indians* (London, 1904), p. 67.

14. *Clues for an Invisible Entrance*

1. Compare the literature on the initiation rites quoted in my book *Ritual* (New York, 1946), p. 92 ff.

2. This follows the translation of Exodus (Chapt. 12–12 ff.) according to Solomon Goldman's *The Ten Commandments,* p. 5.

3. *From the Stone Age to Christianity,* p. 262.

4. *Israel from its Beginnings to the Middle of the Eighth Century* (New York, 1932), p. 179.

5. *Israel, Its Life and Culture,* IV (Copenhagen and London, fotoprint, 1953), p. 662.

6. *The Covenant at Mount Sinai* (Leiden, 1939), p. 16.

7. *Ibid.,* p. 18. Compare the same writer's book, *The Religion of Israel* (Leiden, 1909).

15. Human Agencies in the Revelation

1. *Geschichte des Volkes Israel* (Leipzig, 1887–88).

2. *Origin and History of the Jewish Religion* in *The Jewish People,* Vol. I (New York, 1946), pp. 252 ff.

3. Compare the quoted book, *The Covenant at Mount Sinai* (London, 1947), as well as *De Godsdeenst van Israel* (London, 1947), by the same author, professor at the University of Leiden in Holland.

4. A. Menes, *loc cit.,* p. 243.

5. *Ibid.,* p. 243.

6. Eerdmans, *The Covenant at Mount Sinai,* p. 20.

7. *Ibid.,* p. 21.

8. *The Ten Commandments,* pp. xii f.

9. Eerdmans assumes that we can hardly conceive of a state of mind identifying our own personal actions with deeds of God. "Yet those who performed a revelation of God by human intermediary regarded the results of their activity as a real action of God." (*The Covenant*), p. 31.

16. The Sound and the Fury

1. "The Shofar," published in *Ritual,* pp. 221 ff.

2. A. C. Haddon, *The Study of Man* (New York, 1939), p. 427.

3. *Encyclopaedia of Religion and Ethics,* Vol. II, p. 890.

4. *Das sociale Leben der Aranda und Loritja-Stämme* (Frankfurt a. M., 1933), p. 25.

5. Spencer and Gillen, *Northern Tribes,* pp. 246, 497.

6. *Ibid.,* p. 497.

17. The Mask of Moses

1. Compare the interpretation of the Menorah as an idol's head in Renato I. Almansi's article "A Psychoanalytic Interpretation of the Menorah," *Journal of the Hillside Hospital,* II, no. 2 (April, 1953).

2. J. Buttikofer, *Reisebilder aus Liberia,* Vol. II (Leiden, 1890), pp. 30 ff.

3. Leo Frobenius, *Und Africa sprach* Vol. VII (Berlin, 1903), pp. 139 ff.

4. For instance, "Moses with the Shining Face," in *Hebrew Union College Annual,* II, 1952, pp. 25 ff.

5. *The Covenant,* p. 97.

6. *Moses und seine Zeit* (Göttingen, 1913), p. 247.

7. Maurice Samuel in his foreword to Solomon Goldman's *The Ten Commandments* (Chicago, 1956).

8. S. Goldman, *op. cit.*

18. *The Ten Commandments of the Savages*

1. Solomon Goldman, *The Ten Commandments* (Chicago, 1950), pp. 26 ff.

2. Compare R. H. Charles, *The Decalogue* (Edinburgh, 1923) and John H. Smith, *The Origin and History of the Hebrew Law* (Chicago, 1931).

3. C. H. Johns' article in *Hastings' Dictionary of the Bible* (extra volume), p. 608, and Alfred Jeremias, *The Old Testament in the Light of the Ancient East* (New York, 1916).

4. *Das sociale Leben der Aranda und Loritja-stämme* (Frankfurt a. M., 1913), p. 58.

5. W. Lloyd Warner, *A Black Civilization,* 2d ed. (New York, 1958), p. 284.

6. E. Casalis, *Les Bassoutos* (Paris, 1860), p. 278.

7. Compare the well-known books by J. G. Frazer as well as Moritz Zeller, *Die Knabenweihen* (Bern, 1923) and Ad. E. Jensen, *Beschneidung und Reifezeremonieen bei den Naturvölkern* (Stuttgart, 1933).

8. C. Ryder Smith, *The Religion of the Hebrews* (London, 1935), p. 33.

19. *Circumcision and Covenant*

1. In *Encyclopaedia Judaica,* Vol. VIII (Berlin, 1931), p. 610.

2. On the taboo at this occasion compare Alfred Ernest Crawley, *The Mystic Rose* (New York, 1927), p. 297.

3. Geza Roheim, "Some Aspects of Semitic Monotheism" in *Psychoanalysis and the Social Sciences,* IV (1955), p. 170.

4. In his article on circumcision in *Encyclopaedia of Religion and Ethics,* Vol. III, p. 679.

5. *Semitic and Hamitic Origins* (London, 1934), pp. 98 ff.

6. Kaufmann Kohler in *Jewish Encyclopaedia,* Vol. IV, p. 95.

7. Louis H. Gray in his article on circumcision in *Encyclopaedia of Religion and Ethics,* Vol. III, p. 662.

8. Berlin, 1907.

9. *The Old Testament against its Environment* (Chicago, 1954), p. 55.

10. Herrera y Tordesillas Antania, *The General History of the Vast Continents and Islands of America,* Vol. IV (London, 1740), p. 1888.

11. *The Religion of the Semites* (New York, 1956), p. 318.

20. *The Confederacy*

1. "Notes on the Poro in Liberia," *Papers of the Peabody Museum of American Archaeology and Ethnology,* XIX, No. 2, 1941, p. 15.

2. B. Spencer and J. Gillen, *The Northern Native Tribes of Central Australia* (London, 1899), pp. 274 ff.

3. *Geschichte Israels,* 2d ed. (Göttingen, 1954) and *Das System der Zwolf Stämme Israels* (Stuttgart, 1930).

4. *The Northern Tribes of Central Australia,* p. 350.

5. Robert H. Lowie, *Primitive Religion* (New York, 1948), p. 68.

21. *The Next Assignment*

1. December 29, 1957 (published in the *American Historical Review,* Vol. LXIII, no. 2, January, 1958), p. 283–304.

2. In my book *The Search Within* (New York, 1956), p. 477.

22. *Attempt at Reconstruction*

1. William Arthur Heidel, *The Day of Yahweh* (Oxford, 1915), p. 55.

2. Josephus, *Contra Apion,* I. 26.

3. Johannes Pedersen, "Passahfest und Passah Legende," *Zeitschrift für die alttestamentliche Wissenschaft,* Vol. LII (1934), p. 161–75.

4. *Geschichte der Alttestamentliche Religion* (Gütersloh, 1912), pp. 325 f.

5. J. Pedersen, *Israel, Its Life and Culture,* Vols. III–IV (Copenhagen and London, fotoprint, 1953), p. 348.

6. Idem.

23. *Commemoration*

1. *Ex-prodigy* (New York, 1957), p. 213.

2. *The Golden Bough,* Vol. IV (*Adonis, Attis, Osiris*) (London, 1919), p. 83.

3. For instance, William H. Desmonde, "The Eleusinian Mysteries," *Journal of the Hillside Hospital* (October, 1952), p. 205.

4. J. G. Frazer, *The Golden Bough,* Vol. II *(Balder The Beautiful),* p. 249.

5. Julius H. Greenstone, *The Jewish Religion* (Philadelphia, 1929), p. 54.

6. Compare the material from Australian and Siberian initiation ritual in Mircea Eliade's *Birth and Rebirth* (New York, 1958), pp. 90, 92, 97, 99.

24. *The Bush Burned with Fire and Was Not Consumed*

1. William Arthur Heidel, *The Day of Yahweh* (Oxford, 1914), p. 109.

2. *Ibid.,* p. 55, footnote.

3. The only interpretation of Passover as a puberty ritual which I find in the pertinent literature is contained in some passage in William Heidel's book, *The Day of Yahweh,* p. 174. This writer points to the thought that the children who have no knowledge of good and evil shall accomplish the Passover which may refer to a *rite de passage* for children, and adds: "Perhaps a rite at puberty." The author refers to the different ages when boys are supposed to reach the phase of maturity or discretion among the Greeks, Romans, Arabs, Persians, and so on.

4. B. Spencer and F. J. Gillen, *The Northern Native Tribes of Central Australia* (London, 1899), p. 274.

5. For instance by Benno Jacob, "Moses am Dornbusch" in *Mitteilungen der Gesellschaft für die Wissenschaft des Judentums,* 1922.

6. *Myth and Guilt* (New York, 1957).

7. *Totemism and Exogamy* (London, 1910), esp. Vols. II and III.

8. *Ibid.,* Vol. II, p. 209.

9. *Ibid.,* Vol. III, p. 415.

10. Geza Roheim came nearest to the thesis presented here in his posthumously published paper on "Some Aspects of Semitic Monotheism," in *Psychoanalysis and the Social Sciences* (New York, 1955), pp. 169 ff., but failed to draw the conclusions for which his material could serve as evidence. Quoting from my book *Ritual* (London, 1931), pp. 156–166, he acknowledged that "Semitic religion is based on the puberty-rite."

25. *Myth and Mystery*

1. Arthur A. Feldman, "Freud's 'Moses and Monotheism' and the Three Stages of Israelitish Religion," *Psychoanalytic Review* (October, 1944), p. 400.

2. Most experts agree that the secret societies displace earlier tribal puberty institutions; for instance, Hutton Webster, *Primitive Secret Societies,* 2d ed. (New York, 1932), p. 2.

3. Webster points out that "the magical practices and dramatic ceremonies, elaborated afterwards into the ritual of a solemn religious cult, which are the chief characteristics of the Greek mysteries, may be traced by the curious student to primitive rites in no wise dissimilar to those which, as we have seen, embody the faith and worship of the modern savage. . . ." *Primitive Secret Societies,* p. 190.

4. *Prologomena to the Study of Greek Religion* (Cambridge, 1908), p. 2.

5. Plutarch, *De Iside et Osiride,* in Theodor Hopfner (ed.), *Orientalisches Institute* (Prague, 1940), xxiii.

6. *Studies in Judaism,* Vol. I (New York, 1896), p. 373.

26. *The Leap Backwards*

1. *The Old Testament against its Environment* (Chicago, 1950), pp. 9 ff.

2. *Einführung in das Alte Testament* (Leipzig, 1932), p. 51.

3. Ernest Wright, *op. cit.,* pp. 24–25.

4. Erich Voegelin, *Israel and Revelation* (Baton Rouge, La., 1956), p. 116.

5. Wright, *op. cit.,* p. 29.

6. It is not unknown to me that most scholars date the Exodus-Sinai story in the late Bronze Age. Yet it is not impossible that the smiths of Midian had an earlier knowledge of the use of iron.

7. Quoted in Leo W. Schwarz (ed.), *Great Ages and Ideas of the Jewish People* (New York, 1956), p. xxv.

8. W. F. Albright dates Abraham's migration somewhere between 1900 and 1750 B.C. *From The Stone Age to Christianity,* 2d ed. (New York, 1957), p. 200.

9. *A Social and Religious History of The Jews,* Vol. I (Philadelphia, 1952), p. 33.

10. James H. Breasted, *The Dawn of Civilization* (New York, 1944), p. 348.

27. *The Advance in Regression*

1. *Hebrew Origins* (New York, 1950), p. 207.

2. *Israel* (London, 1932), p. 37.

3. *How Came Our Faith* (New York, 1949), p. 202.
4. *A Social and Religious History of the Jews,* p. 312.
5. *Geschichte des Volkes Israel,* Vol. I (Stuttgart, 1932); *Ueberlieferungsgeschichte des Pentateuchs* (Stuttgart, 1948); *Das System der Zwölf Stämme Israels* (Stuttgart, 1930).
6. John Bright, *Early Israel in Recent History Writing* (Chicago, 1956), p. 84. In the same volume, Dr. McCormick, professor of Hebrew and of Old Testament Interpretation at the Union Theological Seminary, Richmond, Virginia, presents a summary and evaluation of the views of North, Albrecht Alt and Yehezkel Kaufmann and mentions the most important recent literature dealing with the origin and early history of Israel.

28. A Holy Nation

1. Th. C. Vriessen, *Die Erwahlung Israels nach dem Alten Testament* (Groningen, 1951), p. 20.
2. Will Herberg, *Judaism and Modern Man* (New York, 1951), p. 267.
3. *Moses and Monotheism* (New York, 1949), pp. 166 ff.
4. Philo, *Biblical Antiquities,* Vol. VI, pp. 285–293, and Josephus, *Works,* Vol. IV, p. 265.
5. Paul Brunton, *A Search in Secret Egypt* (New York, 1936), p. 178.
6. "From the earliest historic times, therefore, the dominant element in Egyptian conception of Kingship was that the king was God—not merely godlike, but very god." H. W. Fairman, "The Kingship Rituals of Egypt," in S. H. Hooke (ed.), *Myth, Ritual and Kingship* (Oxford, 1958), p. 75.
7. It gives me great satisfaction to learn that a biblical scholar as remote from my views as S. H. Hooke of the University of London, who is a protagonist of the so-called Myth and Ritual school, comes to similar conclusions in a recent book. (See his *Myth, Ritual and Kingship;* Oxford, 1958, pp. 11 ff.) Professor Hooke acknowledges the tradition that Moses spent the first part of his life in the environment of the Egyptian court and was familiar with the ritual pattern whose center was the divine king. Moses spent then some years among the pastoral tribes in the steppes of Midian where he had the experience of the Burning Bush. The new conception of the nature of God was "wholly incompatible with the conception of the Egyptian divine king." This "might well have produced in him a strong revulsion against the whole ritual system of Egypt and especially against anything in it that implied the making of a man into a god." *Ibid.,* 11.
8. See article on "African Societies" (p. 290) in the *Encyclopaedia of Religion and Ethics.*

9. Frazer, *Totemism and Exogamy,* Vol. III (London, 1910), p. 547.

10. See *Encyclopaedia of Religion and Ethics,* s. v. *"Secret Societies,"* p. 304.

11. See N. W. Thomas, *ibid.,* s. v. "African Secret Societies," p. 288.

12. *Ibid.,* 299.

13. Mircea Eliade, who follows the initiatory elements in primitive Christianity (*Birth and Rebirth,* New York, 1958), points out that the sacraments separated the novice from the crowd "and made him part of a community of the elect. . . ." Just as the Christians called themselves saints and "the chosen," the Essenes regarded themselves as "initiates" (p. 117). Both considered themselves as set apart from the rest of society because they had been initiated.

14. A. Powell Davies, *The Ten Commandments* (1956), p. 22.

15. The Deuteronomic reform did not end the controversy. Cf. William F. Bade's *Old Testament in the Light of Today* (Boston, 1915).

29. *The Name Ineffable*

1. Ernest Jones, *Freud* (New York, 1951), Vol. III, p. 351.

2. "Freudian Theology," part 2, in *Psychoanalysis,* 1953.

3. "Aspects of Semitic Monotheism" in *Psychoanalysis and the Social Sciences* (ed. Muensterberger), Vol. IV., p. 212. K. L. Parker shows that the Euahlayi worship Byamee, a colossal man of mythical times whose laws the Euahlayi obey and who now lives in the sky. *The Euahlayi Tribe* (London, 1905), p. 67.

4. Ernest Jones, *Freud,* Vol. III, p. 351.

5. *Der Gott der Väter* (Stuttgart, 1929).

6. Salo Wittmayer Baron, *A Social and Religious History of the Jews* (Philadelphia, 1952), 2d ed., Vol. I, p. 43.

7. George Foucart's article on "Names" in *Encyclopaedia of Religion and Ethics,* Vol. IX, p. 133.

8. J. H. Breasted, *The Dawn of Conscience* (New York, 1934), p. 350.

9. *Op. cit.,* p. 415.

10. *Secret Societies,* p. 287.

11. In his article on "Secret Societies" in *Encyclopaedia of Religion and Ethics,* Vol. XI, pp. 287 ff.

12. Will Herberg, *Judaism and Modern Man* (New York, 1951), considers the covenant the central event in the redemptive history of Jewish faith.

13. *Theologie des Alten Testaments* (Leipzig, 1933), Vol. I.

14. *Die Ernährungstraditionen Israels* (Giessen, 1928), p. 37.

15. *Inspiration and Revelation in the Old Testament* (Oxford, 1949), p. 153.

16. *The Old Testament against Its Environment* (Chicago, 1953), p. 55.

17. *Das Buch Josua* (Tübingen, 1958), p. 108.

18. *Law and Covenant in Israel and the Ancient Near East* (London, 1956), p. 24.

19. *Israel from the Beginnings to the Middle of the Eighth Century* (New York, 1932), Vol. I, p. 152.

30. *God's Incorporeality*

1. J. W. M. Whiting, *Becoming a Kwoma* (New Haven, 1941), p. 90.

2. *Moses and Monotheism,* p. 182.

3. *Ibid.,* p. 187.

4. Dr. A. B. Feldman of Philadelphia has suggested to me that the emphasis put on words (abstractions) instead of images may have led to the result that poetry and music were the arts in which Jews were most at home. Dr. Feldman supposes that exaltation of the ear in culture means coordinate exaltation of the larynx therefore the devotion of the Jews to speech. (Private communication.)

31. *The Birth of a Collective Super-Ego*

1. *Moses* (Amsterdam, 1953), p. 225.

2. My theory is here opposed to that of Elias Auerbach who asserts "We do not know what Mosche thought, but we concluded from the consequences what his thoughts had been" (*Moses,* p. 225), but is at least in its implications also different from Freud's concept which sees Moses only as a follower of the heretic Pharaoh Ikhnaton.

3. *Moses and Monotheism,* p. 135.

4. "On the Exceptional Position of the Auditory Sphere," *International Journal of Psychoanalysis,* XX (1939).

5. "Die Augen glauben sich selbst, die Ohren anderen Leuten."

32. *The Return of the Repressed*

1. Henry A. Bunker, "Psychoanalysis and the Study of Religion," in *Psychoanalysis and the Social Sciences,* III (New York, 1951), p. 28; also Geza Roheim in various publications.

2. See my "Puberty Rites of the Savages," originally published in January, 1915.

3. *Op. cit.*, p. 30.

4. *Christianity and the Children of Israel* (New York, 1948), pp. 146–47.

5. Quoted by Eckhardt, *op. cit.*, p. 146.

33. *The Living Past: Retrospect and Prospect*

1. Quoted by Geza Roheim, "The Passage of the Red Sea," *Man,* Vol. 23–24 (1923–1924).

2. H. I. Junod, "The Bulemba," *Folklore,* XIX, p. 284.

3. Article on "Baptism" in *Encyclopaedia of Religion and Ethics,* Vol. II, pp. 367 ff.

4. *Birth and Rebirth* (New York, 1958), p. 115.

5. Article on "Baptism" in *Encyclopaedia of Religion and Ethics,* Vol. II, p. 409.

6. Num. Shelah. Sifra 109a.

7. *Kitab al Khazari* translated by Hirschfeld (New York, 1927), p. 115.

8. Will Herberg, *Judaism and Modern Man* (New York, 1951), p. 257.

9. *Die Jüdische Bewegung* (Berlin, 1916), II, pp. 123–124.

10. J. G. Frazer, *Adonis, Attis, Osiris* (London, 1914), 3d ed., p. 212.

11. Hugo Hepding, *Attis* (Giessen, 1903), p. 167.

12. *What is History?* (New York, 1953), p. 17.

13. *Geschichte des Volkes Israel* (Leipzig, 1952), Vol. I, p. 270.

14. *Birth and Rebirth,* p. 10.

15. *Ibid.,* p. 17.

16. "Initiation among the Pijtjandjara Natives of the Mann and Tomkinson Ranges in South Australia," *Oceania,* VI (1955), p. 222.

Index

205